Choking on Marlon Brando

Choking on
Marlon Brando

A Memoir

Antonia Quirke

The Overlook Press
Woodstock & New York

This edition first published in the United States in 2007 by
The Overlook Press, Peter Mayer Publishers, Inc.
Woodstock & New York

WOODSTOCK:
One Overlook Drive
Woodstock, NY 12498
www.overlookpress.com
[for individual orders, bulk and special sales, contact our Woodstock office]

NEW YORK:
141 Wooster Street
New York, NY 10012

Lines from *Betrayal* by Harold Pinter reproduced by
permission of Faber and Faber Ltd.

'Creep' Words and Music by Thomas Yorke, Edward O'Brien, Colin Greenwood,
Jonathan Greenwood, Philip Selway, Edward Hammond & Mike Hazelwood
© 1992 Warner/Chappell Music Ltd and Rondor Music.

Cataloging-in-Publication Data is available from the Library of Congress

Manufactured in the United States of America
ISBN-13 978-1-58567-915-7
ISBN-10 1-58567-915-1
10 9 8 7 6 5 4 3 2 1

For Ilana Bryant, best girl in New Jersey

ACKNOWLEDGEMENTS

Many people have been very kind and helpful to me during the writing of this book, but I shall limit myself to two acknowledgements. Two JL's. Julian Loose at Faber, whose idea it was in the first place. And James Lever, without whose editing this book – quite simply – would not have been written.

'You live in a dream and the dream is a cage,'

Said the girl, 'And the bars nestle closer with age

Your shadow burned white by invisible fire

You will learn how it rankles to die of desire

As you long for the beautiful stranger,'

Said the vanishing beautiful stranger

PETE ATKIN AND CLIVE JAMES,
Beware of the Beautiful Stranger

'You have to have a little faith in people'

MARIEL HEMINGWAY,

Manhattan

PART ONE

Mademoiselle Depardieu

1

First I was a sperm and an egg, and then I was an embryo, and then I got born. After that I was a baby and then I was a toddler. This is coming really easily! Then I was ten lying in bed listening to the unmistakable cadences of a man and a woman arguing downstairs. I lay there harrowed by the growing conviction that the voices didn't belong to the radio but to my parents, and trying to will a snatch of music to prove that it wasn't. But it wasn't likely to be the radio at this time of night, and we didn't have a television in those days. The muffled fight went on, and on, until it was no longer bearable. I got up and crept down the stairs towards the living room, where my parents were curled up together watching a man and a woman arguing on the eight-inch black-and-white which they sometimes borrowed from next door when something especially good was on. I can remember the luxury of my relief. I can also remember how the two of them looked altered by the shifting light, made younger by it. And instead of being sent back upstairs I was invited on to the sofa to watch with them. It was a film, a famous film, with a title so romantic it seemed to contain all the scale of adult life: A Streetcar Named Desire.

(Forgive my presumptuousness in telling you all this, by the way, but if I don't I'm going to lose my husband.)

I had never seen a movie before. Not one. I had lived ten years absolutely untroubled by the knowledge of such things. I suppose I'm a bit stupid, really. 'That's Marlon Brando,' my father said. 'He's the best actor in the world.' I watched, delighted to be up late, being initiated into the privileges of adulthood, studying this Marlon Brando, this *actor*, who was now at the centre of a brawl. Some men put Brando under a shower, the women fled upstairs, and Brando began to cry. He walked outside the house in his wet T-shirt, and I saw him – like Blanche Dubois sees him when she first comes to the Kowalskis' apartment in Elysian Fields, like audiences first saw him, tormenting Jessica Tandy in the original Streetcar in the Barrymore Theatre on Broadway in 1947, like Tennessee Williams first saw him, in his original stage direction: *Animal joy in his being is implicit in all of his movements and attitudes. Since earliest manhood the centre of his life has been pleasure with women, the giving and the taking of it, not with weak in-dulgence dependently, but with the power and pride of a richly feathered male bird among hens.*

I saw and I saw and I still see. I like to revisit all my favourite bits of his face, to tour them. The folds over the corners of his eyes which make it seem as if a force is pressing down on him, as if he's subject to a doubled gravity. There's a kind of thumbprint on his brow where something powerful has marked him. The Golden Gate mouth too beautiful not to be disgusted by the ugliness of the human speech it must form.

The curve where his jawbone meets his neck, seemingly the locus of all the strength in his head. The T-shirt torn so that it hangs off one shoulder like an emperor's toga. Brando was calling upstairs like a tomcat: 'Stella!! STELLA!!!' The thunder-clap volume of his voice had the power to hurt.

'What's the matter?' my father was suddenly saying. And something did seem to be going wrong with me. Air was coming in but it wasn't going out. Brando sank to his knees before Stella, burying his face in her thighs. Everything was beginning to shut down on me. My breathing had become an alarming fish-pant. 'Don't ever leave me, baby! Don't ever leave me!' the best actor in the world was murmuring, semi-audible under my breathing. My parents had forgotten the film and ferried me to the kitchen table where my father quizzed me about things I might have eaten. Maybe I'd had a peanut-stuffed lobster stashed under my pillow? I couldn't muster the breath to reply. Time was beginning to thicken and deepen. I could see very clearly the fur coat of dust on our never-used fondue set. My mother gave up trying to open the airways in my throat with a spoon and called an ambulance. It was all happening very far away – I was dying, peacefully. And like a stone in the shoe of my peace was the fear that was beginning to harden into a certainty, that although dying wasn't so bad I would not be able to bear the humiliation of having my mother know *why* I had died. And she knew perfectly well. She understood precisely why I was gasping like a dog on a summer's day while next door in New Orleans Marlon Brando was smashing crockery. By the time the ambulance arrived, I had stopped hyperventilating and had to listen, suffused with shame, as my parents tried to talk their way round what had happened. Everybody was standing about lying their heads off. But what would the ambulance men have said if they'd known the truth?

'Marlon Brando, Mrs Quirke? Do you think that was wise? We've had two Montgomery Clifts and a McQueen tonight already.'

This was the formative incident of my childhood. We lived in a tiny hill village in the South of France where every Saturday old Claude would lead his donkey Napoleon up the winding rocky path to the village square, laden with dusty old reels of film. The loveable village blacksmith, Rémi, would set up his projector facing the whitewashed wall of the church, Claude would feed in those magical strips of colour and light, and everyone would abandon their baking and games of pétanque and come rushing into the square agog with excitement to see the wondrous spectacles: Police Academy 6, Porky's, Evil Dead 2, Conan the Destroyer and Turner & Hooch.

I had been banned from the magical screenings in the square since I seemed so overwhelmed by the power of these 'movies'. Yet old Claude took pity on me and allowed me to climb up his ancient olive tree from whose branches –

Alright. It wasn't the formative incident of my childhood. Life isn't so neatly patterned. But the first time I saw Marlon Brando, I nearly died.

2

Some time afterwards you could have found me standing outside Blackwell's bookshop in Oxford with my elder brother Saul and my younger brother Ben, all three of us holding up the books we had just bought with our pocket money so my mother could take a picture. Ben's book was called Where Do I Come From? and Saul's was called What is Happening to Me? My book was called Who Am I? Who am I? I'm a girl who loves actors.

We lived next door to the writer Jan Morris, and one day my mother said to me, 'Antonia, listen, I've got something to tell you. James from next door is now Jan. So if you see him wearing a dress, tell her how pretty it is.' And I thought: *Isn't that nice?* Anything to do with sex was nice. Sex had our respect. The defining struggle of my father's life had been between the Catholic priesthood and my mother. Sex had fought with God, as an equal, until they could both see each other's point of view. The children were the winners. And so we liked sex. As a nurse, my mother tended to turn everything into biology. 'That bit at the top,' she would say, when Ben and I were in the bath, 'is Ben's *fore*skin. And those are his testicles!' Bodies were nothing to be ashamed of. At fancy dress parties Saul and Ben and I went naked as Adam, Cain and Eve, saving on the price of costumes. We carried an enormous brown-and-yellow-striped home-knitted snake that was otherwise used as a draught-excluder. When we grew too old to go as Adam and Eve, we attended parties as Pollution, dressed in black and trailing empty cans of tuna while our new brothers and sisters nakedly paraded the snake. We were eco-friendly. The stickers in our car said 'Nurses Against the Bomb' and 'Goats Rule'.

When my father became a psychologist, we moved to Manchester and lived in a modest house with campaigning students as lodgers, and the children kept coming: Patrick, Suzannah, Luke and Molly. 'Do you know what Mum and Dad are?' Suzannah asked me and my friend Mischa, as the three of us whiled away an afternoon inserting Crayolas into our vaginas. 'What?' '*Perverts*, that's what they are.' '*Perverts*,' I whispered to myself, rather liking the sound of it. Mischa's glamorous Australian mother Jill wrote the questions for University Challenge among piles of textbooks in her kitchen. It was not a happy house. Jill drank, and kept a bitter eye on Mischa's father Bruce, who came and went in a chocolate Jaguar, supposedly dealing antiques from the boot but mostly parked around the corner with the woman from Thresher's.

Right off the bat, my mother wasn't keen on Mischa, having caught me leaning up against a bureau inhaling on a pencil and saying to Ben: 'You are a cold-hearted prick who wants to see me hanging from a tree in the garden.' I had been possessed by the glamour of adultery. The atmosphere at Mischa's was always one of potential murder. The phenomenal *scale* of the arguments. The range and randomness of the information spilled, the strength-regathering silences in between. When she wasn't working, Jill sat stiffly in an armchair in the study, her dark hair falling to her waist in one solid piece like a bin-bag. There she would relay the drama down the telephone to Bamber Gascoigne.

'Oh, thank *Christ*,' she said when Gascoigne picked up at the other end. 'Bamber – he's here! But he's pissed.' Bruce, sober, handed her a glass of water and some aspirin. Jill looked up at him and spoke, low, into the phone. 'He's making me take some pills. *I don't know what they are.*'

On Tuesdays I rushed from my convent school to join Mischa and Jill watching Johnny Weissmuller being Tarzan on the television. Weissmuller would come down a tree like a Greek statue and rush off in his flank-flashing pants to meet people at the *escarpment*, a place we mysteriously never saw.

'Those shorts look like they just about cover his *scrotum*,' I noted.

'Christ,' said Jill in her boozy voice, 'you Quirkes with your goats, and your Song of the Volga Boatman.'

It was at Mischa's that I saw my first videos. One was called My French Lover and involved a man and a woman carrying a big plastic doll with a moustache into a bedroom and then getting under the sheets and laughing like maniacs. I seem to have blanked the rest. When I told my parents about this, I was banned from visiting number fifteen again. I slipped off in the rain to tell Mischa but she was calm, like someone used to having the ends of things spelled out and then revoked on a daily basis. '*Je reviens*,' I said, a line I'd picked up watching Emmanuelle with Jill.

3

Because Mischa and I weren't allowed to see each other we kept in touch by writing letters that Ben would deliver. Mischa had become very beautiful and began first to sign off as Marilyn Monroe and then to write as her. I responded as James Dean, and the two doomed stars began an affair. This grew into a very serious correspondence which required a great deal of biographical knowledge. I had a stack of Dean biographies and books of photos of him. (It never occurred to me to watch any of his films.) But Mischa was a couple of years older than me and when she went to try her luck as a trainee teacher in Tokyo, she wrote to me as herself rather than Monroe, as if Marilyn had *dumped* Jimmy – which offended Dean. He wrote to her from the set of Giant throughout those fraught early months of 1955. He was bewildered, hurt, jealous of Joe DiMaggio and suspicious that she might be forming an attachment with a playwright on the New York scene. But nothing came back from Tokyo, just chatter about food and friends. Was that what drove him to such near-suicidal recklessness? He burned her old letters. He'd be dead within the year.

4

I got four C's and an E in my GCSEs and failed the rest. But because I spent most of the next year recovering from an operation on my hip I didn't have to go to school and just sat in my room reading. I got four A's at A level. I convalesced in the arms of Antony Sher's Year of the King (about his Richard III for the RSC) and Simon Callow's Being an Actor and Stanislavski's Building a Character, and back to Year of the King, flicking ahead to my favourite bits, which were always about what Sher said to Roger Allam at the Arden Hotel bar. Nothing more comforting than that sense of the extended family which actors thrive in. Year of the King is just about the happiest book I've ever read, the most soothing, which is not what Sher meant at all, but there you go: actors' first neurosis is that acting is just too much fun to be art. *I* wanted to be in the Arden Hotel bar with Roger Allam.

So I decided I was going to be an actress and auditioned at the Contact Youth Theatre for a play called Don Juan Comes Back From the War and got the part of a bisexual dress designer who dates Don Juan after meeting him in a café in 1920s Vienna, gets dumped, strips and throws plates at his head. I petitioned my mother to hire me a sunbed so I could appear on stage with the tan I felt the part required, but she flatly refused. 'You are what you are,' she said.

On stage, I felt I had mainlined into acting. The aperture opened wide and I saw the abyss. 'Listen, you *bastard*,' I had to say, fetching a photo of the Don out of a drawer. 'Our child is gone. That's right. Gone. Vanished. And I can never have another. Who was it I reminded you of, hmmmmmmm? Go on. Tell me. *Who was the bitch?*' I took a needle, poked holes through the photograph's eyes, lashed out furiously at a table, and thinking *what the hell, I can do anything* picked up a chair and broke its back off by smashing it against the floor, and then leaned up against the wall, panting.

I got a glimpse of what I would be like as an actress: a nightmare. Acting was shocking. It was more than just the power of having other people look at me, or the power of being another person. It was the utter freedom and violence and irresponsibility available. Don't think I'm saying that the performance was any good whatsoever – I just thought: *I could easily spend my life in the service of this feeling.* I'd come off stage weeping uncontrollably and sink into a kind of post-coital woolliness that lasted until we got to the pub where none of the rest of the stage-school cast would speak to me because, presumably, they all found me completely terrifying.

My family came and were stunned by my noise and rage as I clomped around on the stage balling up my fists like someone who'd been well and truly screwed over. In the car on the way home, my father turned round and said, 'I'll never believe you again.' And for a moment I had an instinctive feeling – something more than just the inculcated social instinct that being an actor is a bit silly – that if I kept this up I would be permanently releasing a sort of person that I might not like. When the next play was cast, my mother pointed out the ad in the local paper, but I said I didn't want to do it. I would have liked to have called this book 'I've Been Marvellous: Seventy Magical Years at the Top', or simply 'QUIRKE: The Autobiography', but I'm not allowed to. I forgot about being an actress and never thought of it again.

5

Let's start with a whole man. Let's lay down a brief marker, an ideal to measure the rest by. Who should it be, this person who, if the movies were asked what a man was, they could reply with? Someone with a bigger heart than Brando. More longevity than De Niro. Less neurosis than Cary Grant. Let's not use Steve McQueen or Gregory Peck or Al Pacino or Denzel Washington or Valentino. Let's use Robert Mitchum as our marker. Why? Because of all actors he explains himself the most, needs analysis the least. He tells you, more than anyone else, that a body is what a soul looks like, that the way you speak and move is all there is and nothing more need be said. You don't explain it, you just love it. In Mitchum's case, the eyebrows like droplets sliding off a windshield and the genius for standing still, as if he is both moving and staying put at the same time. The way his gaze comes at you through the second set of transparent eyelids he seems to have, like a crocodile. The upswing in his voice as if he's continually stopping himself from drifting off. The mysterious depth of experience implied by so many of his gestures as if he is laughing at the smallness of movies compared to life, which goes back forever. All great movie stars know that they will bore you in the end. Avoiding being boring drove Brando nuts. But the anxiety of being boring never crossed Mitchum's mind. The virus of boring-anxiety – which all actors carry – never made it past his anti-bodies. He is the undiseased. And, having read more pages on Mitchum than I have on anyone in this book, I've learned two things: 1) I have nothing whatsoever to say about him, and 2) nobody else does. So let Robert Mitchum, like a post driven into the ground to stake a claim over a landscape, be our marker. I like being silenced by him. He shuts me up like the right answer. He simplifies everything for me until I can think ah, Bob Mitchum, so that's what a 'man' is, is it? Got it. And what an amazing thing! *Just look at that.* Aren't they amazing, these 'men'? And so many of them! It's raining bloody men! Let me tell you about a few others . . .

6

After my A levels I got a job selling insurance at Scottish Amicable in Manchester where every day I was convulsed by psychosomatic illness. But the job was useful because it enabled me to pay for all the drugs which my boyfriend and his friends liked to take.

'What are you talking about? What are you *on*?' my mother asked one day across the kitchen table.

'Ecstasy!' I beamed, happy to inform.

It was 1989 in Manchester and, had I but known it, my boyfriend was very cool. I had seduced him by the length of my jumper. I hadn't seen my own hands in eighteen months. He was a musician called Mark who looked a bit like Peter Firth in

Letter to Brezhnev, I thought, and I adored him. I loved him. There was nothing else. But when he suggested that we should go to bed together, I was baffled. It was as if he had suggested that we move to South America, or that we weren't English at all, but French. Or aliens. A bizarre and totally irrelevant suggestion. Sex was abstract and ever present but it never actually *happened*. Like maths. I was horrified by the voice-over on Betty Blue which insisted that the principals had been 'screwing for a week'.

'*Screwing* for a week! *Screwing! Screwing? Screw-ing!* Skerr*eww*-ing! For a *week*? Can you imagine?'

'Yes,' said Mark.

I would roll around the floor of the Hacienda in a three-hundred-person embrace while Mark talked record deals with an old man who used to hang around called Tony Wilson. 'Very pleased to meet you, Shaun. You too, Manni,' I would say at five o'clock in the morning out of my tree on ecstasy and speed before removing Mark's hand from my thigh. Just what kind of girl did he think I was? What was he *on*?

Eventually, I acceded to Mark's request. 'Tonight, on the 12th December 1989, I, Antonia Quirke, became a woman,' I thought tremulously to myself. Or had I? A couple of days later I thought: 'Tonight, on the 14th December 1989, I, Antonia Quirke, almost certainly became a woman.' The day after that I thought: 'Bloody hell. *Bloody hell!*' and proudly munched my way through half a packet of Anadin. I was immensely lucky to have Mark as my first boyfriend. My first love. He had great talent as a musician and the dedication to back it up. He was as sincere and grave as any prince in an Oscar Wilde fairy story and bought me a ring whose inscription, *love you baby blue*, obliquely thanked Beatrice Dalle for her help in binding us together. In his blue and serious gaze I was wide open. I was invisible, I had no secrets to conceal. That's young love. Not because it's the first time but simply because you are young, before Life thins into that pointed little thing, A Life. Before time turns your life into a one-woman show.

On the strength of my convalescence-assisted A levels, I got a place at UCL to read English, which gave Scottish Amicable the excuse to sack me they had long been looking for. As I descended in the lift from the fourteenth floor for the last time, the nausea and palsy which had gripped me for a year unclenched themselves floor by floor until I arrived at reception and walked out into Piccadilly a new person. The only truly strange thing that has ever happened to me. It was like I'd been sacked into reality. Everything around me suddenly came into its full life. The traffic sounded out, the shadows of sandstone buildings on dusty concrete became delicately blue, sunlit Georgian granite sprang into heat, the Pennines showed up, windy and bright and in focus thirty miles away, and I felt for the first time, in the nicest way, like I was on my own. I have never felt more well than I did at that moment. In this lofty mood I was reluctant to take money off my parents for university and told them that I had won a 'special grant' to cover my costs in London, which I hadn't. I wanted to do it on my own, like Melanie Griffith in Working Girl. The afternoon I arrived I managed to get a job at Habitat on Tottenham Court Road for six days a week, and at a pub in the evenings, leaving me absolutely no time for lectures or tutorials, but I reckoned I could work around this if I chose only those courses where you don't have to do any thinking (like Phonetics) and stole all the books I needed from the Waterstone's on Gower Street.

'How's college?' my father would ask at Christmas and Easter, then at the Christmas and Easter after that, and I'd think: *Don't ask me.*

But I couldn't go back. Midway through my first year, Mark's band had got to Number 3 in the charts with a dance hit that went 'If there ain't no love then there ain't no use'. When they went on Top of the Pops I stood at the back of the studio smiling a false smile with the other girlfriends and watched him on stage working his keyboard as soothingly as if he were peeling an apple, knowing like you know there are dead flies in the cutlery drawer that I was not built to be a popstar's girlfriend, with girlfriendly skills. While I could hardly grasp the idea that something as infinite and boundless as he and I could have an end, I knew that knowing that meant that somewhere it had already ended. Lessons, by definition, are always too late. In the furniture department at Habitat I listened to couples arguing on sofas with their eyes squeezed tightly shut in frustration and watched the streams of students pass the windows, wondering how to enter their lives.

One day I was walking from Maple Street down to Oxford Circus to buy strawberries from the stall that used to trade outside the chapel on Tottenham Court Road when I realised that a man had been following me for the past ten minutes, so I turned on him and demanded an explanation. He had a red flick like Eric Stoltz in Some Kind of Wonderful.

'How else am I going to meet you if I don't follow you?' he said.

I simply could not discover the flaw in this logic. I was so completely stumped for an answer that I went home with him to his flat near Russell Square where his flatmate shared his bed as if this were a *ménage à presque trois*. The thing about being innocent is that you can never be quite sure what constitutes seediness and what doesn't. I thought: Russell Square! This is where Ted Hughes used to live when he was first going out with Sylvia Plath! It seemed to open the city for me, unlock the

British Museum, and all the print shops on Coptic Street, and the tall white sycamore-shaded houses of Bloomsbury, and the pale yellow Peabody Trust flats blooming among them, and the little square off High Holborn with its bronze of Gandhi sitting cross-legged; and beyond, all the pubs on Theobalds Road outside which young lawyers in their first suits anxiously smoked, looking pressed for time, and then the Regency terraces of the Gray's Inn Road and the flops of Euston. I had been asked home by somebody and – lo and behold, so to speak – I was home. London. So I kept going home with people. And Mark turned up one day to find he had been deceived. It was the usual sad end to first love. You don't leave them for anyone, you leave them for everyone, and it was as messy as hell. The violence of breaking up was infinitely more surprising and disorientating than losing one's virginity. Mark floored it down the M6 to splinter my door, but somewhere under my own hysterics I was reassured that love was all it was cracked up to be. Telling you this makes me feel old, but it's true.

In my third year an American entered the Man in the Moon in Camden where I worked and told me that he was looking for a place to live. 'I've run into some trouble back home,' he said in a Texan accent. He was the first American I had ever met and seemed almost supernaturally exotic. I brought him home in much the way that Elliot brings home ET.

'Who is he?' my flatmate Susie said.

'He's an American!'

'But *who is he?*'

'He's an *American!*'

When I got home from the pub, I would get into bed with Wilson and ask about his life in Salado, Texas. His voice was a McConaugheyan velvet coat. He wasn't a man, I now saw. He was just a kid like me. A handsome Texan boy with a twist of a harelip that turned my heart over. In the mornings he would physically open my eyes to wake me. He got a job as a binman and started bringing back gifts for me from work, like out-of-date pancake mix. So I made out-of-date pancakes, and delicious they were too. But I didn't know what to do with the other salvage, like the little wheels off discarded roller-skates: I cleaned and polished them and put them on the mantelpiece as one might arrange an exhibition of totems of a collapsed society. I couldn't understand why he cried so much through-out that autumn until he eventually told me about his trouble back home. He had shot a man dead for two hundred dollars: 'I didn't think it meant I would never be able to go back,' he said. It was so dark I couldn't see his face.

'After I did it, I went up and looked at the body, even though they'd told me not to. He had this small tattoo on his arm. Of a Swiss chalet.'

If it was just acting, it was just acting. And if it were true, then he couldn't be any more unhappy than he already was. The city closed in, black and orange at four o'clock, a world of buses wheezing through puddles, a world covered in leaf mulch or car-shit which seemed as bleary and smeared as if you were seeing it through an uncleanable windscreen, the conditions of life such that you could do nothing but shrivel under them, never quite clean, never quite dry, and all scrawled over with an illegible graffiti of fear, about money, for Wilson, and of guilt about Mark, who had burned everything I had given him in the front garden of my parents' house. Being sacked from both Habitat and the Man in the Moon allowed me to get a job in a travel agency where the more regular hours let me make it home to Wilson before his binman's bedtime. He feared sheep and had to be reassured of their absence from Hampstead Heath.

'Sheep'll watch ya,' he said. 'It'll always watch ya, like it watches everything.'

Bonfire Night shook him something terrible. The smell of the fires in the parks around Muswell Hill, the blackened sparklers on the pavements, the bins full of charred fireworks and ash, the way it seemed to extend for a month of random bangs and shrieks – a season of *burning* – threw him into prayer. He knelt at the foot of the bed in the posture of the child on the bookmark I had received at my First Holy Communion and gave himself up to a terror of hellfire, craving God's forgiveness. It stunned me. I wanted him to leave, to get away from me, but I knew that I would pay if I asked him to go. I loved him. Yet I had no margin. I envied God the many mansions of His house. It was easy for Him to forgive and accommodate Wilson, yet He never would. At the end of every day, Wilson opened the curtains and looked up at the starless winter sky, and actually – *out loud* – thanked his lucky stars that he'd found me. I betrayed him then by wishing him away, much worse than I had ever betrayed Mark. I was learning another lesson – that not everybody grew up accustomed to love, and those that hadn't couldn't defend themselves from those that had. But Wilson was a ship going down in a black and cold city, and I wanted only to escape the vortex of his sinking.

By February, he had stopped talking entirely, merely dribbling a yo-yo up and down for hours on end. At the travel agent's I sold round-the-world tickets to students in my year who looked at me like they recognised me but weren't quite sure how. It made me feel like a ghost. By April, Wilson started to talk again and told the Anabaptists in whose basement off the Archway Road we lived that he was a professional gigolo. They wanted us out. Doing my exams was like writing cheques

I knew were going to bounce. On a spring day, while I was basing my Chaucer paper around the one couplet I could remember – 'And as thou art a fightul lord and juge / Ne yeve us neither mercy ne refuge' – Wilson had a fight with one of the Anabaptists and cleared out for good, leaving his passport behind in the pocket of his one good winter coat.

7

The single greatest performance by a British actor in the 1990s was by David Thewlis in Mike Leigh's Naked, as (say the following very fast from the back of your nose, like John Lennon) *a cheeky fucking manky Mancy monkeh called Johnny, a hyper-articulate autodidact ignoramus – are you following me, love? – who flees the north and ends up dropping off the radar enfuckingtirely in London, because it's just such a great warm welcoming fucking carnival out on the streets in the Big Shitty, knoworrimean, that he practically perishes from stuffing himself with the free poxy fucking marzipan the pearly kings and queens are giving out, are you with me, love? Peachy fucking creamy.*

Johnny talks like this all the time. He takes a linguaphiliac delight in polysyllables and goes at everyone like a razorblade with his half-baked conspiracy theories and his patchy under-standing of Nostradamus and the Book of Revelation and Chaos Theory – a performance which is *forensically* accurate about a certain type of smart-arse Mancunian educated at a time when comprehensives still did The Odyssey and Paradise Lost. I *knew* this Johnny. I had met about *six* of him. Undefeat-able in argument, destructive, self-destructive, too clever by three-quarters, both frightening and irresistible to women. And Thewlis's creation was a note-perfect capturing of a type no one had ever captured before, a type whose essence was that you could never capture him, whose whole *raison d'être* was to evade capture. This was *news*, a new species for the zoo, grabbed from the world so gleaming and fresh that the rest of the film and indeed the rest of Mike Leigh's work – which we all regarded as the acme of realism – looked like a cartoon.

Thewlis's Johnny has those beautiful wrist-bones which you want to grab to stop his even more beautiful hands from slapping you. His voice quarries out every bit of music contained in the Manchester accent. The mouth beneath the ratty overbite is incapable of anything but sarcasm or supersincerity. That fast, straight-backed walk, like a cursor gliding along a line, looks like the walk of someone walking out on you. And all of these – hands, voice, mouth, walk – are fuelled by that peculiar youthful delusion: integrity. Only when you're young are you so hounded and harried by the fear of being fake, as if a single lie will curse you forever. The God of Integrity wants you to keep running, to never do anything twice, to worship the present tense, to reject comfort as a Siren. He is a cold god who would only really be happy if everyone were on their own, and only the young dream of him. But Thewlis is ten years older than Holden Caulfield, and Johnny is ten years deeper into hell, drowning in north London, in Bounds Green and Southgate and Edmonton, among those tall houses whose white stucco looks like icing in a Richard Curtis movie and like armour plating in Naked. It wasn't wishable-away, this performance, like Travis Bickle in Taxi Driver. Thewlis turned the film into a horror flick for the lower middle classes. He scared the living daylights out of me.

8

Two days before the end of my final term, I was stopped by a Modern English Language tutor on the stairs of the department after finding I had failed my degree. He asked, a little hurt, why I had never been to one of his lectures in three years or, indeed, to anyone's lectures or classes whatsoever.

'Is it drugs?'

'Well, no. I just haven't washed my hair for a while. I've been a bit all over the place.'

'You're sure it's not drugs? It's *always* drugs. Sure? Well, why didn't you come and see me? Everyone else does – the place is swimming in doctors' notes. It's exams.'

I figured what the hell and told him everything, including how I'd been sacked from the travel agent's for absent-mindedly selling forty tickets to Glastonbury on a coach that didn't exist, and he looked at me, still very kindly, and said that if I'd come and told him about all this a month ago he could probably have bumped me up to a Pass, though some of my papers had been truly terrible, he said, really, for shame. 'You just wrote "no time to finish!" at the bottom of all these blank pages.'

Through the window of his room, where he had ushered me, you couldn't quite see the Waterstone's where I had stolen the books. I told him about that too. He nodded and said nothing, leaning forward in his chair with his hands latticed on his knees, occasionally unfolding them to hand me a tissue and looking down at my feet, dirty in their sandals, so that I could cry unwatched.

'It's too late to do anything about all the paperbacks. But

since you've clearly never opened the textbooks, you can simply put them back, can't you?' he said, as gently as Denholm Elliott chiding Helena Bonham Carter to be a better person in A Room with a View. 'What are you planning on doing now? Isn't there anything you're interested in doing? Something you particularly like?'

I couldn't stop crying long enough to reply. Where was Wilson? Who was going to protect him?

'Nothing you like? Nothing you love doing?'

'I like the movies . . .' I said, uselessly.

He asked if I'd be interested in a work placement on a local paper where he knew the deputy editor. I said I didn't think I'd make a very good journalist, but he looked so pained I immediately changed tack and agreed, putting on a face that I hoped suggested I was worthy of redemption. Later that week I did what he advised about the books, like a tooth fairy – one that leaves Bauer's Grammatical and Lexical Variance in a heavy bag by the lift. As I made my way out of the shop, an assistant pursued me with the bag.

'But I don't want it!' I said.

'Well, neither do we, to be honest. We have trouble *giving* this stuff away in the holidays.'

So I went round to Foyles and left it there instead.

9

From the top, then. Very, very fine, dry blond hair which conforms to the shape of his head and, as he has aged, looks like a wig or the helmet-like hair you clip onto a Lego man. Good hair for a David Lynch. A forehead which is still miraculously smooth, the skin very tight to it, the bone very tangible, the first great curve of his head a section of a sphere. His whole face is full of spheres. The eyebrows are faint and fall away. The bridge of the nose is where there has been an impact of pain. There are two, not deep, vertical lines which, taken with the declining eyebrows, make him look harrowed. The curve of the eyeballs is very visible under his eyelids – his face has started to become beautiful. And unusual. He cannot seem to open his eyes very wide, as if the eyelids have too far to travel back up the curve of the eyeballs. The eyes themselves are ethnically unplaceable, a speckled pale blue. Under them are deep pre-Raphaelite shadows (which in time have become real pouches). These shadows are immensely beautiful. And now you begin to see just how exquisite the face is. The nose is incredibly fine and straight, a nose which ladies in Beverly Hills might pick from a catalogue. The ears are sleek to his head: he looks like a bird. In the hollows beneath the cheekbones, like ripples playing on the underside of a bridge, lines of beauty continually form and reform. Everything about the face keeps getting finer – you feel you could crush his bones like a sparrow's bones. The outline of the lips is as sharp as the outline of a baby's lips. The cut in his top lip is like the V of a child-drawn seagull. There is a gap between his teeth which adds to the general feeling of sickness – again, you notice how beauty and sickness are bound together here in this pre-Raphaelite way. The lips are red, like the lips in a Tennyson horror poem. They might be poisonous. Take the head in your hands and turn it to a three-quarter profile. It's heart-shaped, and the line that runs from his forehead to his sharp chin, full of double curves, is the most beautiful thing you have *ever* seen. You're at a loss to say why – it's explicable by mathematics, no doubt – but that line looks like the definition of beauty. And everything is amazingly smooth and golden. A sick beauty, made of gold. The *most* beautiful: Christopher Walken.

10

My mother was confused about what I should wear on the first day of my work placement at the Camden New Journal, torn between recommending a formal skirt and blouse and actually wanting me to wear the uniform of, say, Alan Dershowitz's elaborately casual team of legal students in Reversal of Fortune. 'It's time to get your shit together,' she said down the phone, pleased, because she believed that working at a local paper meant that I was in effect working against the system. 'It's your job to get the truth out there!' she reminded me. 'It's your job to sniff out the truth!'

Propriety won out, so I wore low blue court shoes, a white blouse with a sweetheart bow, carried a neat handbag, and was very nervous on the way to work. It is important to communicate the extent of my ignorance. Getting on the bus, I looked at the change in my hand and thought: *What is money? What do banks do?* Seeing the headline on someone's newspaper, I thought: *What's the Cabinet, exactly? I know they're Major's advisors, but are they actually MPs?*

Inside the Camden New Journal – and there was no one to stop me from walking on in, no one around very much at all – was a room with grey walls and no discernible floor, just layers of newspapers and food wrappers, cake boxes, sandwich cartons, cigarette sleeves, flattened Cup-a-Soups. There were several desks constructed out of piles of back editions on which cigarettes had been left to burn out: the desks were singed but had never ignited because the newspapers were damp. The room was a *shrine* to the cigarette. All around were styrofoam cups hedgehogged with butts, and the three-bar electric heater was encrusted with bits of charcoaled tobacco and frazzled stands of hair where people had stooped down to spark up. Through the frosted glass of a raised office I could make out someone sitting low in their chair with their head back, not moving. Asleep? The only other person in the room was a man of around forty with a floor-length yellow coat talking into the phone in a Liverpudlian accent under a poster of Ivor Cutler. He beckoned me over.

He was the ugliest man I had ever seen. He had fine wavy reddish-brown hair which curled beneath a long pointed chin. His pale skin was covered in sore-looking freckles and from his cracked lips dangled a dead roll-up. He looked like a fox in the late stages of heroin addiction, or someone kicked off the set of The Name of the Rose for being too credibly medieval. *He looked like David Thewlis.* Cradling the phone, he plopped the roll-up in a carton of milk, and smirked at my handbag.

'Got everything you need in there? Got all your little pencils?'

He *talked* like David Thewlis. He rolled his chair to the side of his desk and sat back in it unashamedly – his shiny green trousers unfashionably high, tight into his crotch like jester's pants, squashing his cock up and tight to the side – and relished my shoes.

'Oooh, how smashing – a lovely little pair of Start-rites!' he said. 'I'm Jim Hewson, the deputy editor – we spoke on the phone. And now here you are.'

There I was. On the lapel of his yellow coat was a little badge that said 'Touch My Monkey'.

'Bring your little pencils. We're going out.'

He took me first to a pub and then down to Kentish Town police station, where he heckled the officer giving a statement about a head being found in Regent's Canal. I was already very drunk and confused and became extremely paranoid when he started to goad the police about being in league with the local gangs. The police clearly hated him. There was bitterness and fear in that room.

'Still trying to get arrested, are you, Jim?' the officer threatened. 'And you, Miss "Quirke". You trying to get arrested now too?'

'You're not going to arrest us, we're white,' Jim sneered.

After that he walked me down to a pub in Holborn, striding for miles like a peacock while I ran to keep up, my feet blistering in my court shoes. The Princess Louise behind Gray's Inn was where Jim liked to dig his stories out of the local councillors who drank there after meetings. Again there was a little pulse of fear at his presence, disguised under uneasy bonhomie. When I got back from peeling off my bloodied tights in the loo, he was smilingly scoffing at a councillor: 'You're fucking her, aren't you? That's why this is happening. He's fucking her. You *dirty* man. What happened to your tights?'

On the way back to Camden we stopped at yet another pub where he drank his dozenth double of the afternoon and regarded the jukebox selections with the stalest disgust: 'Why the fuck do I ever drink in here when all they've got to listen to is Freddie Mercury and his harem of stockbrokers?'

I could not reply because I fancied him too much even to open my mouth.

11

Jim was a communist. Everyone at the Journal was a communist. But Jim would never agree with the other communists, which seemed to make him immensely popular among them. People would come round and get sidetracked into spending long, hero-worshipping hours by his desk while he was unbelievably rude about them to their faces. Among these people were a group called the Chartists whom Eric Gordon, the editor, expected every Friday for a serious discussion involving the whole office. Eric was a communist too and had travelled to China as a journalist in the 1960s to help out with the Cultural Revolution. When he had objected to what he was seeing, the authorities had put him and his wife and child under house arrest. For five years. In a room that measured ten feet by twelve. And he was *still* a communist.

On Fridays when the big hitters rolled up, everyone was expected to contribute. Jim, whose hair seen closer up now seemed the colour of curry powder, would dazzle the room while Eric listened through the frosted glass to his protégé, too knowledgeable and wise to condescend to mere pyrotechnics. These were terribly detailed, recondite conversations as abstruse as the discussions on scripture during which I had been equally silent throughout my childhood. There was still the vexed issue of the Twentieth Party Congress. There was serious present business to do with Central America. There was the question of getting Stalin's twenty million victims down to something more manageable, like twelve million. There was *always* 1917 and Trotsky. While Jim waltzed through the upper echelons of theory and practice, I kept my head down and watched his elegant freckled fingers draw their merciless distinctions. Only once did I ever score a success, when the subject had moved to the First World War.

'I don't know, but John Reed always seemed right to me,' I said. 'The First World War was about prophets.'

Jim, who was not to know that I was only aware of this because I was a fan of Reds, flashed me a vulpine grin which sent me floating up Parkway that evening eight feet off the ground. I had won a smile from a man who knew how to repair the flaws in dialectical materialism.

12

Not Reds for Warren *Beatty* – what kind of book do you think this is? For Jack Nicholson! Warren *Beatty* . . . The man with the loveliest, slowest pulse in cinema versus an actor who is forever trying to hoodwink you that his heartbeat is faster than it actually is. The guy who always acts less handsome than he is versus the preener: you're always mentally cleaning up Nicholson's face and mentally trying to ruffle Beatty's. The vulnerable versus the unhurtable. The living versus the dead. Nicholson is the greatest actor since, let's say, the time between the Beatles' ninth LP and the birth of Zinedine Zidane, whose work is founded on a sense of humour. They're not terribly funny, those geniuses whose names end in 'o', are they? Here are ten more words to kill any smile – Sean Penn, Kevin Spacey, Dustin Hoffman, Edward Norton, Gary Oldman. Serious business, great acting. Nicholson plays a small role in Reds as the playwright Eugene O'Neill being manipulated by

Beatty's lover Diane Keaton into thinking he's seducing her. It's all rather sad and Chekhovian. She tells him that Beatty has gone away, leaving her to get on with her own things here in this beach house on Long Island.

'What are they?' he asks.

'What?' says Keaton.

'The things that you have. That are yours. What are they?'

– this in his Nicholsonian way, turning over every word, holding it up to the light, inspecting it, and then judiciously pondering whether to place it, with great delicacy, in the world or just to, what the hell, smash it.

'If you were mine,' he goes on, 'it would just be you and me. And it would feel a lot more like love than being left alone with your work.'

By this time you're pretty much rolling around on the floor clutching your ribs and screaming *stop! stop!* though there is nothing ostensibly there in his delivery except O'Neill's love, his courage in declaring himself, and the glimmer of an accusation against Keaton's way of life with Beatty.

But you're killing yourself, because everything Nicholson says is given its sense by how near or how far it is from the pure delight that makes up his soul. Not sniggering mischief, as people always say of him – *delight*. It's what makes him so tragicomic. Nothing he says isn't a fuse burning towards some dynamite-pile of hilarity. And he makes brilliant use of its absence, sparingly, and devastatingly, like in the two scenes in Five Easy Pieces (his best film) when he walks out on Karen Black. You think: *My God, where's it gone?* He reminds you of just how much you've got to lose, of how high the stakes are. Everything he does in his early films is to do with the frustration of this delight. You've got to be a comedian to be a tragicomedian. He'd be brilliant in Chekhov. Brilliant as

Astrov in Uncle Vanya, the still-not-disillusioned doctor not a million miles from his not-quite-yet-disillusioned pianist in Five Easy Pieces.

It's so *close*, this delight. All you have to do is laugh and the world will be full of it. And in his early films Nicholson keeps trying to tickle the world and failing to make it laugh. Meanwhile, *we're* laughing our heads off. Even to know that delight, in a perfect world, would be the proper response to life is a simplicity beyond most of us. It's not something that any of those other great actors mentioned above seem to have worked out. Do you know how rare this is? This innocence? Why you keep thinking Jack is a boy? It makes him one in a million. It makes him able to tell the story of the loss of innocence which *nobody*, only great artists, can do. What an absolute privilege to watch the young Jack liven up Easy Rider (he's the only utopian in it!) and talk you through the fall in Five Easy Pieces and tell you what you're leaving behind in The Last Detail. Amazing, amazing. It's the heart of Nicholson – that his essential self remembers innocence, remembers, no matter how scuffed, a prelapsarian world. And that's why the revered and lauded three-time Oscar winner is very, very underrated. Yes, *you heard me*! Jack Nicholson is underrated.

13

10 October 1993
The elephants, who have not been getting on with the new rhino, slept through the exhibition which was being held in the

elephant house at the zoo last
night (Monday) by an Israeli
artist who arrived in the country
only yesterday (Monday) before
returning to Tel Aviv tomorrow
(Wednesday).

'No wonder you failed your fucking degree,' Jim said.
'Nobody cares when the artist is going back or what the rhino
thinks. You want to know who was there and how long it's
on for. See?'

'Got it. Except – what's wrong with the rhino exactly?' I
wanted to keep him talking.

'Even if the rhino's doing the elephant's wife, we don't want
to read about it. That's not the fucking story. You've got to *find
the story.*'

But I never could – two-hundred-word pieces unstoppably
ballooned, like Rufus Sewell, into vast paunchy monsters,
and then were brutally slimmed down again (like Rufus Sewell)
by brisk sub-editors. And the Journal, for all its apparent slap-
dashness, was a very serious little operation, with a sinecure
on the Local Newspaper of the Year Award. Eric knew what
he was doing, always running the necessary campaigns and
magnificently inclusive little obituaries of local burglars and
tramps. So I was aware that it was something of a test when
he sent me to talk to a woman who was staging a protest in
Arlington Road about the poll tax. It was an important story
and I had a sense that I might actually be sacked, and never see
Jim again, if I couldn't find it.

'Where the fuck have you been?' said Jim when I returned
five hours later.

'I think Mrs Norman's a bit paranoid,' I said. 'She thinks the
FBI are watching her. But – it's actually quite interesting. There

were two guys in a dark car watching the house the whole time I was there. Wearing *ties*. In this weather? It does seem a little strange. And get this – she keeps getting letters from the library asking her to return a book on J. Edgar Hoover. *But she never took it out.* So I wrote down the licence number in case you want to follow it up.'

I was demoted to theatre reviews.

14

'What's the date, the first?'

'Look at the paper. Oh, no, wait, of course it's the first – it was Halloween last night. What's the matter?'

'River Phoenix is dead. It looks like an overdose.'

'Poor kid. Deliberate or accidental? Bet it was coke. Coke and booze. Bet it's a John Bonham. What's the matter with *you*?'

What's the matter with me? Nothing. There was nothing to show that he was ever going to be great. In fact, you could pretty much guarantee that he wouldn't have been. But he wasn't Andrew McCarthy Jnr, or Ralph Macchio, or C. Thomas Howell either. He wasn't Björn Andrésen, the vision from Death in Venice, who was never going to be an actor. On the other hand, he wasn't Jean-Pierre Léaud. But he broke your heart. He was weak and soft and seemingly always in tears. In Running on Empty, a pretty good film which he made at the age of seventeen in 1988, he was the sort of teen dream that sends girls sobbing to their bedrooms, and yet there was nothing confected about him. He plays the son of parents on the run from the FBI, so he has to keep moving from town to town, leaving his friends and first girlfriends behind. It's an amazingly immature performance for one of his age, as they never say. It's so not mature. It's brilliant. When my little sister watched Titanic she was inconsolable for weeks. 'There's no one like Jack!' she would wail and I'd think *yeah, kid, that's right. There* is *no one like Jack. They just made him up for money.* But there is someone like River Phoenix, sweetheart. Phoenix is an open wound in Running on Empty, with clumsy hands and an uneasiness with his own new beauty (he'd been a chubby kid – Stand By Me), and a bloom of puberty still on his cheekbones. Large stretches of his performance look like perfect honesty, too natural to call naturalism. He *was* Romeo, and no one can ever get Romeo right, because by the time you've cast him the actor's got too old. Running on Empty isn't a good performance by an unfortunately doomed actor. It's a true moment caught in time. The moment when you feel more than you ever have or ever will again: the Romeo moment. *There he was.* And you can't pay an actor a higher compliment than that. He broke your heart. And the date was 31st October 1993.

15

On Mondays he would go down to the police station and then the Princess Louise, coming back late and maybe even sleeping in the office. On Tuesdays he would usually go down to Paddington Green CID to get stories there and spend the evening at a public meeting. On Wednesdays he was busy putting the paper to bed. Thursdays and Fridays – that was my chance. The long, long weekends he disappeared. If you'd have been there, you'd have wanted to be his friend or his lover, if only to turn his fire outwards from you. Jim was the first principled man I had ever met, my father apart, sardonic and fearless like Sydney Carton. He was the first *man* I had ever met. But I hardly ever saw him now, and had no real reasons to engage him in conversation. So I became more besotted. The sentence 'Jim's putting the paper to bed' could incapacitate me for an hour. Yet he was as oblivious of me as an actor on a screen, and one always falls for those who cannot return your gaze, the blithe, the unaware, the one across the lawn.

In the single-figure audiences at the pub theatres where I was sent to review plays and where the actors could detect my gaze, I yearned for Jim and for the remove of the big screen, where actors moved in innocence of my eyes. My first plan was to impress him with the commitment of my reviews. I found out a lot of statistics and waved them at him like breasts at the pub on Thursday.

'Did you know that there are 38,000 members of Equity, and at any one time only 13,400 are actually in work? It's *shocking*.'

'In what way shocking?'

'It's union-bashing, isn't it? Listen, these are *working people.* If there are fifty fringe theatres in London and they've got a cast of, let's say, an average of six per play, then that's, uh, 300 people, and if the Equity minimum is £85 a week, then that's 300 people living on a pittance. Eighty-five pounds a week!'

'That's more than twice what you earn, love.'

My other plan was simply to write such astonishingly unforgettable reviews – reviews you could poke your eye out on – that notice would simply have to be paid. They were skull-crackingly bad. But they *looked* quite good. About a monologue on Virginia Woolf I wrote: '"I am mad! I hear voices! Not only that, I write them down!" That is, I suggest, what the character wanted to say. But where in all of this is our delicious wine? Our great little knitter?' The worse the plays the more free I felt to woo Jim with this unique voice. And so it became a kind of competition. The more terrible the plays were the more terrible the reviews were. It was a contest of terribility. I wafted my pen around like Isadora Duncan, desperate for a glance from him. And one day he did call me over.

'Listen, Sally. You've got to stop writing these reviews or Eric's going to sack you. And if he does that, you're fucked.'

I could feel the wind from Naked tugging at me, trying to tear me off London and suck me up the Archway Road towards the motorway and the oubliettes of the North. I also thought: *He's noticed me.* I wanted him. I even want him now, as I write, a painful need, never since matched, to touch him, though he was like a jagged piece of corrugated iron which would cut you no matter how you held it.

16

Glyn Maxwell has written some fine poetry and some bewilderingly wonky plays, but when Jim found out that there would be free drinks after a production of a new Maxwell play at the Battersea Arts Centre he decided to tag along. As we were leaving the paper an ad-boy laughed at the idea of Battersea.

'Your drinking's changed, mate,' he said to Jim.

'It's not my drinking that's changed. It's your non-drinking. You might have stopped; I'm just carrying on as normal.'

At the interval Jim said he was going to leave and I tailed

after him to the box office where he was demanding his money back and the girl was refusing to give the refund. He loomed over her like one of the inquisitors in Dreyer's film of Joan of Arc.

'I can only refund you if you found it offensive in some way,' she said.

'I found it offensive in every way. It was shit.'

'I can't refund you for that. Did you think it was sexist?'

'No, it was just fucking terrible, and I'm going now and I would like my money back.'

'Did you think it demeaned any minority group?' the girl said. She was trying to open a pathway to a compromise. 'Did it offend you racially?'

'It offended the entire fucking human race. Is that good enough?'

Jim's aggressiveness felt to me like something from an earlier time, when people were rougher and less touchy, when less offence was taken and given, when people were less proud of the masks that they wore. It seemed that Jim's aggressiveness almost relieved him of the burden of goodness – it *was* his good manners, doing you the courtesy of withholding nothing. Or perhaps I was making excuses for him. As he sailed down Lavender Hill in his yellow coat, leaving his disdained wake behind him, I hurried after, raising my voice to ask if this behaviour usually got him anywhere with women.

'Yeah, lots – some fantastic ones, actually. Sometimes they let me fuck them. But usually they just want to tell me about their suicide attempts.'

What a horrible man! He crouched down to do up a shoelace and, since he was briefly my height, with his tongue half out of his mouth in a bite of concentration, I stepped forward and put my mouth around it.

17

And this was brave. This was acting. It sometimes seems as if a romantic history is the history of the removal of the need for courage. As you get older, you only need it for leaving. And even the braver of us – among whom I do not number myself – only use our courage two or three times in a life. It takes too much out of you, until you don't have enough to lose really to call it courage any more rather than heedlessness. So I stepped forward and lost my courage virginity. I would have two or three more to lose only. He reorganised his mouth and kissed me back as he straightened up.

And when we went back to his flat at the top of a tower block by Mornington Crescent, I was bouncing around like Zebedee, not only in the delight of possession but in the joy of having created it all myself. *I did this!* I thought as his puritanical flat revealed itself to me. *I made this!*, and this, and this hair, really the colour of rust right up close, and the taste of it too, and these collarbones and these elbows, and these ribs, and these grooves between his belly and his hip-bones, and even these jokes he's cracking causing me to look momentarily up, and these thighs and long shins – all of it magicked up by my courage. Anything I did, like this, and this, and that, and that again, I had brought into being!

Love runs through you and uses you as a device to get what it wants, and when you're in love you're simply keeping pace with it for a moment, briefly allowed to lope along at the front where everything that comes into view is new.

18

Let's get something straight. The most embarrassing film to like, if you're English, is Withnail and I, Bruce Robinson's failed-actor comedy with Richard E. Grant and Paul McGann. Even the BFI Classic on Withnail begins with much blushing and a statement that to admit to a liking for the film is to declare oneself unfit for adult company. Let's get another thing straight. If Kind Hearts and Coronets is not the funniest British film ever made, it's Withnail. If Kes is not the most touching British film ever made, it's Withnail. No film at all is as *loved* as Withnail, and if your hatred of students extends to dismissing that love then you're probably someone whose response to films stops at something like 'intense admiration'. In fact, bugger Kind Hearts and Coronets, it *is* the funniest film in English. It's also a better film about the sixties than something like Blow-Up and, very indirectly (it's a subtle movie), an exceptional film about homosexuality.

The model for Withnail was a failed actor called Vivian MacKerrell whom Robinson knew. But Robinson is a failed actor too. He had parts in Zeffirelli's Romeo and Juliet and other bits and pieces before turning up, extraordinarily handsome, as the object of Isabelle Adjani's *amour fou* in Truffaut's The Story of Adele H. (great movie!). He's pretty good. He's really very good. All he gets to do is simply be there while Adjani's wave breaks over him. You'd have to see it, if you haven't already. But after that Robinson's phone wouldn't ring. So he became a writer and did The Killing Fields before Withnail and directing. Then he sort of failed as a director. He continues to sort of fail as a writer. Is there any profession in the world with as high a rate of failure as acting? As the movies as a whole? This is a book about successes (apart from me, obviously) and all the actors I mention share a common trait, because being successful *is* a trait – they're all one kind of person, whereas partial success or failure is various.

Why not Bruce Robinson? He had a beautiful wide mouth wittily ironised by the quotation-mark lines around it, enormous cool, even greater charisma, talent (see Adele H.), brains, training (RADA), star quality (if you'll excuse the cobwebs on those words), and he talked, well, the guy talked and still talks like the greatest talker in the English language.

'Vivian was too smart to get a job – an intellectual, erudite man. He'd go to an audition to play a priest, read up all this cackle of theological bollocks and then say, "It's very strange you should be considering me for this part because before I became an actor I was considering the priesthood." And they knew it was nonsense, so he'd never get the job.'

Just one of the quieter bits from a twenty-page interview he did in 1995. Not a great story, but what is that word 'cackle'?

Another bit, reluctantly endorsing capital punishment for rapists of children:

'Dead him, is my view.'

Concerning a Spielberg project about a psychic woman and a child killer, which never got off the ground:

'It's as black as your hat. This woman bounces off the lino of hell.'

The lino of hell? 'Black as your hat' I'm pretty sure is a phrase. But nobody uses it any more. It's remembered or rescued language. What a great phrase anyway, *black as your hat* – I hope it comes back. But 'the lino of hell'? 'Dead him'? A 'cackle' of something? You know who he reminds me of? William Shakespeare, that's who. That's what Shakespeare used to do instinctively, that black as a hat, lino of hell thing. He'd make something up ('the multitudinous seas incarnadine') and then let the groundlings know what he meant ('making the green one red').

I love Bruce Robinson, and all this is merely to remind you of what a great guy he is, this failed actor. Because it's not just the RADA boys who 'only' make a dozen films who are failed actors. It's not just the RADA boys who make no films at all who are failed actors. It's not just the boys who didn't get into RADA but still managed a lot of acting who are failed actors. It's not just the boys who were bloody good in the school play but didn't bother taking it any further who are failed actors. It's not even the boys who were *OK* in the school play but didn't bother taking it any further who are failed actors (like me). It's the boys, that is to say pretty much everyone in the world, who stand in front of the mirror one day, just once, casually, and think *shame I'm no actor*. They're the failed actors too. Most of this planet consists of failed actors.

So the parting scene at the end of Withnail and I, with its dramatisation of the sorting of the successful from the failed, I find as universal as Rick and Ilsa on the tarmac in Casablanca. The 'I' character is moving on, off to Manchester to play the lead in Journey's End. Withnail wants to walk him through Regent's Park to Euston, but it's raining cats and dogs and 'I' would rather have a quick clean break. He refuses the wine which Withnail presses on him and asks him to go back, and Withnail, perhaps realising for the first time that he will never play Hamlet (one of the film's motifs), turns to the wolves of the zoo, those same wolves which gave such comfort to Ted Hughes and his children after their mother killed herself, and gives them 'I have of late, but wherefore I know not . . .' Then he turns back through the rain towards Camden, where, if he looked to the right he'd see Park Crescent, where Robert Donat left his milkman's cart in The Thirty-Nine Steps, and if he turned his head further he'd see the cul-de-sac of St Andrew's Place where Glenda Jackson gave Salome's Last Dance for Ken Russell. And then he'd walk past Chester Terrace where Bette Davis scared the kids in The Nanny and down which Robert Redford would drive in Spy Game: all the successful actors. I is a success. I is saved. I wanted to be I, but Jim was I, I thought.

19

Jeff Sawtell, the film critic of the Journal, was so much of a communist that he wore navy blue Cultural Revolution pyjamas all year round, adding only a scarf in winter. 'If you like your brew in a mug,' he said to my excited inquiry about Four Weddings and a Funeral, 'then it won't be your cup of tea.' One got the impression that Jeff thought Jean-Luc Godard was a lickspittle bourgeois dog. A liver disease was making him progressively weaker, however, and Eric had nowhere else to turn but to me. I was thrilled, a thrill vitiated only by the lingering suspicion I had learned reading Jeff that movie reviewing was a branch of Marxist socio-economic theory.

'Will this do?' I asked Jim, showing him my first ever review, of a Richard Gere movie called Mr Jones.

It read:

> The screen persists in portraying the mentally ill as remarkably gifted on the side. Not only is Mr Jones a virtuoso pianist, he

is also a whizzkid mathemati-
cian and mind-reader. This kind
of publicity does mental health
organizations like MIND no
good whatsoever.

Umbraged social comment, that was the thing. Plus the
MIND charity shop was three doors down from the Journal.
I practically killed myself trying to work out why the incon-
testable Pulp Fiction was somehow despicably pro-capitalist.
Also, you had to write something about *guns* – God knows
what, but something about how a gun was in some way very
similar to a camera. I knew it was in that kind of area. And
there was nobody I could ask at the screening-rooms, where the
atmosphere seemed strangely furtive and even shameful, as
if one were in a municipal library where near-derelicts came
to get out of the cold, and lovingly fold the newspaper into
columns. Always, there would be four or five very old critics
no longer attached, as far as one could see, to any particular
publication, always in macs, always carrying little briefcases as
blazons of busyness, grey and indeterminate as pigeons and
vigilant over their rations of the free chocolate digestives, with
which the pockets of their macs bulged. The husks of critics.

It was only to visit the screening-rooms that I left Jim's bed.
There was the need to earn enough money not to be swallowed
by London; and there was my lover telling me to stick a bottle
of champagne on his tab at Liberties Bar on the High Street
and get my arse round to the twenty-third floor. We didn't
tell anyone at the Journal – although Eric, with his tactful
omniscience, probably knew – and so we were wrapped up as
close together as any adulterers. In bed, Jim always seemed
doubly naked. It was the only place where he was divested of
politics. Restored to his yellow coat, with a bottle of Teacher's,

he was back on: 'Have you ever noticed that the first screen on a cashpoint is actually pleading with you, saying PLEASE INSERT YOUR CARD? Fucking *beseeching* you to spend your money?' And I would attempt to reflect this kind of thing in my reviews of movies like The Little Mermaid.

I came to know the pleasant tattiness of the Soho screening-rooms; the bulk of Philip French of the Observer's trainers, which he wore as though to speed himself breathlessly down Wardour Street from one classic to another. I came to know the little inset ashtrays that still survived like a memory of fifties luxury in the seats' armrests. The yellow cashmere scarf that the Evening Standard's Alexander Walker would wear with its admirable implication that a film deserved the compliment of your having dressed for it. I came to realise that nobody had one of those pens with a light that you always assume movie critics use. And then back through the winter to Jim's flat to wait for him.

He drank all the time. What he was was a 'high-functioning alcoholic', as they say. And even this, even the companionable imperfection of sleeping with someone who's a bit of a mess felt like a freedom, a liberation from the tyranny of physical perfection, so that I came to know him more fully than I would have otherwise. I was happy, and I thought Eric was maybe going to keep me.

'That thing about the First World War you said. About John Reed,' Jim said to me one night. 'Do you really think that?'

'Well, of course. It was all about prophets. People like Lenin, and Trotsky.'

'Sorry, *Lenin*?'

'Well, obviously. But even people like Wilfred Owen, you know. Marcel Duchamp.'

'Profits, Sally. John Reed said the First World War was about *profits.*'

20

Jim wasn't ugly at all, I discovered. Faces are like poems – the longer they take to puzzle out, the better, and Jim's was ungettable. It grew in power and meaning every day I knew him. How did the eyebrows rhyme with the mouth? How did the nose get to the cheek? Men with incoherent faces very often have beautiful hands (as a rule, the reverse applies too – either the hands or the face must be more beautiful, and you rarely get the two together). And Jim had sensationally beautiful hands. The tiny network of cracks in the webbing between his fingers was always grouted with pale skin-dust. They were highly coloured like the flank of a rainbow trout, pink and blue stippled, and had the unconscious elegance of Donald Sutherland's – the Gold Standard of manual beauty (incoherent face – see?). And the hands did beautiful things. What was sarcasm in Jim's mouth was softened to wit in his fingers. Using all five fingers of his left hand simultaneously as bookmarks for different pages of the paper, he would tear articles out in right angles with his other hand. He would seem to describe a simple expressive gesture in the air, and the four locks on his front door would fall open. Oh, beautiful dexterity! James Dean was a show-off with his hands, which were the most muscular parts of him. That's why people couldn't stop taking photographs of him – he was always grabbing attention by fiddling with some prop (bongos, a recorder, a cape, a camera). He was a prestidigitator. A hand magician – that very boyish accomplishment. The early turning point of Rebel Without a Cause is Dean dexterously snatching Buzz's knife in mid-air and there is always the bit in Giant when he's under pressure to sell the land he's inherited on Rock Hudson's ranch.

He's playing with a rope and leaning back in his chair, not focused on the other people in the room. Playing with the rope implies: *I was happiest in the company of myself as a child.* He keeps on playing with the rope, and gets up and walks to the door, still playing, then he flicks it and it forms a knot in mid-air. And although it seems a kind of corrupt, even irrelevant thing to do, so obviously a scene-stealing gesture, you can't help but think: *Jesus, that must be acting.* Or magic. (In the next scene Dean's showing off with his hands again as he sits on the platform of an oil tower, complicatedly putting one hand down between his legs to take all his weight, then transferring the weight to the other hand – like a monkey, little feet, massive sternum, or a gymnast on the rings, with the shakiness of a flower in time lapse. It's not fluent or graceful – it looks like he's demonstrating the resistance of the air, that oppressive weight Dean always seemed to be bowed under. And which his hair strove up against. Hair which looks like a cartoon of dreams of a better world rising from a head.)

21

Even with my new salary of £60 a week, I still felt a bit of an interloper at the screening-rooms. I had never, for instance, been to one of the lunches that were occasionally thrown for visiting directors or stars, until, hurrying out of a screening one day, I overheard someone discussing a lunch that was being held down the road for Oliver Stone to mark the release of Natural Born Killers. Feeling very much that I owed the Journal some *news*, I went along to try and gatecrash.

The party was being held in a private room upstairs from the restaurant. There was lots of sail-bright white linen and untouched fruit juice in iced jugs. Completely on his own, looking plaintive and even a bit lost, sat Mr Stone, so I went over and sat next to him.

'What paper are you from?' he asked, exhaling a plume of blue smoke.

'The Camden New Journal.'

He nodded. 'Is that like the Village Voice?'

'Oh, yes. Very much.'

A tall and extremely beautiful Oriental woman came over and sat next to Stone, with a cigarette which was successfully impersonating her own slenderness.

'Are you with the film?' I asked her.

'No. I'm with Oliver.'

Then Stone began to talk in a very low, slow voice. He didn't really pause at any point so I started to take notes.

'Who are the *real* killers anyway? Is it *really* Mickey and Mallory? Or is it the *media*? And who are the media? It's just another a word for *us*, right? Are *we* the real killers?'

While Stone talked, I wrote down his thoughts in big swirls
and hieroglyphics and loops across pages and pages of notebook. A strange thing had happened. I think I must have been
pretending, to both Stone and myself, that I knew shorthand.
Which I don't. A couple of times he looked down at my notes
and then caught my eye and I returned his puzzled look with a
calm one, reassuring him that this was indeed an obscure but
ingenious system of European notation.

'. . . If you think about it, a camera is just another kind
of gun. They're both machines you shoot things with, yeah?
What I was *trying* to create in NBK was a *thinking man*'s action
film. It's like the anthropologist meeting the so-called "primi-
tive" tribe. They think that when he takes a photograph, he's
actually . . .'

Before I caught the bus back to Camden, I rang the Journal
and told them to pass on the message to Eric that I had an
exclusive interview with Oliver Stone. They were absolutely
bowled over, and literally held the front page for my return. I
would be safe at the paper from now on, I felt. But when I read
back over my notes on the bus, it was like trying to decipher
the markings on the cave walls at Lascaux. All I had was – well,
it wasn't English, anyway, just pages and pages of *drawings*,
which in their own way did seem somehow to capture the
essence of Oliver Stone's conversation. You could have *ex-
hibited* them, maybe, but not published them. They were quite
undecodable. If I showed this notebook to Jim or Eric, having
promised them an exclusive, I would be finished. Inconsolably,
I nibbled the top off one of the mini pizzas I had pilfered from
lunch, trying not to think of the disappointment and even
contempt with which they would greet this fresh foolishness,
and decided to leave the notebook on the bus. But what if they
rang the bus company and got the notebook back, with me all

the while palely cheering from the sidelines, saying things like: 'Oh, thank God'? I dumped it in a bin and prepared myself for a performance of which I was incapable. But it turned out that none of this mattered in the slightest because when I got to the office I found that Jim and Eric had finally had the fight about Jim's drinking which I should have realised had been brewing for years, and that Jim had either been sacked or had walked out – no one could tell – and had gone back to Liverpool. Had gone to his flat and cleared out. Had gone. Gone.

Many years later somebody gave me a poem because they knew how touching I found the end of Withnail and I, though they may not have known why.

> In Camden rain falls heavily
> On elephants and wolves and him in
> The greatcoat. 'Man delights not me,
> Nor woman neither. No, nor women
> Neither.' Nor even wolves. Stop now:
> Make that heartbreaking little bow,
> Reshoulder your rain-loud umbrella
> And drink the last of Monty's cellar –
> One can quite reasonably say
> That you will never play the Dane,
> Chin chin. So so long wolves, the rain
> Was artificial anyway.
> The city's a machine which tries
> Us; sorts the Withnails from the I's.

22

nce upon a time there lived a family of ogres called the Noltes. They were enormous, and even the smallest of them still looked as big as a mountain. He was called Nick. Being so small, Nick felt different from the other ogres, but he also felt different from all the other people he came across, because he was still an ogre. So Nick was never quite sure who he was. Was he big, or small? This was something he thought about all day. He realised he knew a secret – big ogres were also small ogres. After all, Nick was both.

One day when Nick was thirty-five, some men came along and said, 'An ogre! Stand there and look ogre-ish while we film you.' Nick did as he was told. In a very gruff voice he pretended to be a proper ogre like his brothers and uncles were. They made him wear a scuba-diving suit and go under the sea, and people saw the film, which was called The Deep, and said, 'Oh, look, a real ogre!' He had thighs like tree trunks, and a neck like a bull, and a chin like a boulder. He was awfully funny and handsome and looked the very picture of a big happy ogre.

Nick pretended to be a big ogre in lots of films, even though he knew the secret that big ogres were really small ogres. Nobody else knew or cared, but to Nick it was very perplexing, because he saw that all big things were really very small inside, and the rest of the space inside big people and big ogres was filled with sadness, dreadful sadness. Which nobody ever talked about, and they certainly wouldn't believe you if you did!

And Nick was the saddest of them all. How could he tell everybody that he wasn't big at all, but very small and filled with sadness, just like they were? He stretched himself up as high as the sun and then toppled over with an enormous crash. His legs and arms turned into stone, and his ribcage too, and his head turned into a great wooden door. He wasn't an ogre any more, he was just a ruin. But when people went in through the wooden door they were amazed at what they saw! On the walls were four great big pictures, of Nick as a painter, and as a horrible policeman, and a frightened lawyer, and, in another one, as an ogre afraid of his father. But the strange thing about all the pictures was that, in them, Nick was very small. Just about the size of your thumb!

'How sad it is in here,' the people said, standing inside the ruin of Nick. 'There certainly is a lot of empty space inside an ogre!' And then Nick stepped out from behind a candlestick. He was just as big as your thumb. Everybody fell silent, and Nick said, 'See how small I am! *This* is what it's really like inside big ogres.' Everybody was very surprised. So they all went home that night and felt happy because Nick was telling the truth, and the truth always makes people happy. So by telling the truth about ogres, Nick had also got rid of some of the sadness inside the people and everybody was very grateful to him. Nick was the most truthful ogre there had ever been!

And they never forgot those four wonderful pictures. (New York Stories, Q&A, Cape Fear, Affliction.)

23

Jim rang me from Liverpool but whatever had passed between him and Eric had cut deep and he was too proud to come back. 'It's the strangest thing,' he said. 'I keep thinking I see you.' And it was the strangest thing – I didn't keep thinking I saw him, but I did feel like he *was* seeing me, or a ghost of me I had shed and seen on to a northbound train at Euston.

London felt empty. Down none of the fifty-five thousand streets of the city was a long yellow coat moving quickly. Some- where, on one of them, was Wilson, if Wilson was alive. How strange men were, how unanchored, that they contained within them this show-stopping *coup de théâtre*. They could disappear. It was the male miracle, this neat erasure, this tidy and total cancelling, the negative of giving birth. Men had secret powers. They were private in a way that women weren't. They seemed to know something we didn't about voids. They were amazing.

24

This is what I did. I watched films to cheer me up when love had made me unhappy. The oldest problem in the world and the twentieth century's greatest solution to it. Plus this was my job, right? Because Eric had actually run my Oliver Stone interview with its two extremely approximate quotes – the only thing I could accurately remember Stone saying was 'Is the Camden New Journal like the Village Voice?' – I'd been given a slot on Saturdays at a local radio station filling in holes in the programming with film reviews. It seemed to get easier the more I steered clear of relating everything to Engels. Another ten pounds. I was closing in on the Equity minimum wage.

I knuckled down. I tapped the fan and it opened. Not directors – who the hell were they? – but *actors*. Whereas some people might see, say, Women in Love and then go on to The Devils because they're interested in Ken Russell, I would see Women in Love for Alan Bates, and then chase after him in Britannia Hospital, bump into Malcolm McDowell there and follow *him* into If and O, Lucky Man! and then back to Bates in In Celebration, and without even realising it I would have seen most of the cream of Lindsay Anderson. Had you asked me if I'd ever seen any Godard, I'd have said, 'Oh, no no no!', even though I'd seen Breathless, Pierrot le Fou and Une Femme est Une Femme during a Belmondo binge and followed him to Is Paris Burning? where I recognised Glenn Ford among the ruins and hitched myself to him through Gilda and The Courtship of Eddie's Father by Vicente Minnelli and some rather duff westerns to The Big Heat where Lee Marvin throws boiling coffee over Gloria Grahame, and then careered after Marvin in everything (he was always brilliant) until we (Lee and I) tracked down the erotically brainy-looking John Cassavetes in The Killers, which got me to Rosemary's Baby – Christ, he's good in that – and a film called Brass Target which had good old George Kennedy in it playing Patton, who in Cool Hand Luke I sort of preferred to Newman and then in Thunderbolt and Lightfoot I even preferred to Clint, meaning that I could no longer avoid The Dirty Dozen, what with him, Marvin, Cassavetes, Donald Sutherland and Robert *Ryan*, who was so fantastic in Bad Day at Black Rock (with Marvin again!) that I went on a Ryan safari, stalking the wounded beast through

Billy Budd, The Set-Up, Men in War and Crossfire, where the mighty Mitchum loomed, and that was me gone, an acolyte in the Mitchum temple, where one day (Cape Fear) I formed an attachment to a mid-ranking avuncular type I saw around a lot, Martin Balsam, that virtuoso of shirtsleeves, who has in fact appeared in every film ever made apart from Trainspotting and Raise the Red Lantern. Balsam's forearms were particularly compelling in All the President's Men (which I can never understand and is anyway not all that good but nonetheless my favourite movie of all time), wherein Hal Holbrook, playing Deep Throat, stank so much of cigarettes that I became passively addicted to him (even his hair looks emphysemic) and got out Capricorn One for another fix – though I had Jeff Bridges by now to take care of and Hoffman and Redford and Robards and Harry Dean Stanton and Terence Stamp from Billy Budd and Gregory Peck, obviously, and Jack Palance who was in Second Chance with Mitchum – and who do you think was running around in Capricorn One, in a flapping tie, but Elliot Gould, trying to rescue James Brolin, who at one point *uses his medallion to break out of his prison*, an action which perfectly describes Brolin's entire career. (In the ruinously expensive illustrated version of this book, the 'Connoisseur's Edition', there will be a full colour fold-out wall chart detailing these connections more lucidly.) It was always the actors. You could track actors through the cities of their films, and they would never disappear.

The best example of how my actor tracking worked is Woody Allen. I developed an enormous crush on Tony Roberts (oh, Tony Roberts!), Allen's microphone-haired sidekick in Annie Hall, and ignored Manhattan (for *years*) in favour of the Roberts flicks – Radio Days, Play It Again, Sam, Stardust Memories (great *thighs*, Tony Roberts) and Hannah and her

Sisters, in which I saw, sort of for the first time, Max von Sydow ('Haf you been kissed tonight? You can't fool me, Lee, I'm too smart!'), whom I hunted down through Winter Light, Wild Strawberries, Three Days of the Condor and The Seventh Seal, during which I tumbled head over heels for the acrobat played by a man called Nils Poppe. Since I couldn't find Poppe in any more Bergman films, I callously discarded the great Swede and sought out Tony Roberts again, who I mistakenly thought had a part in Allen's September (even better than Gene Kelly's thighs in a way – he's *taller*) in which I saw Sam Waterston, who I went on to fancy even more in Capricorn One of course and even more, so meticulous and lonely-seeming, in The Killing Fields, which had the effect, I remember, of splitting me in two directions – towards Malkovich and also towards Patrick Malahide, who happened to be on television at the time as Casaubon in Middlemarch, in fact it was on tonight, *oh, good*!

In short, I didn't get out of the house much. I was promiscuous. The actors just kept on coming, and it's not like when an artist rearranges your head leaving no room for others and you go into a Dylan phase or a Ted Hughes zone or a Godard jag. It's a broad church, the church of actors. The Church of the Beautiful Strangers. It's always got on my nerves, the affected way with which some people try to lay claim to a kind of screen monogamy – 'I'm a Monica Vitti man.' Oh, you *liar*! Monica Vitti and not Claudia Cardinale? Not Sophia Loren? Such fidelity! 'For me it was only ever Gary Cooper.' What and *not* Gregory Peck? Ooh, you lying cow! Watching movies simply is a promiscuous experience. The voracity it breeds! That quantity of quiddity compressed and quickened and sent at you! It's a little bit mad, isn't it, to hold a faithful flame for the one you've picked, when no such choice is required of you? The sane response to a rainbow is not to pick your favourite colour. And it did make me happy. If you'd have seen how happy I was, going through my stack of Lee J. Cobb videos like so many digestives, you'd have called me sad. But I really was sad. Because I really was happy.

25

Perhaps it was the result of a slight difficulty in adjusting from one reality to another, but when one Saturday I saw one of the production assistants at the radio station reveal a Quaid-cobbled stomach as he changed his shirt, I determined to doorstep him in an effectively cinematic fashion, which is to say like Sean Young in No Way Out or Ellen Barkin in Sea of Love, that is, in nothing but a fake fur coat and a pair of heels, thinking *keep it snappy, keep it flirty, keep it The Big Easy*, as I rode the tube to his flat on the Edgware Road inside which Tom, the Quaid-cobbled production assistant, asked me why I had such a guilty look on my face, to which I had no reply other than to attempt to shrug the coat to the floor, struggling with the buttons in an un-Sean Youngian fluster which none-theless carried enough weight of intent to make him, maladroit himself, lurch towards me and sort of accidentally knock me to the floor, where, after rather a while of polite tussling, he scrabbled for a condom and put it on, tentatively, like he was potting a cactus, and, once inside me, became oddly static, allowing me to observe his beautiful silky hair (of a paler, more delicate red than Jim's, hard to describe) and wonder, with steadily diminishing enthusiasm, whether he were doing some sort of tantric sex on me, a semi-debacle which I amended a week later with a twenty-year-old trainee chef who had curls like James Frain and who, to my horror, turned out to be fifteen in the morning (that skin, I *knew* it!), an offence which I assume, perhaps overconfidently, the police will regard as having happened a long time ago etc. etc. should they ever read this or subpoena my diary of the time, which records that I attempted to remedy, and then – what do you know – remedied the child-chef-non-semi-debacle over the following few days with several other *legal* (take note, police!) men, the last of whom was an ethical banker with a garland of rose-tattoos around his neck, just low enough to be invisible under a T-shirt, with whom I enjoyed a lovely fortnight before his tetchy tutting at Walter Matthau's casual, rather gentle sexism in The Odd Couple drove a wedge between us, leaving me with nothing to show from the fling except an American acquaintance of his called Ilana, from New Jersey, a chestnut-bright young woman simultaneously hard and soft like all the great movie stars, with whom I felt I was going to be permanent friends, and who in fact set me up with a Canadian who lived alone, bald as Kurtz, in a condemned house on Plimsoll Road in Arsenal which he had decorated with the most staggering murals of Ganesh and Shiva and Vishnu and other gods whose names he must have told me but I have since forgotten, and who comforted me the day I was diagnosed with cervical cancer by making me watch In the Heat of the Night, which did indeed help keep my spirits up until I received a call from the hospital two days later informing me that they had mixed up their smear tests and I wasn't going to die after all – a relief which had the paradoxical effect of somehow sundering me from the Canadian and propelling me into a, no doubt, easily explicable series of one-night stands over the next ten days, as England rolled past their opponents in the European Championships on a growing wave of belief that this time, finally, they were going to prevail, and I found myself considering the question of promiscuity and wondering about the motives of the promiscuous, maybe 50 per cent of whom are Don Juans, mere number-crunchers, and maybe two-thirds of whom are sex-addicts and maybe nine-tenths of whom are frightened of commitment, and for maybe four-fifths of whom promiscuity is an index of their unhappiness, and wondering what proportion simply *liked a lot of people*, could simply be marked down as slow learners, could be thought of as just needing lots of lovers, lots of lessons, before they understood about their own capacity to absorb other people, such as the apple-picker from Somerset whom I attempted to console after Gazza had stretched to make that Sistine Chapel contact with the ball in front of the gaping German goal (which he would never, never do, freeze-framed forever in memory a millimetre from redemption) and who had been so thoroughly consoled he broke, that very night, into his estranged father's house in Greenwich where we lived an idyllic life for three weeks before the police, called by a neighbour, arrested us, sending me on my way that afternoon with no charge against my name but with a note from the apple-picker in my hand which read, 'Good luck with everything and, well, just don't put people off by making too great a display of yourself and by overdoing things' which, although with hindsight I can see that he was on to something, royally pissed me off at the time: so much so that it was rather self-consciously in defiance of this advice that I went out and overdid things a bit, thinking *it's not me that's doing this, it's the movies* as I learned about the absolutely crucial importance of beryllium to the Russian economy, and what it was that banks did exactly in the bed of a precious metals dealer, and just how hard it was to be an amateur boxer in London if you were from

Paris, and that blue Y-fronts are acceptable underwear among Brazilians, and that being an officer in the British Army does not preclude a high intelligence, and even softness, and that 'good in bed' is pretty much a meaningless and vicious term imposed upon life by a public discourse that revels in encouraging neurosis, and that the anxiety I felt in the company of a dimple-chinned Sinn Fein man (whose smoke-and-mirrors face seemed to incarnate all the shape-shifting of his political life) with whom I conducted a stop-start affair at this time was different from the kind of nervousness I had felt around Jim, because Jim's violence was social and unconcealed whereas the Sinn Fein man's was something altogether more unreadable, so that I felt, when I was with him, like William Hurt faced with the opaque obelisk of Lee Marvin in Gorky Park, to the extent that even though I idolised him, I would come over with a fit of the vapours like Michelle Pfeiffer's Madame de Tourvel in Dangerous Liaisons whenever he undressed me, causing the affair to fizzle out, and I thought, about that time, how incorrect it was that the promiscuous should be thought of as jaded where they were really innocent, that they were not so much fools slow to understand the fact that human variety is far from infinite, that the exploration should be in oneself rather than of others, but a different kind of fool, happy in the illusion that human variety *was* infinite – having said all of which, and despite the fact that I was hardly Catherine M. (and doubtless sixteen-year-old readers will at this point be asking themselves, 'Where's this promiscuous patch she keeps talking about?'), I must have been feeling a slight lesion of identity, a slight blurring of definition, a slightly *stretched* kind of feeling, because when a man with curly hair and a long nose asked me who I was one night in a bar, I surprised myself by saying, and almost meaning, 'Oh, just some girl.'

26

Marcus Denning was an actor who had appeared in a series of adverts for instant coffee in the early 90s as a thirtysomething vet who goes to work in the country because, as he tells his mother in the first commercial: 'I'm a vet, Mum. I belong in the country. Country air, country people, country ways.'

No sooner has he arrived ('But I haven't even unpacked yet!') than he is doing something indeterminate to an ailing but photogenic cow. 'That's that, then,' says the kindly yet curmudgeonly farmer. Marcus, transmitting with great delicacy a millisecond of umbrage, counters with: 'A coffee would be nice ...' (the *embedded catch-phrase*). But the farmer doesn't have any!

'Good job I brought my own,' Marcus says, still cleverly conveying a scintilla of urban disdain for rural hospitality. Fences are mended over a cup of instant at the farmhouse table. Indeed, so taken is the farmer by this metropolitan concoction that he threatens to retain the jar 'until next time'. Marcus now has to convey, in one-and-a-half seconds,

- shock
- reflex urban possessiveness
- the softening of that possessive impulse as he comprehends the farmer's disguised compliment
- and soul-deep satisfaction as he realises he's been accepted, thus escaping the surly bonds of his transparently suffocating maternal relationship

Don't knock the ad actor, master of micro-technique. So recognisable was he as this vet at the time, that he'd come out of his house the week before I met him to see a group of people standing round an injured bird, and they'd turned and looked at him, clearly expecting him to do something about it. He'd even been in the News of the World under the headline 'RAT VET LOVER – Coffee Vet Cheats!' when an ex-girlfriend sold her story about how he'd left her for another woman.

The girl who he'd left the kiss-and-tell artist for, he told me, used to lounge around in front of the telly and would, bored, shout through to him in the kitchen, 'Come on, Maz, shove it up my box!' Marcus was a master of that very thespian accomplishment – the unimaginably dirty one-liner, or indeed any story to do with sex, and over the next year I would ask for my favourites again and again. My very favourite was a story about a friend of his whose sex life with his wife had deteriorated to the point where sex had become a once-weekly treat scheduled for the weekend. One Wednesday night, Marcus's friend had reached out to touch his wife on the hip as they lay there in bed and the wife had turned to him and hissed: '*IS* it Saturday?' The best storytellers always know how to make your flesh creep. *Is it Saturday?* became a catch-phrase between us, the sort of totem lovers use to ward off bad luck when they're rich in love themselves.

They're exactly the kind of dirty stories Brian Blessed might tell to break the ice at a read-through. But they used to make me laugh and laugh, putting my hands together with a satisfied clap: 'Tell it *again*, Marcus . . .!'

Marcus's family were aristocratic and deeply eccentric. His maternal grandfather had been an hereditary baronet ('rare as rocking horse shit these days') and the whole lot of them (mother, father, three sisters and Marcus) went around on motorbikes. When Marcus had been younger, they used to go on nudist holidays together on their motorbikes, the kids in sidecars. The family had once been invited to a drinks party on the compound to which they went, naked, on their motorbikes. Their hostess, wearing an evening gown and pearls, ushered them into a room full of similarly dressed people. Marcus insisted on leaving, but his father was mortified and ticked him off for being so rude. 'Rude?' Marcus sobbed. 'Aubrey, we're *naked*.' It was like a grand trumping of my own Adam and Eve indiscretions with the draught-excluding snake. He'd do an impression of Aubrey getting back from the party, sitting on the stairs with his balls out, sighing, 'I met a *wonderful* couple. *She's* seventy-one and has just taken up the piano and is already on grade 5. *He's* just designed the postgraduate centre at Maidstone General Hospital. Such a *lovely* airy room . . .'

Aubrey was a GP who operated an out-of-hours service and used to take calls during the family's suppers, which Marcus relayed to me: '*Mister* Coombes, if you think I'm coming out to provide digital manipulation to your wife's recalcitrant stools, you can *think again!*' 'Tell it *again*, Marcus . . .!'

He had a cousin called Marie who had won Best Actress on the Edinburgh Fringe six years earlier for playing Nora in A Doll's House. She'd received a fan letter from a man who maintained that her Nora was the only English one he'd seen who retained a hint of the phonetic hardness of Ibsen's Norwegian. 'In short,' it said in a PS, 'you were so good I pissed my cords.'

And each time he told it, the letter would get funnier and funnier, and he'd do a perfect little impression of Marie's face falling as she got to the bottom of the page.

Aubrey was posh, but his dreamy wife Janie was incredibly posh. She was a twin, and fiercely proud of it, as if it were a personal achievement. She and her twin sister Duzz (Dorothy? Dolores? Dusty? *Doris?*) once volunteered to have tests done on them at the Great Ormond Street Hospital and arrived there expecting to be fêted and shown through to a buffet, only to find literally hundreds of other twins in the corridors. Already somewhat put out, they were poked and prodded and urine-sampled and thoroughly out of temper when Marcus and I went to pick them up:

'Goodness. *What* a day!'

'What did they do to you?'

'It would be much easier to tell you what they *didn't* do.'

'What didn't they do?'

'Well, they didn't *fuck* us.'

I had been *there* but I would still be asking him what had happened: 'Oh, tell it *again* . . .!'

And they were like this all the time, each one of them, his father, his mother, his sisters, his brothers-in-law, his five-year-old niece with her imaginary friends Dot Com and Direct Debit. It wasn't as if Marcus cherry-picked these stories, it was normal. The first time I went to visit the clan in Dorset for the weekend, Janie came downstairs to breakfast holding an enormous vibrator and asked me in the nicest possible way, as if it were a paperback that she'd found on the stairs, 'Antonia, my love, is this yours?' I demurred and went for a wander around the house, the rooms upon rooms, a colossal ballroom with just a single bed in the corner and a bowl out to catch the leaks from the ceiling. A nursery in the attic entirely filled with an ancient train-set. A four-poster bed with tights blatantly knotted around each post. In one of the corridors I ran into Aubrey: 'Oh, hello! I've been walking around the house and do you know *everybody* is in bed with their lover. It's *marvellous.*'

That evening over dinner, the family tirelessly berated Marcus's brother-in-law for failing to go down on his wife, Marcus's sister Jennifer. The indictment lasted well into coffee.

'But *why?*' Janie kept saying, gripping the brother-in-law's hand, genuinely distressed.

'We're not trying to make you feel bad; it's just *so unfair!*' It was Jennifer's vibrator which Janie had been hefting over the breakfast table. 'Oooh, can I borrow it, Jen?' said Marcus's other sister, Harriet.

Next morning Marcus flew me back to London himself, in his yellow two-seater aeroplane which he kept at the BBC flying club at Denham.

27

What is love? Let's ask Barbra Streisand.

It's like going to the movies, and we see the lovers on screen kiss, and the music swells and we buy it, right? So when my date takes me home and kisses me . . . (This is The Mirror Has Two Faces (1996) and she's playing a professor of English at Columbia University who is adored by her students but, being plain, can't attract a man of note, although in about fifteen minutes she'll be approached by a maths professor played by Jeff Bridges who, cynical about long-term love, will suggest they marry purely for companionship. Bridges has come to spy on her, here in a student-crammed lecture hall the size of the Coliseum. Crammed with more than students, actually: there are people standing at the back, suggesting that perhaps even the janitors, or tutors from other disciplines, are gatecrashing Streisand's Nurembergian weekly address.) Barbra, in black dungarees and big specs, continues – *and if I don't hear the Philharmonic in my head I dump him, right?* From the students, appreciative, democratic laughter. It's the one lecture they've been looking forward to all week, and note-taking has been superseded by the desire simply to drink this all in. *Now the question is, why do we buy it?* Cut to the leonine Bridges, whose gravitas suggests that this is truly an exceptional college lecture and he is responding to it as one should to a serious con-tribution to the social sciences. Unfortunately his pager goes off, causing a rapt black student to look daggers at him, and he is forced, reluctantly, to drag himself away, looking perplexed yet intrigued. Had I reviewed The Mirror Has Two Faces, I might have been tempted to write something like: *Jeff Bridges looks as if he wishes he were elsewhere.* It's a classic reviewer's white lie, designed to let a favourite actor off the hook. Can you really imagine it: 'Jeff! Can you *please* concentrate?' Yet it appears in reviews all the time. Here's one, from a review of Chicken Tikka Massala, a 'British Asian comedy', in The Times a while back (May 2005). The reviewer, Wendy Ide, wishes that she'd been somewhere else rather than watching the movie, and 'from the bloodless crushed look on Chris Bisson's face, I'd say he feels the same way'. Can it really be the case? It's a kindness. But in The Mirror Has Two Faces, I submit, we have a genuine once-in-a-lifetime example. No beautiful teen asked to fall for Woody Allen could ever have looked so stunned and reluctant and nauseated as Jeff does looking at Barbra Streisand. Rent the DVD and if you spool to the final credit sequence where Streisand and Bridges kiss and dance on the street, you'll notice that Bridges suddenly makes a break for it and runs to a taxi – and even though Barbra drags him back for another clinch, it unmistakably looks like the great Bridges has miscalculated by a mere twenty seconds how much time he must spend sentenced to this *mishagas* and is trying to get the hell off the set of what, to extend this digression, I further submit, is the worst film of all time, worse even than Peter's Friends or Maybe Baby. Worse even, possibly, than The Godfather Part III. A little charge goes off in reviewers' heads when it becomes apparent that such a possibility is in the offing. I have sat through screenings of Battlefield Earth, The Brylcreem Boys and Sex Lives of the Potato Men, and felt the electricity in the room, the silent commencement of an unspoken inter-critic competition to write the most freakishly abusive response. It's a perk of the job. And this *really is* the worst scene in the worst film ever made. *We buy it because whether it's a myth or a manipulation, let's face it, we all want to fall in love, right?* Cut to student with a red rinse, solemnly nodding. The blond guy in front of her looks a little confused, not because he can't follow, but because of the intellectual head-storm Barbra has whipped up in his cortex. *Why?* (Streisand's accent is becoming increasingly twangily Brooklynite.) *Because the experience makes us feel completely alive! Where every sense is heightened! Every emotion is magnified! Our everyday reality is shattered and we are flung into the heavens! It may only last a moment, an hour, an afternoon, but that doesn't diminish its value. Because these are memories we will treasure for the rest of our lives.* (Or resent, of course. Or possibly be tortured by.) She pauses, and takes off her spectacles, enjoying a well-earned breather while the camera moves towards her, triggering an unusual effect: the closer we get to Barbra, the less visible she becomes, so smudged and blurred and vaselined is the film texture. *I read an article a while ago* – she flicks her hair from above her left eye with an unacademically long and manicured fingernail, and one wonders momentarily if those nails were ever the subject of battles at executive level before wearily realising that Streisand is both director and a producer – *that said when we fall in love we hear Puccini in our heads.* (God, *Puccini*? What kind of article *was* this? Not Noam Chomsky in the New York Review of Books, surely?) *I love that.* Balding mature student with moustache and cricket jumper raises a fist in salute and silently mouths the word *yes* like a tennis player who has just aced a volley. *I think it's because his music fully expresses our longing for passion in our lives and romantic love.* Shot of a transfixed bank of female students in polo necks and tweed jackets, almost tearful, as if they were watching David Helfgott swing through the Rach II. *So, the final question is – why do people want to fall in love when it has such a short shelf life and can be devastatingly painful? Stacey?* She points to a female stooge in a lumberjack shirt who offers: *'It leads to propagation of the species?' Ray? 'Because psychologically we need to connect with somebody?'* Barbra cedes Ray's theory with a nod, but points to a third student – *Cath?* And suddenly it dawns on us that this woman knows every single one of her students by name. Cath stands up to put her full weight behind her answer – *Is it because we're culturally preconditioned?* The camera pans to Barbra, who smiles. (One imagines that the Reverend Gary Jones gave the same smile to his doomed acolytes minutes before the Jonestown Massacre.) *Awawall good answers, but way too intellectual for me.* There's a near-hysterical buzz in the room, and the viewer is already anticipatorily cringing at the by now completely inevitable bathetic definition that Barbra is unswervingly heading towards, like the Titanic towards its iceberg. *I think because, as some of you already may know, while it does last* – again, the smile, and one's sinking spirits now register the absolute certainty of an incipient deflationary profanity (a scientific curiosity: studies among both rats and humans have shown that if you stab somebody at this point in the film then they will actually *pull the blade into them*) – *it feels FUCKING great!* The room erupts into wild applause. Joseph Fiennes has just pulled off Romeo and Juliet. Cuba Gooding Jnr has just followed his touchdown with an amazing little dance. Liam Neeson has just won the Second World War. And Barbra raises a thumb up to the crowd and shouts *Thank you! Thank you!*

She's right about one thing of course, but it doesn't feel like Puccini.

28

To me it felt more like this:

Jeremy Irons says *I've been waiting for you* and Patricia Hodge says *What do you mean?* They're in a bedroom upstairs in a smart house; music is thudding below. *I knew you'd come* he says, and she says *I've just come in to comb my hair.* He says *I knew you'd have to comb your hair. I knew you'd have to get away from the party.*

He's drunk but he looks like he means it. She laughs – he's her husband's best friend and there is absolutely nothing whatsoever about her which suggests that flirtation or infidelity has ever crossed her mind. So when she asks *Aren't you enjoying the party?* and walks amusedly to the dressing table to pick up her hairbrush, she is just humouring an old friend, no more, no less. He just comes out with it. *You're beautiful. Listen. I've been watching you all night. I must tell you, I want to tell you. You're incredible.*

You're drunk.

Nevertheless. Irons delivers this word beautifully. It is a beautiful word to say, after all. *I was best man at your wedding. I saw you in white. I watched you glide by in white.*

I wasn't in white.

I should have had you in your white before the wedding. I should have blackened you in your white wedding dress, blackened you in your bridal dress before ushering you into your wedding as your best man . . .

She looks headmistressily unbothered by the situation. *My husband's best man, your best friend's best man.*

Irons ignores this. *You're lovely! I'm crazy about you. All these words I'm saying – don't you see they've never been said before? Can't you see? I'm crazy about you. It's a whirlwind. Have you ever been to the Sahara Desert? Listen to me. It's true. Listen. You overwhelm me, you're so lovely.*

I'm not!

You're so beautiful – look at the way you look at me!

Patricia Hodge gives us this woman's easy talent for coping with such situations. Fending off this kind of approach, we see, has always been one of her more instinctive accomplishments. *I'm not looking at you!* She is kind but stern.

Look at the way you're looking at me! I can't wait for you. I'm bowled over. I'm totally knocked out. My jewel. He puts his hand near her hair as though it's radiating heat. This isn't a pitch or a line, although I have seen several actors play this speech of Pinter's as just that. Nor is it a drunken error, as Douglas Hodge had it at the National Theatre in 1998: Hodge is supposed to be good in Pinter but he never plays *against* Pinter, which is what Irons is doing, rather than nudging us in the ribs to tip us off to what the author really thinks of these avowals. You could do this scene so many ways. But for Jeremy Irons, no editorialising, no standing apart. This is actually happening. The actual magic. It's magic.

I can't ever sleep again. Now, listen! It's the truth! I won't walk! I'll be a cripple, I'll descend – I'll diminish into total paralysis. My life is in your hands, that's what you're banishing me to – a state of catatonia. Do you know the state of catatonia? Do you? A state where the reigning prince is the prince of emptiness, the prince of absence, the prince of desolation. I love you. She makes some footling objection, looking as pale as Patricia Hodge has ever looked. You want to reach into the scene and pinch her cheek, raise the blood to the surface. *I adore you. I'm madly in love with you. I can't believe that what anyone at this moment is saying has ever happened. HAS EVER HAPPENED. Nothing has ever happened. NOTHING. This is the ONLY thing that has ever happened. Your eyes kill me. I'm lost. You're lost.*

No she says. But her brain is beginning to register depths of feeling which have been slumbering under her marriage for years, for *fifteen* years, which this man has disinterred for her.

Yes.

Well, that's Pinter. The film is the backwards-running Betrayal (1982) and this, the final scene, is the start of the story, a trick which the last decade has become rather addicted to copying. It's one of the greatest love scenes ever filmed because it does something which you almost never see. This is where, if you don't have a script like Pinter's, you have to cut away (to bedroom or breakfast) but here we actually witness the woman falling in love with the man, and you can see it because you can *see* Irons hypnotising himself, enchanting himself. You can see the actual magic.

Of course Irons has this quality of doomed romanticism – there is in his face something tending towards sickness and his teeth look a little brown – which makes him perfect for old-fashioned romantic parts. His best bit in Brideshead Revisited was being dumped by Julia Flyte, sitting on the stairs, embodying the pain of love: *I don't want to make it easier for you.*

I hope your heart may break. In The French Lieutenant's Woman (another Pinter script, which I've always cherished for presenting the actor's life as an idyll, with Irons and Meryl Streep both playing actors, lounging around on beds doing the crossword and at garden parties in the sunny 1980s) he says to Streep: *Why did you leave Exeter? You told me you loved me; you showed me your love. Answer me! Are you saying that you never loved me? You must say, 'I am totally evil, I used him as an instrument, I do not care that in all this time he hasn't seen a woman to compare with me! That his life has been a desert without me. That he has sacrificed everything for me!' Say it!* In Damage he gets damaged by Juliette Binoche. And naturally Betrayal ends unhappily. They should sell a three-disc DVD box-set of these sad stories called The Jeremy Irons Grief Trilogy. *I'd* buy it.

The thing is, I just can't take my eyes off Irons's face in any of them. And I mean that literally. I just can't take my eyes off him. There is a quality of mesmeric handsomeness in certain actors which simplifies the experience of movie-going to the point where the aesthetic pleasures of bone-structure photographed over an hour or so are enough entirely to satisfy you. And it's a kind of acting available – among a multitude of hunks and dreamboats – only to a tiny minority of the shockingly beautiful. Faces so beautiful that you get a tension between the idea of a movie being a story and it being moving portraiture. It's weird – your appetite for looking at these faces seems never to be sated. Were Last Tango in Paris twelve hours long I'd still be shovelling Brando's face into my eyes. How can we tear ourselves away?

Into this category put: David Bowie in The Man Who Fell to Earth (1976) – a good example since it is one's riveted gaze on Bowie's indescribable beauty alone which holds a somewhat bitty film together. Christopher Walken in everything. Billy Crudup in All the Pretty Horses, a face somewhere between the young Sinatra's and Montgomery Clift's. Rupert Everett in Another Country, handsomeness raised to an almost comical level. Bruce Robinson in Truffaut's The Story of Adele H. (1975). Paul Newman in Cat on a Hot Tin Roof, fighting against it. Rutger Hauer in Bladerunner, looking like a sane Klaus Kinski. I can look at Hauer for hours, unable to believe that nature has done something so complicated as a face and made so few mistakes. That throughout the whole delicate process it hasn't made a single error.

And Kinski, of course, handsomeness gone insane; a grotesque exaggeration of handsomeness, as though every feature on his face is trying to out-handsome the others. Alain Delon in Rocco and His Brothers, obviously. Adrien Brody in The Pianist, like someone from a different breed of men, taller, nobler and more hairless than us. Robert de Niro – just that once, but undeniably – as the young Vito Corleone with his otter-slicked hair in the section just after he has assassinated Don Fanucci in Godfather Part II. Buster Keaton, proving the point about mesmerism – without those good looks our concentration on his smooth, logically unfolding routines would be lessened. Gary Cooper. One feels amazed and almost grateful that people so physically gifted should condescend to have talent at something else as well. These are the hypnotists.

And Jeremy Irons's brand of hypnotism is the suffering of love. We are prettier when we're happy, but often we're more beautiful when we suffer. And we hate the beautiful because we don't believe that they do suffer. Watching Irons suffer, you see it especially in his slender and muscular throat – his expressive Adam's apple, those tortured tendons, that clavicle, the paper-knife jawbone. I love Jeremy Irons's *neck*.

So to see him capsized, hyperventilating with joy, in that scene with Patricia Hodge is doubly delirious because we so rarely see him laugh. And that's what love is. It's a total surprise. It's not what you expected. It's a relief from those decades of consciousness which try to kid us that they're enough to be going on with.

29

Happiness in movies is a bit like love – the camera's always cutting away. You hardly ever get to *see* it. All you get are those ultra-casual but ever so slightly speeded-up kitchen sequences over breakfast just before Harrison Ford's wife gets murdered by a terrorist, or his kid gets crushed by a hit-and-run HGV. Instead we have happy montage sequences, like the one in Manhattan where Woody Allen dangles a hand into Central Park lake and comes up with an armful of muck. Woody was the master of these sequences. So *happy* they've been playing on the inside of millions of skulls for twenty years.

Marcus was a magician. When his face became known to the children on the street after playing the 'marvellous' dad in a children's TV series about twins living on a farm, kids would come knocking on the door to speak to him, and he'd go outside and sit on the wall and do magic tricks for them. One day a little boy knocked on the door and asked to meet 'the wizard'. Though I was always asking him to do tricks for me, he only ever did once. At Brixton Lido he found a small tin alligator behind my ear and I was as pleased to get it as Diane Keaton was to get her toy skunk from Woody Allen on the beach in

Play It Again, Sam: *Oh, it's lovely, it's beautiful. A plastic skunk! I'm so touched, I don't know what to say . . .*

Marcus was like David Niven, a natural actor, one of those effortless guys always two seconds away from winking at the camera, passing themselves off as a minor aristocrat (or in Marcus's case cunningly passing himself as the sort of guy who might pass himself off as a minor aristocrat) and giving the impression that acting was a ridiculous profession. Acting was slumming it, but, having wound up doing it, it was one's *duty* to keep everyone around you on set or in the rehearsal room amused. Niven tells us in his autobiography The Moon's a Balloon that his impossibly difficult debut in a speaking part was as a poet called Leo who has to enter a room and single-handedly raise the tempo of a dull party ('Oh, Leo's wonderful, isn't he!'). Well, that was Marcus. Single-handedly raising the party up.

He appealed to my longing for a slightly anachronistic post-war world, a world of digs and mucking in, and even had a phrase for making the best of things – you put on your 'good grace cardigan'. He sent me a telegram from the Isle of Arran where he was playing a vicar in a television film about a post-man travelling around Scotland on a pushbike: *Shower, shave, 18 mile journey to set, big hearty working breakfast – kippers, porridge, 2 gallons of tea – laugh politely during half a dozen humiliating impressions of me drunk the night before. Into frock, wrapped by nine. Arran is some sort of wintertime hibernating Lanzarote and clearly home to all sorts of pixies and goblins and sprites. You could set the Tempest here if it weren't for the accents.*

Into frock, wrapped by nine. I couldn't resist it. I was fifteen years old again with my leg in plaster reading Year of the King, thinking that the world of actors was the ultimate fun, such a luxurious, well-stocked life. I had entered my mumps book.

When Marcus got back, I found a Polaroid in one of his pockets of him dressed as a granny, with a handbag under his arm, being a Good Company Member, jollying everyone along.

Soon after we met Marcus bought a house with a little room at the back that he turned into a study for me. 'Let's call it the Quirke Memorial Library,' he said and went out and had a sign made for the door. 'I hate shopping,' he said, 'so we'll do it all in one day.' At John Lewis he bought three beds, three sofas, ten luxury towels, six Egyptian cotton duvet covers, spare duvets filled either with goose down or silk so that people who came to stay could choose whichever they preferred, two big televisions, Moroccan rugs, silverware, a tumble dryer that reduced the hot air into a pellet that it delivered at the end of the cycle, and a little art deco dressing table made of mirrors which I'd briefly admired. I was like Woody's kid in Manhattan, getting spoiled with the bigger of the two model yachts. I'd known Marcus was posh but I had no idea he was *rich*. It was the coffee ads. Adverts are incredibly lucrative for actors because they're effectively buying your face, and by being the coffee vet Marcus ran the risk of not being cast in much else because people would keep expecting him to stick the kettle on. Though he had been banned for speeding, he bought me a red-and-white-striped 2CV to teach me to drive in. One November day before I'd even got around to applying for a learner's licence, or insurance, or the correct registration documents, we decided to risk it and went on a trip down to Eastbourne. On the way back he bought a painting of a sheep at a gallery – a sheep standing there like a Stubbs horse, watching you, like Wilson had said they did – and stopped at a garage for some coal and wood to make a fire when we got home. Marcus was driving when I smelled something odd.

'It's a bit late for them to be burning the fields,' I said.

Looking down, we saw flames licking the steering wheel.
Marcus pulled onto the hard shoulder and tried to put the fire
out with his coat sleeves but it was impossible, there was smoke
everywhere, so, yelling, we fled the car with the painting, and
stood on the bank watching the 2CV being taken by the flames
like a roman candle – the canvas roof burning like paper, the
firelighters and wood and coal making a bonfire in the boot –
and being neither insured nor legal, made a run for it up the
hard shoulder and over the bridge to the other side of the
motorway, like Jeanne Moreau and Oskar Werner in Jules et
Jim – the single greatest happy movie – moving as quickly as
we could with the painting across the fields, finally hitching
a lift to East Grinstead station. It's those expensive lobsters
scuttling away in Annie Hall that everyone really remembers as
the apotheosis of happiness. The mess that you can delightedly
turn your back on because the present is so much fun.

Marcus couldn't work on any British adverts while he
was still the vet, but he could still go to India to be twinkly
and reassuring about beer, or to Spain for spectacles, or to the
Maldives for indigestion tablets, or to Germany to make a car
commercial for a Hungarian director who used German as a
second language and English as a third.

'Lazlo thinks every language but Hungarian is just *foreign*
and completely interchangeable. So when a word escapes him
in one he just moves to the other ... *Und when you see ze car
you look at it and you are eshtambaumflot, OK? Allez vous en!* So
I say *No Lazlo, wait! I'm not sure what* ... and he shouts *No,
Marcus, nein! Zis is not vat I'm asking. Eets my fault, my English
is gebrochen. You come out and you are zer funny yah? Oui!
My liebchen actor! And then you see the car and you are eshtambaumflot. So I say Ah! Now, that's the problem Lazlo, the thing
is...*'

I loved it when he dissed directors. That's actors' favourite thing in the whole world by a *mile*. The randomness of a travelling life suited him. It's what The Moon's a Balloon is all about: telling dirty limericks at screen tests; trusting to luck and leading a life that seems like a sequence of unlikely but successful throws on a roulette wheel. He never got lost in translation like Bill Murray. He wanted news, data, details. Having left school at sixteen, he was something of an auto-didact and slightly nervous about his academic knowledge, like a lot of actors (Michael Caine, for example, or, on the other hand, James Woods, who went to the prestigious MIT and never stops bringing it up in interviews). So he had something to say about everything. Rochester's love poems, the number zero, sport, China, the life of Jesse James, fish, trade routes, gold panning, whether or not my brother Ben should come down to London to try and make it as a singer. He made a reading hut in the garden, on wheels so you could turn it slightly away from the sun, where he would tinker or get stuck into a textbook.

It's not like Marcus wanted concentrated deference; he wanted stories back. I was still clinging on to my film page at the Journal, but had managed to snare a new job, reviewing books on the breakfast show at Greater London Radio, setting competitions and giving away the prizes – reissues of classics, cookery books, screenplays, poetry, dictionaries, all sorts – so lots of information came my way, stuff I could talk to Marcus about, odd facts and figures that pleased him. I would go to the hut and feed him information as though he were the ravenous Sarlacc, Return of the Jedi's great fanged Pudendum of the Sands.

'Did you know that Boadicea is buried under Platform 10 of King's Cross Station?' I asked.

'Did *you* know that the word *slang* comes from the Scandinavian *sleng* from which the English *sling* is also derived, which makes slang both literally and metaphorically a thrown language?'

'Do *you* know that at Stonehenge they used to sacrifice women to the dung god?'

'Really?'

'Yeah. And Diego Maradona nearly drowned in a cesspit when he was a kid. That's what gave him his will to win.'

Marcus encouraged me to talk about old lovers. Men, in my experience, *contra* what you might read in the women's glossies, never do seem all that threatened by the rivals of the past (though conceited women like to fool themselves that they are frightening the comparison-haunted boys). I was shy about mine but he told me all of his, and made up more, from outrageous fantasies about losing his virginity in his sleep to things I still believe are true, like the time he was the magician at a fortieth-birthday party on the Isle of Man and stuck his cock up the Birthday Girl and five of her friends.

'In 1988?' I asked. 'In 1988 I was collecting postcards of James Dean and thinking that my thighs looked so much better in plaster.'

'Open those thighs to fate and withhold nothing,' he joked, after e. e. cummings. (Actors were all big on e. e. cummings after Barbara Hershey read out that poem in Hannah and her Sisters.) 'And if you can withhold nothing, conceive a man.'

Pillow-talk. That was something Woody was brilliant at. Or just slobbing-around-the-house talk. Watching him eat Chinese food with Mariel Hemingway, it occurs to you that Manhattan's subject simply *is* a straightforward happiness. Even the Divorced Fathers and Sons All-Stars that Woody's character plays touch football with look like happiness.

'Are you having good orgasms?' Janie asked me one hot March day the next spring. Jesus. We were at Bletchley Park looking at the Enigma Machine with her and Duzz and their elder sister Chips. Marcus had gone to get everybody ice creams. 'I *do* hope so. I mean if there's one thing I'd really hope Marcus was good at, it's that. Are you? *Are* you?'

Duzz and Chips turned their attention to us.

'What's this about orgasms?' said Duzz, delighted. 'Janie, are you talking about the Hussar again?' The Hussar was a Hungarian count who'd been a friend of Janie's father in the 1950s.

'No,' sighed Janie. 'But he was a *wonderful* lover.'

'Oh, *wasn't* he . . .' agreed Duzz.

After a while Chips leaned forward and said, 'Marvellous *rhythm,* but definitely N.S.I.T.'

'Oh, Chips! You too?'

'You didn't know? Of course!'

'Well, I think that's *marvellous,*' Janie said. Aubrey wasn't at Bletchley because he was overseeing the final technical rehearsal of L'Elisir d'Amore. Every year he staged, and performed in, an opera at the family house – the Seldon Park Opera.

'What's N.S.I.T.?' I asked.

'Not Safe in a Taxi.'

We had to hurry back to Seldon because there was plenty to do in advance of the opera. Duzz and Chips had painted the sets, Harriet had done the programmes and the signs around the lanes which read 'S.P.O. THIS WAY!', to which Jennifer had attached the traditional balloons. Wise Marcus, with an instinct for self-preservation, restricted himself each year to designing the lighting. Seldon Park Opera was the event around which Aubrey based his year – he travelled to Glyndebourne and Garsington to nick production ideas and visited a voice coach to brush up his *tessitura*. It was serious. The whole village was expected to attend and the family would file in last to take their seats in the centre of the front row in full opera-going fig.

Then the lights were dimmed and someone pressed the play button on the stereo which provided the orchestral music. Aubrey couldn't sing. But nor could anyone else. Duzz shook and wept with not entirely suppressed laughter throughout the performance, drowning out the quieter passages of the Donizetti, or those not infrequent parts where the singers had forgotten their lines and would sketchily busk along. The two-headed fox-fur stole she wore seemed to animate with her trembling, making the foxes dance over her breasts. Marcus inclined his head in a sustainably credible attitude of connoisseurship. I used my nails on my palms and tried to think of famines and prison camps. My ball gown was sodden with sweat. Four hours later, still high from the standing ovation, Aubrey fretted over certain imperfections. 'I was *ready* for it, but I just couldn't seem to hit it. That *bloody* E. Maybe tomorrow ...' The Seldon Park Opera always gave three performances and many of the audience went all three times. That night, with Marcus, I gave in to the longest and most nearly dangerous fit of laughter I have ever known.

Extended families. The party at the start of Hannah and her Sisters, lit by Sven Nykvist – people have been trying to match that party's happiness ever since.

I loved Marcus so much. I loved his slight campness and blaséness about life. A wiser person might have seen how strong his need to perform and to conceal was, but I was not wise. I loved his nice cynicism, his eyes as blue as just-lit gas and his long, friendly nose which he used as a prop – he could droop it a good inch to make a woeful face. I loved that he was always looking for the maximum quantity of drama he could make from his own life, was always looking for the story – it meant that in a way all time was redeemed. This was a guy on whom nothing was wasted. A bad day could always be turned into a good anecdote, and I would listen to him refining things as he went from person to person, forming and shaping, not lying or exaggerating even, just telling it best. It struck me then as incomparably polite – to make that effort.

Marcus commented now and again during those days that I was very quiet. Me, who had never been particularly quiet before. And yet I was quiet around Marcus, not simply because he talked a lot, but because I was just looking and learning – like Horatio around Hamlet, like Watson around Holmes – noticing how the space and everyone in it adjusted happily around him, just as the rooms tilt around the storyteller in Broadway Danny Rose, in Bullets Over Broadway, around all the happy tables in Woody Allen movies. I settled for a time into the role of reviewer of *Marcus*, a sort of archivist, and discovered that – even more than I'd previously imagined – I had a temperament disposed to admire.

I can't truthfully defend Woody Allen from the charges laid against him, which make it so *embarrassing* to like him, that he can be pseudo-intellectual, that something like Hannah and her Sisters is self-satisfied and unaware of its own privilege and alright if you've got the money. But I always thought that what he was *really* like was Frank Capra (that's why films like The Purple Rose of Cairo, Sweet and Lowdown or Radio Days, set in the thirties, come so easily to him). He could make you happy. He knew what good times looked like.

30

So you wait and you wait and wait and you wait. And then you wait some more and George Clooney turns up. And you think: *So close, but not it.* Not the thing itself, without reservations. And then you wait a bit more. You begin to worry. What if this wait is like the wait in a Kafka story, which will be endless? And then Russell Crowe is suddenly there, like the last great chance of the movies. Crowe is The One. He may not be in three years' time – there are worrying signs – but he has been ever since LA Confidential (1997). And that it's been nine years already and the thrill of his potential is as fresh as ever is tribute to his range, his openness, his greatness. I remember the equation from school: *Momentum = mass x velocity.* In other words, a bull has more momentum than a bullet. That's Crowe's greatness on a blackboard. You could go further and say: *Art = mass x velocity.* A symphony, a Shakespeare play, an epic poem: the things you'd want to do if you could do anything, *great* art. The point is to recognise greatness as a quality distinct from talent or brilliance. Crowe isn't about talent or brilliance – his greatness conceals them. That's what greatness does.

Look at his mass and velocity in LA Confidential: the heaviness of his thought processes, the speed of his temper, the weight of his stupidity, the rapidity of his violence. Crowe's 1940s cop, Bud White, is in a rage because he's not smart, and he knows that the only way to stop being in a rage is to be smart. But he's not smart, because he's in a rage. It's as good a description as any of what it's like to be human. Look at his hatred at being outwitted by the clever people who run the world when he goes to visit the dressing-gown-wearing David

Strathairn. It's like all of Raymond Chandler in a scene. Look at his face when he tells Kim Basinger he'd like to see her again and she says, 'Do you want a date, or an appointment?' and he's too stupid to work out the answer so he just says, 'I don't know.' You see the speed with which his brain has run up and down all its blind alleys and, coming up with nothing, has told him what he is – again. Look at the way he gets trusted with a back-of-the-neck shot to transmit fury. Look at the way he turns the scene of pillow-talk with Basinger from a post-coital conversation into that lovelier thing, an intimate conversation in bed, *just by turning on his side* (heavily and quickly). Remember? That moment – when you realise that there are greater intimacies than sex – that's the moment, just there, with your cigarettes, so often, when love starts. It goes without saying that he's a complete sex bomb. That very natural body that looks like it's never struggled against its DNA . . . only his head.

Crowe's the only current non-comic actor you could seriously say deserves to have films built around him, like adventure playgrounds he can't break. Needless to say, half an hour into LA Confidential, I wanted to run down the street punching the air shouting *Yes!* You wait and you wait and you wait and you wait and then . . .

31

It often happens to women that their wedding day is the only day in their lives that they're taller than their husbands. Having committed herself to something 'sleek and modern', Ilana eventually took her position next to Ross under the *chuppah* in the usual meringue and veil, and an operatic turret of American hair around whose ramparts white roses, clematis and lilies climbed, topped with a mist of gypsophila as if her summit were occluded by low cloud. She looked gorgeous, like a Steel Magnolia. As her bridesmaid, I'd had *my* hair weirdly back-combed. I looked like the Sydney Opera House. It was the first wedding of a friend I'd ever been to, and yet that didn't seem significant. I suppose it was becoming clear to us all that none of the rest of us expected to get married before we were thirty. We were just becoming aware that we were deferrers, and that was fine. Hugh Grant was a deferrer.

The New Jersey cousins examined English change critically in the sunlight (Ilana's father had used computer-modelling to calculate that this was statistically the day of the year most likely to be fine).

'This is worth something,' said Ilana's Aunt Blanche, holding up a one pound coin. 'The rest is garbage.'

'Hamlet's last line in America,' Marcus said to me. He couldn't help himself. 'See over there? On the other side of the moat? The little summer house?' he directed the knot of American relatives he'd already collected. 'That's where Coleridge used to take drugs, before he went into battle.'

'Which battle?'

'Waterloo, actually. But he was too stoned to know it.'

I didn't really approve of his Simon Callow in Four Weddings and a Funeral act. To me, Europeans were ignorant in comparison with Americans, who knew how to pursue happiness – who had invented the movie star.

'Marcus, you can't tease those nice old ladies.'

But it was all too good to waste – the guests, this Oxfordshire castle where the wedding was being held, the lost children screaming in the maze, the little fish lounging in the moat, the day itself, the summer, England, being alive. Paradise. I'd been here before and I think everybody felt it too – the rom-com nature of the day's perfection made everyone a bit self-conscious, I think. I wasn't a fan of those post-Four Weddings movies, though. They weren't about being in love, they were about being in a communal garden reading Captain Corelli's Mandolin, preferably in London. They were about mortgages and makeovers and *setting up your own business* and were all obviously going to end in violent rows about dirt in the coir carpet ten years down the line. (Martha, meet Frank, Daniel and Lawrence – and then get the hell out, quick!) I liked things like Crossing Delancey, and Educating Rita, and Indiana Jones and the Temple of Doom, and Moonstruck, and Ferris Bueller, and Gregory's Girl, and Tootsie, and The Graduate, and Withnail, of course. Romantic comedies which weren't all about restaurant openings and white stucco houses and the South bloody Bank. They were about romance, and comedy.

'We were going to go to a Registry Office but we didn't have the guts,' Ilana said cheerfully. We were briefly hiding out in the castle's kitchens, among caterers and crates. 'So I seem to have ended up with the full Brideshead.' Ilana's Anglophilia made me feel protective about her – as if it were her weak spot, or not so much that as a condition. Chronic, gently progressive, treatable but never curable. And now conversations were beginning to turn important and unbreakoffable; every so often someone would fall out of a boat; Marcus was upstairs going through the finer points of mullioned windows for an architecture student. I'd changed into a strapless red dress and was watching Ross and Ilana being chaired about the dance floor when I overheard someone say, 'Yeah. Lisa Simpson without the brains.' They didn't know I was there as I was concealed behind one of those fences of wine bottles that form on tables at the end of weddings. But that was *me* he was talking about – with my blonde spikes, general sort of yellowish aura, small stature and red dress. *How dare he?* I'd been chatting cheerfully with him not five minutes ago, a messy clever type called Jonathan Marr. Who the hell did he think he was? So I went over to take a picture of him with my disposable. His face fell. 'Smile,' I said. 'Though you may smile, and smile, and be a villain.' I'd never have had the nerve to say something like that if it hadn't been for Marcus. I wouldn't have known what to say either. He was the sort of person who could equip you for life.

32

'He sings he dances he acts he's a real entertainer like Liza Minnelli! he's actually *really talented* and I'm not just saying that he has a way with words he could talk you into buying a house without a roof he's irresistible! people *cannot resist* him you know I bet you've seen him on TV he's had guest spots on NYPD Blue and Homicide and he did the Garry Shandling Show twice? and he was *totally* hilarious *and* he's read personally for Barry Levinson and Don Simpson? and Simpson was going to give him a lead in this romantic comedy that his new production company . . .'

So babbles Natasha Gregson Wagner to Heather Graham at the start of James Toback's improvised 1997 movie Two Girls and a Guy. The boyfriend is Robert Downey Jnr. He's Heather Graham's boyfriend too, it turns out, the two-timing louse.

While the two girls hide in his apartment, plotting their revenge, Downey Jnr enters, unaware that he's not alone, and, for six minutes, sings Vivaldi in both a baritone and an achingly pure soprano, leaves two hilariously dirty messages for his girlfriends ('I am ready to perforate your every orifice with my tongue. I am *hot*'), makes a pretty good stab at the fugue sections of the Vivaldi ('Cum Sancto Spiritu, in Gloria Dei Patris!'), calls his agent ('What happened with this job? Didn't I get it? Why? Too talented as usual?'), improvises a pant-wettingly funny and insulting piece on the piano for his agent's ears ('Bend over and take it like the pig that you are for offering me this job' goes the refrain), turns into an aged Latin cabaret announcer announcing himself, and sings – show-stoppingly – Jackie Wilson's 'If You Don't Know Me' into the mirror. He's irresistible. He's *totally* hilarious. Like *my* boyfriend.

May I gush? I love his face from the bottom of my heart. Like Pan's face, with big unapologetic features, a touch simian, like a compact Jerry Lewis, like a *toy* Jerry Lewis with its sprung head pushed in. I love the way it looks corrupting but not corrupt, the impersonations of propriety it stages while slipping you filthy little winks when the cops are looking the other way, the perpetual intimation of some unspeakable but somehow fun-for-all-the-family deviancy, the Gogolian pleasure taken in the fecundity of lies. RDJ as the Government Inspector! As Tartuffe! And if you haven't seen him in Wonder Boys (2000) do, and if you don't like it, write to my publishers and I'll refund your DVD rental fee – I mean that quite sincerely.

And the terrible irony in Robert Downey Jnr being made an emblem of self-destructiveness – in his being the only major actor of his era branded (in both senses) with drugs whilst snowdrifts of cocaine bank up on the sidewalks of Beverly Hills – is that he, the scapegoat, cannot be made to look like a cautionary tale. He looks like a walking advertisement *for* drugs. Everyone knows that in the last analysis most drugs are just poison. But there should be a special dispensation for anyone who's really good on them. You'd have to go to court, stoned, and prove that you actually were brilliant company. If you couldn't, you'd go to jail, like Richard Dreyfuss. But if you could, you'd get a renewable five-year licence and we'd be allowed to hang out with you, like Hazlitt around Coleridge. Forgive me if this sounds naïve, but it is, I think, the most brilliant solution to the global drug problem yet devised.

As a boyfriend you'd imagine he'd be lazy and spoiled but his moods wouldn't last long, and you'd love it. He'd be needy and mendacious, and you'd love it. He'd be too high tempo to cope with and would probably forget all about you for the occasional fortnight, and you'd love it. He'd forever be apologising with that tear-sheened look he always has in his eyes, aghast at what he'd done, again, and you'd love it. Can you imagine losing someone like Robert Downey Jnr? Can you imagine trying to leave him? There are many super-talented yet joyless people, but the ones who revel in the delightful surprise of their own talent, like Bessie Smith, or Godard, or George Best, or Walt Whitman, or Jack Nicholson, are the true irresistibles. *Brilliance* is a suspect quality, tending, as it can, to turn inwards instead of out, as genius should. Tending to get drunk on itself. Tending not to be a good caretaker of itself. But we're not talking about wasted promise here – Downey Jnr has already *done* it, if you've ever seen his tour de force in the otherwise tedious Chaplin. Two Girls and a Guy is a tour de force, too. And there'll be more, without a doubt. Brilliance, if it means anything, means talent that comes easy. It's not as burdensome as genius, or as hard won as excellence. Brilliance is fun. And fun is usually trouble.

33

It was just after Ilana's wedding that Marcus landed a big part in a prime-time sit-com in which he played a divorced son who'd given up his dreams to look after his Alzheimer's-afflicted mother. And just before the show the announcer would say something like 'Comedy next! How to keep your mum, but lose your marbles!'

Here's a snippet:

Marcus, making his away across the kitchen in the background pauses and sniffs.

Marcus

Mum?

His mentally ill mother, in the foreground, is spraying plants.

Mother

I'll be with you in a moment, Andrew! I'm just giving these a good spray.

Marcus shuffles towards her, nervously sniffing the air like Mole on the riverbank. He sees what she is doing and his mouth drops open, then raises his hands in a gesture that says 'you got me'.

Marcus

But WHY are you using DEODORANT?

And that was it. Unbelievable! Like a show about someone with MS who keeps us in stitches by *dropping things* all the time. It was like Beckett, without the jokes. Marcus would get home and say, 'God, I can't cope with this crap,' and for the first time I saw a lack of confidence. And his disappointment – because sit-coms, truly, are where you can get to do most acting. Who are the best actors in the country? The most revolutionary in their discoveries of subtlety and delicacy? Ricky Gervais. Paul Whitehouse. Chris Morris, and the actors he uses, those barely-known wizardly nanotechnicians like Mark Heap and David Cann. That's acting. But when journalists called to interview Marcus over the phone – as they increasingly did, since he was, after all, the BBC's new boy – he'd manage to steer them away from the show and on to his current pet subjects. Listening to him from the other room I'd applaud his cunning.

'. . . for a billion seconds to tick by takes thirty-two years! But the thing is we don't really have a feel for what a thousand is. A billion, after all, is only a thousand times a million.'

Then . . .

'Of course in the Darwinian sense we need to have a feel for numbers such as how many cows can I see, how many berries am I holding, but nothing much above thirty or so, and it's only very recently in terms of evolution that we have even started talking about billions . . .'

And even . . .

'The thing about lemons is *that nobody actually knows where they come from . . .*'

If it was something I'd told him I'd feel encouraged, and if not, redundant, becoming really quite superstitious about these things, thinking to myself, 'If he says the thing about lemons he loves me and if he doesn't, then he doesn't, and what am I going to do then?'

34

In this world my hard-won 'career' shrivelled into 'the little film thing on the local paper Marcus's girlfriend has for pin money'. I had become a housewife, which, frankly, was *ace*. 'Yes, I *will* get Marcus to call you back, but if you'll excuse me I've just got to check on my casserole.' Then I'd check on the casserole and wander through the different rooms of the house feeling all that cubic yardage of owned air on my skin like silk. The silence of the street in the afternoon was disorientating, like the silence after a war. But Marcus was such a blaze, so in demand, that I couldn't help but nurture everyday worries of being left behind. I thought of Suleiman the Magnificent and the humble Roxelana.

Then one day I got a call from Radio 4 asking me if I had anything negative to say about Al Pacino.

'Well . . . he shouts a lot these days.'

'Anything else?' They were craving negative things about Al Pacino.

Not really. By 1996 Pacino had totally lost control of his voice. When Kay tells Michael that she's taking the children in The Godfather Part II and he makes his great speech beginning, 'Do you expect me to let you go?' he played his voice like an oboe. A beautiful wind instrument. By Heat (1995 – 'What am I, an *owwwl*?') he was like a guy on the electric guitar. The producer wanted me to do a series of five-minute profiles of actors for a film show on the radio called Back Row, so called to complement the weekday evening arts programme Front Row, which they also wanted me to review films on. The Camden New Journal was free, and people read it.

'But if you do Back Row, you can't do Front Row,' said the producer, 'so you'll have to choose.'

'Can't I do both?'

'No, it's front or back, I'm afraid.'

(I couldn't wait to tell Marcus *that*.) Not to put too fine a point on it, *fucking hell*! All I'd ever done was fail my degree and be too incompetent to hack it as a reporter, and now someone was offering me the best job in the world! It was a licence to re-watch old favourites, *for money*. Harvey Keitel, for instance, was an obvious excuse to see Taxi Driver one more time. Doing De Niro would, naturally, necessitate another quick reassessment of Taxi Driver. Albert Brooks? Well, it would probably be unprofessional not to study his thirty or forty words in Taxi Driver. This was film-reviewing at its purest. This was *diligence*. There on the John Lewis sofa watching Travis Bickle for the ninth time in two months, wearing the profoundly inconvenienced expression of the hard at work.

They recorded them on the morning before broadcast, so I'd wake up early, turn on the video, and watch a scene in bed with Marcus. It was illuminating watching movies with him. Where the rest of us see stories, he saw a lattice work of technical decisions – blocking, dialogue edging, shooting across the line.

'Notice how Spacey stops when he leaves the office and hits the mark he's going to have to hold to talk to Jonathan Pryce.'

Spacey's hair looks like spill-proof carpeting I would write, and then cycle down Regent Street to the studio.

'It can't be too gushy, Antonia, it's got to be accurate.'

I tried not to be gushy, but kept finding reasons to be thrilled about everybody. I'd begin with the ice-hearted intention of eviscerating someone like Kevin Costner, or the egregious Penn, or square old Denzel Washington, or Brad Pitt or Bruce bloody Willis. And then you end up re-watching Tin Cup (stupendously easy and natural performance) or Carlito's Way (in which Penn, playing a coke-addled slimeball lawyer, has a moment – do you remember? – on a late afternoon lawn pleading with Pacino to help him out, in which everything you've ever felt about cocaine is contained). Or Cry Freedom (I love Washington's posture; nobody stands like Denzel Washington. Gregory Peck did thirty years ago). We're too quick sometimes to discard the stars we tire of – like, let's face it, Schwarzenegger, who was once inarguably a brilliant young Terminator – and we blank out the thrill that once came off them. I was in love and I gushed.

Though I couldn't think of *anything* to say about Brad Pitt.

35

A word about Willis, who's been slaloming in and out of respect for the past twenty years. Treasured for his cameos or quieter stuff, his Sixth Senses and his Players and Pulp Fictions, and derided for his grubby-vest bollocks, in Die Hard Willis did something that no performer of his era has ever managed. It's when he's in the ventilator shaft, in dire straits, and he sparks his lighter, looks into the camera and says: 'Come out to the coast, we'll get together, have a few laughs!' That's how lively and puckish and foxy and trusted Willis was after his reign as David Addison in Moonlighting: that it should seem perfectly natural that he should be allowed to make an aside to the camera in the middle of an action movie. It was his *act* that people wanted. Bruce has *grace*. How can you not delight in all the variety of his gun-holding? His work with lighters? His smudge-wearing? His moonwalking backwards-sidle? An action film is a dance; usually a comic dance. You've got to be a clown, up in the class of the great silent boys. Willis had the best 'pre-explosion look' among his peers, for instance – he could always make you laugh in the second before something blew up. Don't knock Willis. He's got *rhythm*. Does Orlando Bloom have rhythm? Does Colin Farrell? No. So shut up.

36

The day of the first recording Marcus ushered me upstairs to the Quirke Memorial Library and asked me to stay away.

'You're *crazy*,' I said. 'It's going to be fine! I want to come.'

'It is shit and nothing can save me. You get *tarred*, Antonia. Flops *tar* you.'

But I went and took a seat in the audience with Janie and Aubrey.

'*Such* a large crowd!' said Janie. 'How nice of them all to come! Are they *all* Marcus's friends?'

'No, Janie, they're mostly just people who asked the BBC for tickets.'

'How *nice* of them! How *sweet*! Marcus must be *thrilled*.'

Not thrilled exactly, no, but certainly gracious and helpful to the other members of the cast, backing the production manager when she asked the audience to laugh *really hard* if they found something funny, so that the show went with a swing. Making comical little begging gestures to us for ever bigger laughs, keeping the audience up between scenes by pretending to smooch with the girl who played his ex-wife. He was a model of capability. Not even I could tell he was hating it. Or only just. Over his face was a pink wash imperceptible to most – shame coming up from the inside, and I felt the same intenseness of sympathy that Marsha Mason feels for Richard Dreyfuss in The Goodbye Girl (1977) when she's watching him on stage mincing around as a camp Off-Broadway Richard III. Because this sit-com, I realised, really was career-destroyingly terrible.

I saw a steel in him those days, an incredible discipline, and suddenly thought that here was a man who was perhaps not trusting to luck at all, who was trying very hard and was used to bending most things to his will. I even began to fear him a little. And not just that, I began to fear myself, full as I was of this overwhelming possessiveness, a possessiveness that began to extend to not really wanting him to go to work because it pissed him off and kept him distant from me, a possessiveness that seemed to spring from my utter incompleteness and as such was stronger than anything I had ever felt, so strong it made me sweat on the stairs when he went out.

37

He looks like a man in a headache advert. The two vertical furrows between his eyebrows as if his head is imploding. The insomniac bags beneath his eyes. The way the eye whites and teeth flash out from the ingrained dust like the face of a savage under war paint. The mouth never fully closed, like he's forgotten how to breathe easily. That's Fred C. Dobbs in The Treasure of the Sierra Madre (1948). One of Humphrey

Bogart's best performances, particularly because it was *Bogart* and this was his first post-'Bogie' part. Dobbs, you may remember, is the gold prospector who strikes lucky in the wild mountains of Mexico but is driven to paranoia about his two partners by his own runaway gold-fever.

'I know what your game is,' says Bogart in that slightly stagey John Huston speech. 'Why am I elected to go to the village instead of you and Curtin? Oh, don't think I don't see through that! You two've thrown together against me! The two days I'd be gone would give you plenty of time to discover where my goods are, wouldn't it?'

'If you think along those lines, why don't you take your goods along with you?' says decent old Walter Huston.

'And run the risk of having them taken from me by bandits?'

'If you was to run into bandits you'd be out of luck anyway. They'd kill you for the shoes on your feet.'

'Oh, so that's it – everything's clear now! You're hoping bandits'll get me!'

It wasn't a 'career move' or a 'reinvention', it was a proper development for Bogart. These days, playing against type for a mega-star is usually described as somebody 'deconstructing their own myth', or if they're not big enough to have a myth it's just 'brilliant casting'. But maybe it's just somebody following the logic of their myth through. The next stage for Bogie – the character isolated by his own integrity, with his Hemingwayan refusal to say much about his motivation or to take credit for his goodness – was the paranoid Dobbs. Dobbs was what a Bogie under pressure would eventually curdle into. All that detachment and disenchantment and unwillingness to trust that made more people want to be Bogie than have ever wanted to be any other star, was really paranoia in the first place. Why is the guy with the gun and the trenchcoat and the utter self-sufficiency *the* Romantic icon of cinema? Because, not to sound too much like a lip-smacking Cultural Studies killjoy, he's a paranoid juvenile fantasy, that's why. And the movies are a juvenile and Romantic form. And Romantics are paranoid. *Dobbs.* I knew Fred C. Dobbs like a Python fan knows his dead parrot. I liked to imagine him mouthing along to The Big Sleep in some fleapit, whispering 'Bogie' to himself in the darkness, feeling tough.

Like I said, Romantics are paranoid. And it was Fred C. Dobbs who growled through my head those days spent sitting on the stairs worrying about the lemons: 'Yeah. So he *said* the thing about the lemons. But he was just foolin' me. Making me *think* he cares. But I'm onto him. He don't love me. Thought he could pull the wool over my eyes! He tried to fool me with them lemons. But I was too smart for him! Right?'

38

'Keep Friday free,' Marcus said. 'I've got something for you that could change your life.'

'What? What thing? God, *what*?'

'You're going to love it. I hope. Well, I assume you'll love it. I hope you'll love it. It's shiny. It'll really suit you.'

'Is it clothes?'

'No, but you can wear it.'

'Jesus, Mum. I think Marcus is going to propose to me on Friday.'

She sounded dubious: 'Well, he hasn't asked Dad for permission, and Marcus has always struck me as the kind of person who *would* ask for permission.' She had met Marcus once and developed a migraine the moment she looked at him, groping her way out of the house to the car and suggesting to me via bloodshot eyes alone that he was wrong in a way too dreadful for words, hence the uptightness.

On Friday Marcus sat me on a chair in the kitchen, knelt down and took my hand. I blushed, and prepared myself to join the ranks. Then he put something in my hand – a small box. Through the wall I heard the woman next door letting her dog out into the garden, and its pant as it rushed down the back steps. I closed my eyes, opened the box, and looked down. It was a digital camera. A very small digital camera, a James Bond kind of spy camera, actually, from one of those strange shops for surveillance operatives on Baker Street, and pretty in its own way and, yes, very shiny and you *could* always wear it round your neck if you were perhaps the sort of person who likes to wear amulets.

I writhed in a spoilt silence until Marcus spoke.

'You said the other day you'd never had a camera and I thought because you liked faces so much you might be a good photographer and . . . could perhaps branch out a little.'

Eventually he got up and idled at the door, obviously wondering why I was looking at him as though he'd just given me a Chinese burn.

Then, two months later, I called him on his mobile phone one afternoon and he sounded very shifty.

'Where are you?' I asked.

'It's a secret.'

'Why? What is it? What kind of secret?'

'I'm choosing something for you . . . something I frankly want you to have because it's time you got serious about the things in your life that you really love.'

'How serious? What things?'

'Wait and see. But it won't be ready till next week.'

This time it was a computer of my own – for years I'd been borrowing one from Eric. So I got a bit more serious about my writing but not nearly as serious as I would have liked to have got about Marcus.

Around the same time, Marcus was on the phone to a journalist from the Mail on Sunday who was interviewing him for a little piece, and they were chatting and I was cooking and Marcus was answering questions like 'Do you like Indian food?' ('D'you know, Indian is *not* my favourite, so many *lentils*, which originally came from sub-Saharan Africa where they were thought of as cattle fodder. Interesting thing about . . .') and what would you rescue first if your house was on fire ('My cigarettes. And a painting of a sheep, which has great sentimental value'). When he said he much preferred Brigitte Bardot to Audrey Hepburn, I nodded, admiring his taste. (God, how I hate Audrey Hepburn, by the way. Not a single word she says is not part of a pre-built cadence. There is *nothing* that is not mannerism. When people say they admire her vulnerability, what they are really admiring is her armour – she is someone who does not seem to be growing or responding or interacting with the world in any genuine way.) So I was cooking away and nodding when he said:

'No, of course! That's perfectly alright of you to ask – I'm single.'

I looked at him, quizzically, and carried on looking like that with my wooden spoon suspended until the interview finished and he put the phone down.

'What do you mean you're single? What am I?'

'Well you're either married or single. And we're not married so I'm single.'

'But you're not single, you're living with me.'

'Yes, but we're not married.'

'But that doesn't make you *single*.'

'It doesn't make me married either.'

'But *you're not single*.'

'If I had to fill out a form and tick the Married box or the Single box, I would be legally obliged to tick Single. There is no box saying "well, we met and she didn't go home" or "hard to say but all her stuff is here". I would have to tick the Single box.'

'But you're not ticking any boxes. You were talking to a journalist and now she thinks you're single!'

'No-oo. She thinks I'm not married.'

'*No*, she thinks you're single!'

'Well, she's right. I am single. But I'm also going out with you.'

'But that doesn't make any sense. Can't you *see* how ridiculous that sounds?'

'Antonia. Are we married?'

'No.'

'Well, then!'

That Sunday the piece appeared, and at the end of it was the line: 'And hey, girls, the good news is – he's single!' Ilana called and said isn't it incredible how those goddamn scum journalists make things up all the time because it says here he's single and I said, well, actually, he did say he was single because we're not married after all, and she said is it because actors have to pretend to be single so as not to put off the fans, like popstars used to, and I said possibly, yes, and she said who did Marcus think I was, Cynthia fucking Lennon?

Then, a fortnight later Marcus said: 'When you finish at the radio can you come straight back?'

'Why?'

'Because I've got something for you. It's getting silly now – it has to be sorted out.'

'What has to be sorted out? *What?*'

It was a car – another 2CV, an extremely pretty white one to make up for the one that burned. Later that month my elder brother Saul got married and used the 2CV to drive away from the reception, with JUST MARRIED sprayed on the back along with some tin cans attached with string. When Marcus and I made our way back from the wedding in the car we didn't think to take any of the paraphernalia off it, so people kept beeping their horns at us and giving us the thumbs up, and Marcus waved back while I sat there, bootfaced, with Fred C. Dobbs chuntering in my head all the way from Yorkshire.

I only tell you these deeply unflattering things to demonstrate how occasionally life can be like a movie you'd much rather not be in.

39

It's not the stills of actors in performance, it's the photographs of them rehearsing. The tubed scripts, the monkey crouches, the director's dozen-fingered hands, the studiedly demotic working outfits (the crinkle-crotched jeans and bovver-boy turn-ups), the indolence and love of sprawling . . . I don't want to be there, but I want them to be there, in the early 1980s, parlaying earnest rants against Margaret Thatcher into a hundred thousand one-night stands. And this ineradicable nostalgia of mine, a half-false, half-fantasised memory patched together from *stills*, is the reason why it remains impossible for me ever to think of Marcus, who was the lover my child-hood daydreams had constructed, without feeling that I had been subject to an enchantment. It remains, crazily, my most defenceless place. And there is always a pulse of shame attending any memory I have, not of having been expelled, like Keats's knight-at-arms awaking on the cold hill's side, but of having been so easy to bewitch in the first place, something I handle by rarely meeting Marcus, and never, ever, going to the theatre.

40

What it was like, was like Serpico (1973, Al Pacino at his most beautiful as the one honest cop, *and* Tony Roberts too, being very funny and stoned, falling to his knees in front of a crisp-machine saying, 'Come out potatoes!'). It's the scene where Cornelia Sharpe takes Pacino to a party and he wanders around charming all the hippies, sitting in a corner with a girl who claims to think Japanese culture and theatre is 'too rigidly *stylised*', and he says, 'Yeah, well . . . ya'know . . . yeah . . . but I think, after a while you get through that and start to appreciate the clarity . . . the authority.' Then he's off wowing some-body else, joking that 'there have been sheepdogs in my family dating back sixteen generations. Dating back to the *Borgias*. The family crest is a sheepdog pissing into a gondola . . .' (which he pronounces 'gon-*dohl*a'). And then he starts dancing wildly (has Pacino ever looked so happy?) and Cornelia Sharpe throws her arms round his neck in a delirium of pride, saying, 'Paco! Everybody loves you! I love you!'

Well, everybody loved Marcus too. And it was now I began to get the feeling that I had competition, particularly in the form of an extremely beautiful and tall girl from South Carolina who had come to London to write a book on 'bondage and the single girl' – or some such waffle about how unsentimental and sexy metropolitan women are – and live with her boyfriend, a quite-famous British intellectual who, for all his dirty talk, rarely wanted to go to bed with her and preferred McDonald's and the multiplex to the sort of upper-crust bohemianism she'd been hoping for. Marcus on the other hand flew his own yellow aeroplane and had a family crest dating back sixteen generations. When he referred to his pregnant sister Harriet as being 'in the pig', I thought the American would die of the thrill. She was always coming around with still-warm home-made cookies – I mean, in little *wicker baskets* – and ogling him in the kitchen. I had been immunised to this kind of thing because just about every girl I knew fell in love with Marcus for a fortnight or so of trips to exhibitions, concerts and lunches, before reluctantly coming to terms with the situation. But the Southern girl was lovely, grown up and sophisticated like an American actress sent over to add authority to a British production.

I had all my unserious curls cut off then, close into the neck and feathered in front of my ears.

'Like Jean Seberg,' said the hairdresser.

'Like Mia Farrow,' said Marcus.

'It's really Kenneth Branagh as Hamlet that I was going for,' I said.

And from then on Marcus called me his Gloomy Dane. His Gloomy Dane. Why didn't he call me his Most Royal? I started to *sneeze*. It was an unusually and reassuringly frosty Christmas – sub-zero temperatures, an inch of snow on the car roofs

– but this was no cold. I couldn't stop. My throat itched, my arms itched, I had a rash round my mouth like Gwyneth Paltrow's ratty little beard in Shakespeare in Love, and two or three times every minute, every hour of the day and through the night, I'd contract into a plosive little sneeze. We moved everything with feathers out of the house and got a cleaner in to tackle the dust, even though I'd dusted every crevice myself. When people came round for dinner I would go and sit in a bath of cold water, supposedly demonstrating both sense of humour and presence of mind, listening to Marcus talking downstairs and considering my arms – violet from the itching. The worst thing was how I terrorised the screening-rooms, putting everybody's back up like a baby wailing through a wedding speech until I dozed off on the antihistamines I'd stuffed myself with. I was sneezing so much I couldn't make it through a single driving lesson. Have you ever seen the magnificent Safe (1995) by Todd Haynes, with Julianne Moore as a Los Angeles housewife who starts off reacting to a perm and winds up hiding out from her mystery ailments in an oxygen tent in the Nevada Desert? I was well on my way to that tent. One of the doctors I saw told me to drink my own pee and – most vehemently – to avoid licking adhesives that contained wheat. This, Marcus found ridiculous.

'How can anyone be allergic to a *stamp*?'

Oh, I did lots of things that annoyed him. Any living thing – flowers, fruit – seemed literally to get up my nose and I would put them straight in the bin. I kept little bottles of pee in the fridge next to his bottles of Château d'Yquem. I threw everything away – keys, cashcards, that week's Radio Times. I bought dishcloths and hoover bags and standing orders to dog shelters from every Tom, Dick or Harry that knocked on the door. I forgot to sieve the port like you're supposed to. I would sit on the edge of the bed with the belt of my fungal bathrobe trailing, blowing my nose on pairs of his discarded underpants.

And though he sent me notes saying things like *there's the rest of your magnificent boeuf dans le frigidaire si tu veux to have with your wee-wee*, I was certain I could sense a turning away. And I was too much in love with him to do anything other than point this out. *You don't love me.* In the supermarket. In the interval. In the bedroom. *You don't love me really, do you, not any more?*

'What do *you* think?' said Marcus, reassuringly, like Jack Nicholson to Karen Black in Five Easy Pieces.

'Are you happy with me?' I'd ask.

'Let's not speculate about happiness,' Marcus said, like Leslie Howard to Ingrid Bergman in Intermezzo.

'I love you, Marcus,' I'd say.

'Ditto,' he'd say, like Adrian Dunbar to Tara Fitzgerald in Hear My Song.

41

In February Harriet gave birth – to twins. We went to Seldon for the christening and I was terribly sick, having been out drinking the night before with Marcus and Ross and Ilana. On the train I threw up out of the window, losing my dignity entirely. 'Jesus wept,' Marcus said. 'Do try and keep it together, darling.' But I was coming apart all over, everything wanted to come out, and it wasn't just the hangover. Aubrey picked us up from the station and drove us to the house crushed together in the sidecar of his motorbike, and I was a little bit sick on my dress. 'Try, for Christ's sake,' said Marcus. 'It's a *christening*.' I couldn't understand how Marcus could be so well. He had drunk bottles of wine, and lager and cider, and some brandy, and some properly sieved port, I had *seen* him.

Halfway through the service I had to leave the chapel and make my way to the family graveyard which gave on to enormous dark-ploughed fields, where the usual crows were strutting down the furrows with their arms behind their backs like invigilators touring rows of desks. I leaned against the headstone of somebody who had once had something to do with Marcus's genes and tried to keep the sick off my shoes. Janie and Duzz weren't the types to frown on this kind of thing. But Marcus was nowhere to be seen, already back at the house, taking care of drinks, working the crowd, anagrammatising the twins' names for the local gentry.

'Dear oh dear!' said Duzz. 'Were you drinking poteen? Was it *iced*?'

It didn't matter. Everything was sliding away from me. I was never going to be coming here again. I could see him at the reception, Suleiman the Magnificent. And really it had been in front of me all along, how he liked new crowds the best, how he had the special terror of the socialite, of crowds of known people, people he'd already won, people with whom there was nothing really left to *do*. In any given room he was the Terminator, with special vision able to discern who should be charmed first, who needed geeing up or rescuing. I *feared* this almost impersonal efficiency. I felt like a five-year-old, beckoned on to the stage by Captain Hook. And I worried that the old thing Guildenstern says about actors – 'they're the opposite of people' – was true after all. They were the opposite because they needed nothing back. They vanished if they weren't giving – like Marcus, my tutor, my patron. Have I not got Marcus across to you yet? Have I failed? Alright. He had a pull-down cinema screen in the kitchen and managed to manufacture an entirely realistic laminated, bar-coded, *holo-grammed* Film Club membership card solely for me, with a little photograph on it. That was just for the look on my face. That is what he wanted above all. The look on my face. That is all you're allowed to give some men.

Around five o'clock, when the party had broken up, I went looking for him. Up and down the corridors, the dozen staircases, through the whole Gormenghastian maze. There were no longer tights knotted around the corners of Harriet's four-poster. Eventually I found a bathroom in the nursery with its door locked.

'Marcus? Marcus, is that you?'

There was a silence – he was turning into a werewolf, perhaps.

'I'm sick.'

'Why? Is it something you ate? What was it you ate? Are you alright?'

'It wasn't something I ate, Antonia, it was all I drank last fucking night. I've got a hangover, that's all. Go away.'

'But why now? Why are you feeling sick now? Have you been drunk all day?'

'No, I fucking haven't. I've been feeling ghastly all day. I've been feeling as bad as you. It's called *acting*.'

That was the straitjacket of the Good Grace Cardigan – you maintained your control and maintained your control until you could slump on the floor with your head against the loo, and finally undo it.

'I've been *trying*, you know? Just go away.'

I didn't appreciate all the hard work that went on behind the scenes, was the charge. I was silly. I wasn't enough fun. I was too young and I couldn't keep up. All I could give him was the look on my face. So I had to go away.

42

How stale, flat, weary, and unprofitable seem to me all the uses of this world – Marcus had taught me that too.

The length of a minute. The length of an hour. The tricks time suddenly starts pulling. The clock's sleight of hand. The way that half an hour after ten past two it's half past one. The length of a *second*. The disappearing fortnight. The year it would take to win him back. The decade it would take to get better. The eternity it took to say 'Nothing' when people asked what the matter was.

Oh, I went to pieces. I cried looking at the happy dogs at bus stops. I cried at the starless sockets on the name tags of burger-bar employees. I cried at the Christian names of streets. Bayswater Road. *Bays-water*. Greenland Road. Rochester Terrace. Coldharbour Lane. The state of catatonia, the state where the reigning prince is the prince of emptiness, the prince of absence, the prince of desolation. I needed things to cling to. The sofa in Ilana's flat. Ilana. Gérard Depardieu. The reassuringness of bulk. Gérard's bulk. His hair. Like his mother had cut it. His mother saying, 'We're gonna need a bigger bowl.' The fat man's grace. The heaviest man, even when he was thin. Les Valseuses, 1974. A body like Irek Mukhamedov's. Dancer's hips. Narrower than you'd think. Swimmer's shoulders. Only 5′ 11″ but he looks 6′ 4″.

Green Card – his fingernail, bitten like a schoolboy's, when he's explaining his tattoos. His *own* tattoos. One on his arm with a heart half coloured, half blank: *This is how the heart is, half love, half hate. People say they love everything, but it's not true. This is my honesty. This is how the heart is* . . . The voice, all throat, all diaphragm, no edge.

At home in the vineyard, fat as a tractor, like a one-man justification of the French way of life. His peasant recipes. Comfort food. Something solid to return to. Pines when he's away from the things he loves. Like Jean de Florette in his tax collector's office – exiled in a state of catatonia. Needs to be loved too much, says his ex-wife. Needs to be connected to the well-spring: wine, Frenchness, the Great Tradition – Molière, Balzac, Zola, Rostand, Hugo, Asterix, Jean Gabin. Thought of as a buffoon in France these days a friend told me, but they'll be shellshocked when he dies.

Bit of a death wish? Six bottles of wine a day. 'When I am relaxed, only three or four.' Five movies in 2004. Wants to die on the field of battle. Like a poet-warrior. Sword in hand, and . . . 'Cut!' An actor muddled up with the greatness of the characters he's played. The best kind. Mark of the true great. The only actor I have ever seriously considered getting on a plane for and driving down to the house to throw myself at his feet, offering everything, offering marriage. Could imagine myself doing anything with him, things I'd never do with anyone else, going completely haywire. *The sexiest of the lot.* Because of his solipsism, his self-centredness. Son hates him, gave an interview about it. Actors eat people. Brando. Laughton. Greedy bastards. Vampires. *Marcus.* The *I Want I Want I Want.* The longing. Cyrano's longing. The insatiable longing of the great artist. My longing. I wanted I wanted I wanted. I wanted him.

43

'When I first came over from NYU to Oxford, all my friends were going, "What are you going to eat? There's no sushi in England. They don't have rice cakes. They put *pineapple* on their bacon." So I'm on the coach from Heathrow to Oxford and I see all these fish bars – fish bar, fish bar, everywhere – so I call my dorm and go, "The English have more sushi than Tokyo! It's like fish bar *heaven*." Then I went into one and saw the pickled eggs . . . not that I mind fish and chips. But it's too late to change now – my mom was always on at me about my weight. When I was a teenager, and I took an extra piece of cake, she'd be like, "How can you do this to your father?" and so what I did was I watered down the whisky in the cocktail cabinet as revenge, only Mom and Dad – who have like *one drink a year* at Thanksgiving – never noticed and then we have this party and I hear this guy saying, "Goddamn Jews, this scotch is two-thirds water!"'

When Ilana came home from work she would sit with me and tell me about New Jersey, rightly divining that, to me, America was a comforting fiction. It killed me that she didn't mind my face, my picked fingers, my slept-in shirt. She and Ross had a little box room in their flat and squeezed in a mattress between the bags of smokeless fuel, albums on vinyl and stacks of tragic videos. The videos said Crocodile Dundee II, Riverdance: The Movie, Dune. They said 'Spare' and 'Blank' and '?' and 'Keep'. The bag I had brought from Marcus's held fewer chattels of mine than mementos of him. There are people who must make bonfires of their exes but I have always retained the evidence, perhaps because I have never felt a true

owner of anything I haven't acquired or inherited from someone else. All my possessions have either been given or stolen.

Looking out of the box room's window I wondered why
Ilana had come here, why any American would come to this
dinky, two-bit town. I thought about a tall, accomplished
woman who carried her cookies in a wicker basket and never
sneezed. In the worst nights, when I felt I would suffocate, I
would hunt for traces of Marcus's breath in the dregs of the
tear-tasting ether from an old asthma inhaler of his which I'd
smuggled away.

I remember an evening when Ilana tried to coax me out
of the box room. Some friends of hers were going to see As
Good as it Gets, but the Lisa Simpson guy would be there, and
I could no longer stomach the idea of Jack Nicholson. I didn't
want to see him at all. *At all.* I felt suspicious now of people
who shone at parties. People loved by absolutely everyone.
Long before As Good as it Gets, Nicholson's tempo-shifts had
become operatics; his menacing sexual confidence, sated sexual
confidence; his quiet unhappiness, noisy happiness; his *delight*,
sniggering mischief. He was loved too much. A great star;
a lousy superstar. His films were like those papal courtside
waves he gave at Knicks games. You could even hear the decline in his name. Jack. Such a simple, modest, snappy name.
But over the years that *a* had hypertrophied into the *a* one says
with Italian-American hands, chin held into windpipe. A fat
Goodfellas vowel, bloated with sappy love. *Jaaaack.* So loved he
no longer needed his surname. Everybody loved Jack, loved
Marcus: *Jaaaack*, I thought, I'm through.

Blank. Nothing. ?

44

I frequently took refuge, as many heartbroken women have done, among my own sex. At the Ladies' Pond on Hampstead Heath I would sit and sneeze among the rock-hard Russian women there. Small-time mafia wives, you couldn't help but think. I took comfort from the forcefulness of the sound of their words. They used to read each other's Tarot cards and twice I had picked out the Magician. *Excuse me, is the Wizard in?* In the tea-coloured water I would swim deeply, gripping the life-rings' slimy ropes at their roots so I could stay down there longer, where I wanted to be, with the slothful, mulch-grazing carp. Zonked fatties ruling a kingdom of sludge. Conquering her native phobia of the unhygienic, Ilana would sometimes come along at the weekend to keep me company.

'I might as well tell you,' she said, one of those days in June, 'because you're going to hear about it anyway. I was talking to someone who works at White City and I mentioned Marcus and she said . . .' Ilana was slowing down, ominously. When she was breaking bad news, her face grew Eastern European, like an understanding Polish peasant from The Tin Drum. 'She said – *Jesus.* She said, "Is he still going out with *that poor girl?*" and I said, "What do you mean?"' Something terrible was about to descend. I braced myself. Marcus had been cheating on me with his leading lady in Scarborough. And Ilana was right, I did hear about it. I never stopped hearing about it. The girl from Scarborough. The cookie girl, of course. A receptionist at the Groucho Club, the cookie girl's *flatmate*, the architecture student he'd explained mullioned windows to at the wedding. And others, going back, seemingly, to about fifteen minutes after we'd met.

And you know, I couldn't help but take my hat off to him. It wasn't in me, then, to tell him he was a cold-hearted prick who wanted to see me hanging from a tree in the garden. He was an actor. And cheating is the one area of life where everybody gets to act, the one area where your acting really counts, and it can be thrilling, more thrilling than the cheating itself. Some people can't cheat, not through any moral decision, but simply because the prospect of acting is too awful to contemplate. They just don't have the talent. And one wonders whether it *is* a virtue to be completely unable to function when dissembling, when acting your head off. Actors always like to think that acting is about giving. But a great actor knows that it's about concealing. Great actors are people with something to conceal – usually their emptiness. Like Olivier. Like Brando. Marcus was simply too happy within that whole world of sudden facial straightenings, and desperate dashes across town, and breathless whispered conferences for you ever seriously to want to change him. He was an actor, and he needed someone to egg him on to ever-greater performances. And that had been me, the movie critic, the straight-man, the groupie.

One place I could go to and cry with impunity was anywhere which was screening the newly released Breaking the Waves. Breaking the Waves wasn't a tear-jerker like It's a Wonderful Life or ET. It was an Eviscerator. When the lights came up, people weren't silently weeping, they were jack-knifed over with their faces in their hands, racked with storms of sobbing. Arid Film Studies types in oblong glasses come to see whether Lars Von Trier had moved on since Europa, sat stunned in their masks of tears. The audience as a whole looked wrecked, like the losing crew at the end of the Boat Race. I saw the film five times. The first time because I wanted to watch the blues. The second because I felt at home in the Hall of Tears. And then again and again and again because of Stellan Skarsgard. Skarsgard was born in 1951 and spent the seventies on stage in Sweden running through the canon. *Lots* of Strindberg. In 1982 he gave a performance as a halfwit in a film called The Simple-Minded Murderer which they're still talking about in Gothenberg and which I'd love to see one of these days. From then it was just a matter of time. You can see him being very frightening as a secret policeman in The Unbearable Lightness of Being, but it was Breaking the Waves when everybody first thought: *Who the hell is that?*

Skarsgard plays an oil-rig worker who marries a sort of idiot savant saint (Emily Watson) whose love is so great she ends up generating a miracle. He's the straight-man to Watson's planet-shaking, award-winning performance (like Tom Cruise opposite Dustin Hoffman in Rain Man). He's got to anchor the movie. But the movie, which is about love, is very complicated. And Christ, he's astonishing. You can feel his breath on your cheek. You can smell his warm ursine smell. He demonstrates about nineteen different forms of love, forever modulating and shifting into each other. He doesn't know whether to protect the girl, or protect himself from her. He's always watching her intently, unsure whether he's a babysitter or a pupil or a teacher or a victim, a sex god bringing a virgin to bloom or an ordinary guy redeemed by a sex genius, or Job caught in the crossfire, or Lazarus lucking out, or Saul going *why me?* on the road to Damascus. He puts them all in, and it's all coherent, clear as his beautiful Swedish enunciation, fluid as his face (*nobody* has as expressive a face as Skarsgard – you could cast him as God or a surf dude). And, crucially, in a film which is always about an inch away from being annoying he's irresistibly likeable. That's the thing about Stellan Skarsgard – you can't not like him. Everybody likes him. A guy who can be trusted. And I owe Stellan, for being vivid enough to furnish me with brief respites from another face. Let's be honest here, girls, if a guy in a suit turned up at your house out of the blue and said, 'Stellan Skarsgard's fallen for you – he knows this may sound a little odd but here's a one-way ticket to Stockholm and an engagement ring: yes or no?' you wouldn't even be going upstairs to change, would you? Let's be *honest* here, girls.

And, incidentally, he's *always* doing this.

45

You shouldn't, the wisdom runs, go out on your own if you're feeling blue. But let me counter that with the observation that although you might not consciously want to meet somebody, it's just about the only time you ever find yourself sitting unprotected by friends in a bar at eight o'clock on a Saturday night (the Curzon, Shaftesbury Avenue) soulfully sipping a drink (a value-for-money pint of lime and soda), thinking profound thoughts (*Who are the Cabinet exactly? I know they're Blair's advisors, but are they all actually MPs?*) and, though you may not know it, generally receptive to the world.

Dan was dark and slim, with a mole high on his right cheek like De Niro's and had, like me, just come out of Les Parapluies de Cherbourg, so it was almost surprising to hear him speak to me rather than sing. He looked more beaky and worried than

De Niro, more like David Tennant, not that I knew that at the time, but he had Tennant's habit of always slightly holding his head back like a man on the lookout, and brown eyes with an underlay of green, like leaves seen through the water of the Ladies' Pond. Dan was a financial advisor, fidgety and very capable, and a little bruised by the fact that his father, a clergy-man, had recently come out to his family, leaving them for a bearded psychologist he'd met on the tube. He had patience, and an adult's conviction that I would come round to him in time. I liked him, although that didn't seem to have anything much to do with things right now. I liked him like I liked George Clooney, because of his adultness. Every time I snuck a look at FHM it seemed it was full of boys in suits, hoping that they looked like Steve McQueen or Sinatra. Then you'd go to Con Air and see John Cusack, or Godzilla for Matthew Broderick, and feel their terrible shortfall of weight. It was like there was a global crisis of gravitas. As if there were an oubliette waiting for men at the end of their twenties from which they'd emerge only as squares – as Kevin Costner or Bill Pullman. Suddenly, the transition from boy to man seemed to have become a fiendishly tricky act of reinvention. And it was to the ageless stars like Cary Grant or Robert Mitchum that the FHMers kept yearning back. Clooney (who is only a year older than Brad Pitt, don't forget) showed up like an obvious answer that had been on the tip of your tongue for years. Here was someone who could separate cool from youth. He had the almost forgotten talent of looking like time was not the most important thing happening to him. Like Cary Grant, he has played and will play a man of the same age for three decades. That age being: no age at all. The Prime. A producer on ER, Clooney says, once came up to him and told him, 'If you keep your head still, you'll be a star.' *That's right*. That's what stardom is. That's cool. To project a fixity of personality in the face of time. You conquer time and you conquer your fear of death: you're a hero. Clooney is a hero where Pitt just looks frightened of dying. (As a *director* that's Clooney's flaw. You don't want adults behind the camera, you want children, like Hitchcock or Orson Welles.)

The thing is, I didn't know any adults. Goddamned Marcus had been brilliant at acting an adult, but he was really Peter Ustinov – a big, happy kid. There didn't seem to be any adults *about* – those very few of my friends who were married weren't terribly happy and seemed already to be looking to eject themselves back into the lightness of youth. Whenever Ross mentioned Ilana, he'd talk Guy Ritchie-ishly about 'getting back to the missus'. And, just as if he were Nick Moran or Jason Flemyng in a Guy Ritchie movie, you couldn't miss the boy-man uneasiness in his voice.

It was a strange thing, but Dan immediately decided that he loved me as much as I loved Marcus, and that he didn't mind that I was in love with someone else and spent my days sitting without a thought in my head, sneezing and holding a miniature tin crocodile. I in turn thought that because I had told Dan I was in love with someone else I could behave as badly as I liked. I had the protection of a disclaimer, I had drawn his attention to the small print. When his best friend came round to show off her new baby, I refused to coo over it, projecting supercilious disdain for motherhood. And when his sister started having visions and was found swimming in the Stour in a smock, like Ophelia, I shrugged and said, 'Sad, but what can you do?' I couldn't bear to be held, but when he did hug me he pretended to worry that he couldn't hear my heart beating.

'That's because my blood is cold and stagnant and doesn't need to circulate,' I said.

'When I was little,' said Dan, 'my mother used to encourage me and my sister to use words like cock and cunt because they were Anglo-Saxon. She was an English teacher.' I never wanted to hear a sentence beginning 'When I was little' ever again. I didn't want someone spring-cleaning themselves, disburdening themselves of their stories ever again, while I was shutting up for the winter.

'And then one day at school my sister stands up and says, "Can I be excused, please? I've got an itchy cunt." So we all got hauled up in front of a panel of social workers . . .'

Even when Dan pretended to strangle me with the telephone wire to cheer me up, I would just lie there lighting my cigarettes with his awkward and poetic love notes. (Don't do it. Don't do it, girls! If you don't love someone, just go as quickly as you can. Don't stop to pack. That's all you can do.)

'. . . and the social worker asked me if anyone had ever . . . hey. Hey, listen. Why don't we go on holiday?'

(And don't go on holiday.)

46

'There's a film festival in Zanzibar,' he said. 'You could write a piece on it or something.'

'I haven't got any money.'

'I'll pay.'

'I don't travel well. I'm allergic to things.'

'I'll pay for all your injections.'

'I'll miss Everyone Says I Love You.'

'Oh, *come on.*'

'No, honestly, it's in the Sunday Times: "Tom Shone enjoys seeing a director out of the doldrums and right back on song."'

I called Marcus and told him I was going to Africa. It was the first time I'd spoken to him.

'You won't see me for some time,' I said, like Grace Kelly to James Stewart in Rear Window. 'Do you want to maybe meet and talk?'

'Africa sounds wonderful!' Marcus merely said. 'It's just what you need, an adventure. How exciting! Just be sure to take malaria pills because there's a strain of it over there at the moment that heats your brain to boiling point. You know a virus is to a person as a person is to a planet? It's *that* small. And if you scale the earth to nought point nought nought *nought* one centimetre – smaller than a bacterium – it will sit one centimetre away from the sun but the nearest star will be *two miles* away.'

I could hear him hunting for some biscuits through the cupboards that for eighteen months I had pretended were mine. I was now someone he shared scientific facts with on the telephone after the ten o'clock news. It didn't make me want to kill myself, but I wanted to be dead.

47

What you do in the movies when you're down is *you take your shoes off* and everything is alright. What's *that* all about? In Third World movies you *get* a pair of shoes and everything's alright. Dan and I went to Stone Town where the film festival was happening in an old Roman amphitheatre, but the projector broke down on the opening night. The World Cup was on and everywhere we went Zanzibarian lads pointed at my Kenneth Branagh crop and said, 'Michael Owen! Michael Owen!' We were the only non-honeymooners there, but because it was a Muslim country I had to wear a ring to disguise our sinfulness. I wore the Betty Blue ring Mark had given me. Oh, I was high-minded! And this is the great performance that all women have access to. It used to strike me, watching rom-coms like Sliding Doors or Maybe Baby that they weren't about love at all; they were about the desirability of being a close-mouthed, frosty, high-minded bitch. Three-quarters of Gwyneth Paltrow's screen-time in Sliding Doors is devoted to her quivering disapproval of John Lynch, and men in general. And girls love it! Maybe Baby is all *about* just how bloody cross Joely Richardson is. It's an ode to female vindictiveness and rectitude. Hugh Laurie thinks he's going nowhere in his life, writes a screenplay about his and Joely's difficulties with conceiving which she vetoes as 'too personal', but rather than committing suicide he goes ahead and sells it and makes something of himself. And that's the movie – *how fucking dare he?* Then we settle in for an enjoyable hour of Being in the Right. It should be *called* 'How Fucking Dare He?' They're violent, these films. And no matter how disappointed in love you may be, your silences, and your 'Nothing's', are just acting. Through the days, I skulked in our beach hut, sneezing. It was never Saturday. Dan slid his awkward and poetic notes, like out-takes from a Julian Barnes novel, under the door: 'In Brazil, there's a man who will carve a mango-wood doll of the lover who spurns you and throw it into the hot soup where the River Blanco meets the River Negro – two rivers, two colours, one meeting line. If it floats into the black, you're fine, she will come to you. But if it floats into the white, then you can forget about your caiparinhas sipped through each other's arms under the Jaguar moon. So, look. He's an Amazonian peasant, this guy. Not even basic postcard comprehension. How on earth am I going to find out which river you are?'

He sat in a chair by the bed pleading with me to get up. Once he brought back a puffer fish puffed up rigid in death, not squeezable as you might expect, but hard as an iron football. But I was fazing out, spending my days in my vast lumber-room of scenes and stars, up in the attic going through my shoe boxes for something comforting. I thought about Spencer Tracy a lot on that trip. And swaddled myself in the comfort blanket of Gene Hackman. Another time-immune adult. Oh, Gene! Oh, Eugene! When he was Popeye Doyle in The French Connection, the Daily Express called him 'the man with the face in the crowd. Hackman is the hope of every fortyish man feeling the first intimations of middle age.' Hackman was thirty-seven, playing Warren Beatty's older brother in Bonnie and Clyde, when he was first noticed. So we have no memory of him as ever young or unformed or callow. But not a dad, never a dad. An older brother, an uncle ('Funny about Uncle Gene, how he never married . . .'), someone slightly to one side, someone whose youth seems to have been another country, scarcely relevant to this long serious business of living and working. That's why he's so brilliant, and so frequently cast, as a workaholic, like in Under Fire (1983, great movie by the way, better than Salvador by a *mile*). Or in Crimson Tide. Or The Conversation, of course.

Working a lot in acting can often be a refuge from the genuine hard work *of* acting. Too many films, not enough thinking-time. When he retired after Superman and went off to repair and drive racing-cars, he had a lousy time, claims that he felt a sort of constant self-disgust, which shows him for what he is. A kid born in 1930, anxious about employment, and not made for childish things like those racing-cars. A goddamned adult! I *love* his peculiar crinkled hair, like a dead or dying animal on the back of his head, his rounded shoulders and his short scuttling stride. I love his jowls when he smiles, his terrifically unhappy grin when he's playing men whose consciences are bothering them. He'd make a fantastic Claudius. He'd have you booing Hamlet.

I kept thinking about Hackman in Another Woman (1988), a dullish movie except for this one little scene where Hackman, who's had an illicit fling with Gena Rowlands, plays his last card at her engagement party. They are at the buffet table, dealing with their wine and cheese. He keeps his voice down because there are people around, and tries to persuade her one last time to forget about her cold-fish fiancé. Rowlands really doesn't want any of this. She bats him away, implying he's drunk, and says: 'He's a wonderful man!' She is slipping through his fingers like the magic beans which James spills before his giant peach grows. And Hackman's character has to drive himself into an uncharacteristic boldness: 'Maybe I was wrong about you. Maybe you're two of a kind. Maybe this conversation is scaring you.' And the more impotent he becomes the more he seeks to hurt her, and the more he seeks to hurt her the more you see his resentment of his own decency, which flags up his violence for the weakness it is. He looks like a hand which, closing around nothing, has become, without meaning it, a fist. Gene Hackman is a hand which, closing around nothing, has become, without meaning it, a fist. But aren't we all, I thought . . .

Marcus had gone because I sneezed, and didn't know who Edward Albee was, and couldn't follow the multilingual puns when his friends came round. But enough. Enough. It's all about gravity really, love. Without gravity you're a planet which can keep nothing in its orbit. And if you have none, you sometimes allow yourself to collapse like a black hole, which is nothing at all; except a complete failure that happens, it turns out, to possess more gravity than anything else in the universe. Or something like that. I wrestled with my metaphors, a girl with an E in GCSE physics.

48

'You know when we were going out I was a jerk a lot and treated you like . . .' Steve Buscemi says to his ex at the end of his own Trees Lounge (1996 – a great film, the best film made by an already famous actor in our time). You can hear the saliva pop on every *t* and *p* that his mouth forms. That amazing mouth. As if he has just stolen (incompetently, of course) an extra set of teeth and is trying to hide them in there. The glistening fangs. The eyelids the colour of raw liver. The face like a puzzle in which you have to find the bits that are handsome and the bits that are ugly – because there are handsome bits all over his face, well bits and unwell bits, as if only half of him is Peter Lorre, and the other half, shuffled in, is . . . Bogart, maybe? Buscemi has the greatest character actor's face ever. He could have been a silent comedian. I defy you not to laugh at the memory of his terrible blood-soaked stagger through the snow to bury the loot in Fargo. When he started out he *was* a comedian, doing stand-up in New York. He should have been billed as a double-act: Steve Buscemi and His Mouth. That amazing mouth, which acts as a Laurel to his Hardy. He's the stooge and the mouth is the one forever getting him in trouble, saying the wrong things, grassing him up as a victim, and kissing the wrong girls. (At which, by the way, the mouth is astonishingly good – Chloe Sevigny for instance is the recipient of a kiss in Trees Lounge which they should use clips of in manuals. I'd pay at least, let's say, a hundred – no, no, no, let's say, two hundred and twenty quid, two-thirty – for a kiss from Buscemi's mouth. Cheaper than a mini break in Paris. Put it like that, it doesn't sound crazy at all. I'll go two-fifty. But not for charity, for *me*.)

' . . . and treated you like . . .'

'Like shit?' the ex replies, not vindictively. She's in a hospital bed, recovering from the birth of her baby by another man. She's his *redemption* – the redemption we've been waiting for since the first frame.

'I know what you're going to do,' Dan said in the queue for a taxi outside Heathrow. 'You're going to call him, *aren't you?' I didn't say anything. Not saying anything seemed to be working out as a way of hurting him.*

'I was really fucked up back then,' Buscemi says.

'Oh, and you've really straightened yourself out now?' says the ex, but fondly again, because Buscemi's face is bloodied and bruised after a recent beating.

'I would if I had a kid,' he says. That's the redemption he's after – even if the child's not his, he'd take care of it. He went out with this woman for eight years. He once was charming, and funny, a loveable wastrel who has been forgiven and indulged all his life, but he must be, what, thirty-five now, and from the first moments of the film we've seen him in trouble, drinking too much in Trees Lounge (the local last-chance saloon) and reduced to driving an ice-cream van. He's clinging on by the finest of threads. If he's not careful, he'll have wasted his life.

I couldn't leave Dan because I could not stop acting. Because acting is addictive. That's why I fear the Gwyneth resentment so much – it's such a hard habit to break. Have you, gentle reader, ever lain like a shadow over someone else's heart? Have you found that, like all addictions, acting consumes every waking minute, that it becomes instinctive, that it's something you start off thinking you can quit any time and end up knowing that it's you or it? You can't stop. The little buzz you get keeping your eyes closed when someone enters your bed, pretending to be asleep while they forlornly stroke your back. The thrill that goes off, acting your way out of that bed at 7 a.m., leaving crushed hopes behind. Then the hit that you get from every item of clothing you put on, from every wearily assembled item of breakfast, the pleasure you take in the contempt that seems, for some reason, to be located in your upper arms. All day, this companion, your addiction, your acting, poison in your veins. Don't act. Life's a struggle against acting, which claims more lives than all the other drugs of the world put together.

'Look. I don't care if the baby's not mine. I don't.' This is Buscemi's last shot. It hurts to watch him.

At one of those kids' birthday parties where the adults all get quietly hammered, I found myself in a kitchen oohing and aahing over the hostess's little daughter's height-chart, growing in pencil on the wall there like a climbing plant. 'You're Dan's Antonia, aren't you?' she said, and cut me dead.

'Oh, Tommy,' Buscemi's ex, his redemption, says. 'Stop. I'm really tired.' Her unwillingness to hurt him is the worst possible thing he could hear. And Buscemi can't believe it. The Mouth opens and closes like a dying fish's. Though he cannot believe that he has been reduced to such a tiny request, still the thread doesn't break: 'You mind if I just sit with you for a while?'

Even that would be enough. The ex says: 'Uh . . . Rob is coming back any minute, so . . .'

Dan was wrong. I didn't have a 'him', except as an empty threat. Looking round the box room, I could see that I didn't have an awful lot.

Buscemi takes it on the chin, as he's been taking it on the chin for a decade. 'OK,' he breathes, coping with this new pain, deflecting it, picking himself up once again. And *still* – because this is a movie – you're waiting for his redemption. Then he twigs. He has wasted his life. I'm telling you, this is an astounding piece of acting, properly bleak and frightening because you never see something like that coming, do you? There's always a redemption round the corner. Buscemi opens his mouth to say something, stops, and then with a little wag of the head, as if he is reciting the inscription on his own tombstone, he says: 'I'm sorry.'

49

In time-lapse Camden Town finally Starbucksed; in a dissolve everybody's pagers were suddenly mobile phones; in a jump-cut I moved from the box room to a bedsit in Bayswater; in a wipe, Kurosawa was gone. There is gentleness in the movies' handling of time. Human consciousness touches the brim of its hat to these edits. Underneath my byline in the Camden New Journal it now proudly stated: 'Antonia Quirke can be heard on Radio 4's Back Row every Saturday!' That was Eric geeing me on – I was a comrade from the Jim era, when the Journal looked like Krook's shop, before it had been forced into non-smoking neatness by the Health and Safety prefects, and he was the loyallest of men. Imagine him as the wise old trainer (Morgan Freeman – oh, just put this book down for a second and contemplate just how stupendous and bloody sexy Morgan Freeman is! Has *anyone* ever been so consistently too good for his roles?) encountering the up-against-it girl (Hilary Swank (or me)) and taking her to a gym where he selects an old cassette marked 'training montage mix' and presses PLAY. So. I made phone calls and read a lot of Pauline Kael with my eyebrows at the back of my head, wondering how one person could be right about everything, all the time, every sentence, every word. I wrote to Geoff Andrew at the National Film Theatre suggesting a season of the Lesser-Known Films of Jeff Bridges, angling for some sort of curatorial job.

'We have in fact,' Andrew replied, 'recently completed a comprehensive retrospective of Bridges which I am surprised you failed to catch. But thank you for your interest.'

I wrote the film page for a little magazine published by a restaurant in Soho which was all about jazz and jazz-related things: 'Gattaca is not a great film, and it doesn't have any jazz in it, but it does have a kind of jazzy look.' I wrote little synopses for the London Film Festival's programme, calling lousy films 'lively' and competent films 'a stunning meditation on love and loss'. I filled in for someone doing the graveyard-shift reviews on Sky. I did all those little reviews which you see on the posters for real dogs, saying things like: '*** Delightful! You will leave the cinema smiling' – Prima. Or: 'Effortlessly stylish. The best gangster flick since Lock Stock' – LBC. Or even one of those suspiciously decontextualised 'Amazing's. I went on Woman's Hour to talk about whether Cate Blanchett's Queen Elizabeth had ever had penetrative sex and in what way that might have diminished her ability to fend off the Spanish

Armada. I passed my driving test. I told Dan how sorry I was for the way I'd behaved and slipped away quietly, though by that time he already hated my guts. And then one day I picked up the phone, and the caller said he had seen me cover the Oscars for Sky and did I want to go down to the breakfast show GMTV to talk about hopping channels? I tentatively agreed, having never covered the Oscars for Sky. London Weekend Television is down on the South Bank over the other side of the water from the Inland Revenue. When I got there I was met by a producer who ushered me up to the fifteenth floor, past people studying OK! magazine like it were a ticker-tape from Wall Street, through to a room and a leather chair so soft it was like sitting inside a kangaroo's pouch.

Over the other side of what looked like an obsidian desk was the Head of Programming at LWT, a man with a face that suggested he had gout and a dose of the pox. In fact that was why I was there. Nobody other than serious drinkers would be up watching Sky Moviebites at four in the morning. He looked at me and chuckled, nodding. 'Yes,' he said. 'Yes. You really *do* look like Anthea Turner.'

(The last time someone had pointed this out to me, he was easing my knickers off in a university hall of residence and saying, 'You remind me of the girl who presents Blue Peter,' like he had finally snagged his ideal. That was a *brilliant* night, funnily enough, which just goes to show.)

Then he said they were going to open the new season with a serious film bit, presented by Lorraine Kelly, in a part of the studio dedicated *totally to film*: 'We're going to have rows of velvet seats, and you and Lorraine sitting there with boxes of popcorn talking about the films of the week. And when we play in the clips, we want you and Lorraine to turn your heads to the camera and then look up as though you're in a cinema and we're going to pan on to your faces for a moment or two and it's going to be fantastic.'

'But will it be *serious*?' I asked, like an actress would.

'Very,' said the Head of Programming, seriously. 'What we want to know is how many buckets of popcorn you are awarding each film and *why*.'

'The buckets of popcorn thing . . . it sounds a little bit cheesy to me.'

'The cheesiness of it all is *essential*. It's cheesy to *draw them in*. You mustn't think the cheesiness is real — the films are what's real here. And you. And Lorraine.'

They were going to do a whole little credit sequence with clips from films, and me talking and gesticulating and Lorraine looking intrigued, and they were going to keep running it through the earlier parts of the show as a trailer. The Head of Programming said he was *dedicated* to the whole concept because he was bothered that there was nobody talking about film properly on the television any more. He was like the marquee of an Odeon proclaiming 'Fanatical About Film!'

'Now Barry's gone we can't be expected to listen to *Ross*. Ask anyone here about his *hair*. And the Kung Fu stuff.'

He said I could talk about anything I liked, anything to do with film, absolutely any kind of film that took my fancy.

'What . . . any film? Old films on the TV? What about . . . Where Eagles Dare?'

'Yep. Just name your price. How much do you want per appearance?'

I got the impression that the Head of Programming seemed to be enjoying this — not enjoying it at my expense, but more in the way that the chuckling old plutocrat gets to wow the orphan by just giving them the toy factory for the hell of it.

'Here's where you take what you're getting at Sky and

triple it,' he said. His face was as wine-dark as an Homeric sea.

'Sixty pounds?'

'Ha ha. Funny. Try again.'

'One hundred pounds?'

'You don't sound happy with that, and I don't blame you. I want you to be happy, Antonia. This is very important to me and to the whole GMTV family. Try again.'

I thought for a second: *What would he do if I said a million pounds?*

'Five hundred pounds!' I said.

'*Deal!*' he yelled back. 'That's one hundred pounds a minute. Well done, girl. *Well fucking done.* Well negotiated! Now what do you think about *that?*'

I thought, here is a man with unbeatable drug connections. I thought, it's nearly two years since I split up with Marcus. I thought, now I can afford to get my teeth done and date Ray Liotta.

50

And then Eric called to tell me that someone at the Independent on Sunday had rung up wanting me to write a weekly film column. 'I didn't give them your number direct,' said Eric, concerned that I might have thought the Sundays were capitalist purveyors of unattainable lifestyle imagery. But I was coming round to capitalism. I was rich!

Things had changed a little at the screening-rooms. There were several new faces. Having left the Guardian to be replaced by Pete Bradshaw, Derek Malcolm was now giving a long valedictory definitive for all-time Top 100 ever (is the Top 100 the moment when you can declare an art-form dead?). Quentin Curtis had left the Telegraph to make a go of it as a screen-writer in Hollywood. The sense of betrayal among the critics was profound. I imagined him partying in cashmere at the Playboy mansion and married to a woman from the 1970s who never leaves the house without her cigarettes and Piz Buin. His replacement Andrew O'Hagan went completely over the top about things. The week I hated a movie called Ratcatcher, he wrote: 'I love this film so much I would find it hard to be in the same room as someone who doesn't.' So I offered to leave and he punched me quite hard in the arm. Colleagues! We were having *critical spats*! And there were the odd celebrity film columnists, like Sebastian Faulks at the Mail. Generally speaking, this kind of writer is treated with light contempt by the critics, especially by the Biscuit Men, who reckon a bloke like that can't have much film knowledge in his tack. Not if he's just written a much-loved bestseller. Tcoh! There's a camaraderie among critics, but it's a slightly ashamed and quiet one. Whether the faces changed or not there would never be stand-up *rows* in the foyer. We're loners. Movie-watchers.

The screening-rooms themselves had changed a bit too – most of them had been made over, with comfier seats and air-conditioning. The new Warner Bros' screening-room had framed photos of old Warner stars on the walls, and a bar which gave the impression that critics might emerge from evening screenings and sink a communal cocktail. Warners put on the best spread in town, and you could munch your way through Holocaust classics. The Columbia screening-rooms had a steel and glass lift, which was always a funny sight: four critics in a Bladerunnerish pod with their plastic shopping bags, not looking at each other. My favourite screening-room was Mr Young's, on D'Arblay Street in Soho, about the same size as you'd imagine Sam Goldwyn's private screening-room might be. Once, they put the reel of a long French film (I forget which, but it had Alexis Loret in it) on the wrong way round and no one noticed until one particular half hour was repeated. The moment passed without comment. It was 2 p.m. on a Tuesday after all and . . . well . . . what else would we be doing if not this?

Just occasionally the critics get antsy. If a film started late there would be moderate tutting, and eventually Alexander Walker, always the take-charge person of the group, would stand up and eyeball the projectionist until it began. Once we waited two hours for The Sorrow and the Pity at the NFT – something to do with the electrics – but because we'd all schlepped down to the South Bank and it was a wet Friday afternoon and we all quite fancied four hours of Vichy atrocity nobody wanted to leave, so we read each other's newspapers and even went out and had a plate of chips together in the NFT café. This was an apex of clubbability.

51

(Just before you go in to the film, you're handed press notes by a PR. These are peculiar things, either a page long with a cast-list and an inaccurate synopsis left over from the original pitch, or about one hundred and twenty pages long in an embossed full-colour folder. There are favourite words: nobody ever makes a film, they 'helm' it. Nobody wins awards, they 'garner' them. Each Academy Award has a paranoid little

™ sign next to it. Everybody on the film is forced into telling lies about it at immense length, and you read these things with a strange feeling of waste as if seventeen months of interviews in hotel suites had been condensed into one solid wodge of bullshit. Take Troy: 'Brad Pitt has so much dedication,' says the fight coordinator. 'He's so focused on the character. I video the fights and then I show Brad the choreography that I'm proposing, and you see his eyes light up . . . it took three months and about thirty people to come up with the way Achilles fights. He has a boxing style, but with the velocity of a speed skater and the agility of a panther.' (Iliad, Book II: *Proud Achilles, like a cat on ice wearing boxing gloves, dealt his fury among the sons of Troy.*) Brad: 'Every now and then you get on a film where everyone seems to be at the top of their game, and I would say that was true of Troy, from the director down.' Wolfgang Petersen: 'What Homer did so very cleverly is that the anticipation for this fight is built up so much that we can't help but feel the weight of how monumental this contest is. Even though we've seen 50,000 soldiers clash against 25,000, the battle between Achilles and Hector is the most spectacular I've ever seen, simply because Brad and Eric are totally *in the zone.*' And all of this is written as if it were a novel. So it says things like: 'Petersen agrees with O'Toole's assessment of Pitt'; or: 'another thing Bloom found particularly impressive about Pitt was . . .' But they're useful to write your notes on. I had a boyfriend who would look at my notes to see how good the film had been. If I'd written 'peas, pie, milk', then it had probably been Troy.)

52

F, late 20s, petite, blonde, smoker, Ldn area, into country walks, animals and movies, wltm M 20–44, solvent, professional, well groomed, good smile, good body, good at running, must be good with kids, must be essentially happy person, must be handsome enough to gaze at for two hours at a stretch, must have a face that always seems to fit the contemporary mould, must not become dated, must be biggest star in world bar none, must understand that the *absence* of personality is what is required to carry a blockbuster, must have that flavourlessness, that frictionlessness, must use these absences as an *asset* so that a major film does not get snagged on the intrusion of personality, must be like a pair of shoes or a sports referee, good to the extent that you're unaware of him, must take *up* the burden of his good looks rather than escape from them or play against them in slimeball character parts like Rob Lowe or Matt Dillon, must be slightly uneasy with those looks unlike Robert Redford or Mel Gibson so that he is perfectly placed to play weak or uncertain or lost people, must have good looks *in excess of his charisma* so that he's at ease playing an ordinary small-scale guy, must be able to live with or even dominate Paul Newman, Jason Robards, Dustin Hoffman, Jack Nicholson, Philip Seymour Hoffman through an honest awareness of his own limitations, must have *tact*, must have energy, must have talent, must have stamina, must be *brave*, must be smart, must be aware of and able to exploit his own shallowness so that the marriage-breakdown scene in *Jerry Maguire* is an unforgettable self-portrait of a guy with something missing, must *absolutely nail* that film so that the reconciliation scene with Renee Zellweger is the best romantic comedy speech since Nick Cage in *Moonstruck*, must examine his own shallowness again in *Magnolia* at an even higher pitch and nail that too, must be the best thing among a stellar ensemble in that whole movie, must be so damn good that he can survive being a slick-seeming, thoroughly spun, successful (ex-*Top Gun*) American pin-up at a time when that puts you first in the queue to be kicked, must have a winning little gesture with both his index fingers as if he's conducting his films, must be the pre-eminent leading man in Hollywood for twenty years which puts him almost in a class of one and doesn't happen by accident, must not be so polite that an average movie like *Collateral* gets away from him in a way that, say, someone cooler than him such as Steve McQueen, would never have allowed, must, if he *has* to make more money, be able to see that there is no love in his *Mission Impossible* franchise, must have more love in general, must have more soul, must have the equipment to get off the top (most climbing accidents happen on the way down from the summit), mustn't be frightened of comedy, must be able to do rage without sounding peevish, must be able to cry convincingly, must play Willy Loman before he dies, a man out there in the blue riding on a smile and a shoe shine (America demands it), must be still braver because he's not a souped-up Brad Pitt but a genuinely great star and you'll miss him when he's gone, must be ever so slightly – just a smidgen, just a pussycat's whisker – better than Tom Cruise. Will travel. Waiting for your call.

PART TWO

Perforated Screening Mechanism

1

The week I find myself dressed as Anne Boleyn for the GMTV Midsummer Madness Special Live! From Leeds Castle I have an annoying conversation in Ross and Ilana's back garden with Jonathan Marr, who refers to the hearty Ross and his sub-five-foot wife as Otto and Mezzo. When I ask him about this, Jonathan Marr says, 'Well, she's Mezzo, so he's got to be Otto hasn't he? *Otto e Mezzo.*'

'What's Ottoeymetso?'

'It's what I'd give you out of ten,' he says.

He is wearing a manky jacket made out of what looks like pressed plastic over his bare chest, and a pair of maroon binend winklepickers – his tennis outfit. He has come to pick up his dog, which Ilana sometimes likes to walk, an enormous black German Shepherd now ricocheting around the garden like a squash ball. I have no idea what he's talking about.

'How do you mean out of ten?' I say.

'*Otto e Mezzo*. The great Italian comedy duo. 8½. I thought you were supposed to be a film critic,' says Jonathan Marr in his tramp's jacket.

I make no comment. I think his clothes are affected and it seems an elaborately insulting mark to give someone out of ten.

'You've seen 10 with Dudley Moore, yeah?' he says. 'Well, it's similar to that, minus one and a half. It's kind of 10 meets Seven. Divided by two. Like 2001, minus one thousand nine hundred and ninety-two and a half. That *genre*.' He says *genre* with a limitless contempt, as if it were French for *dogshit*.

What particularly piques me about this conversation later is that I *have* seen 8½, about five times – it's just that I call it 'The One with the Spacerocket'. Marcello Mastroianni always looks to me like a skull cracking urbane jokes about its late owner. I love the feeling he gives me, of a headachy three o'clock, and low grey hills with the chance of rain at the horizon.

Jonathan Marr's dog turns out to be called London and is the mascot of his Sunday league football team London Fields, named after the Martin Amis novel. This I find highly pretentious.

2

tobey /tō'bi/ *adj.* (**tobier, tobiest**) **1** Curiously detached in a trance-like way, apparently hyper-receptive to the wonder of the universe, usu. of US high school male seniors, occ. of freshmen ['That guy's not a creep, Willow, he's way tobey' – *Buffy the Vampire Slayer*, season 7, ep. 14, 'Never Judge a Guy by his Trenchcoat'], *der.* from

Choking on Marlon Brando

Tobey Maguire, US screen actor; **2** *pejorative* falsely projecting hyper-receptivity, etc. ['Carlton's kid brother had this tobey look which made me want to smash my Tanqueray glass in his face' – Easton Ellis, *The Duplicitors*], poss. *der.* from *Hamlet* III. i ,'To be, or not to be . . .', the implication being that the tobey ('to-be-y') look is an attempt to co-opt the soulfulness and fatalistic intellection of the Prince of Denmark. Also the removed air of someone turning suicide over in their hands. Term orig. after *The Ice Storm* (1997) ['Totally Tobey Guys Free Wall-Sized Pull-Out!' – *Seventeen* magazine poster supplement, Oct. 97], leading some commentators to observe that the numb/internally hyper-receptive quality of **tobeyness** has its roots in divorce-related trauma. A 'tobey guy' is typ. high IQ or near-genius, solitary, but distinct from other peer groupings (Goths, nerds, *Matrix* addicts) in that he gen. excels at schoolwork, feels connected with nature and has usu. a wise younger sibling with whom he likes to hang out. Indeed, tobeyness can be seen as a response to Goth nihilism: it is quintessentially tobey to write limpid but not untalented short stories beginning: 'The summer my father left we decided to cut down the old . . .' ['The lack of physical dynamism – that hanging-armed, straight-backed posture which seems to *impersonate* simplicity, *qua* Maguire's work in *Pleasantville* (1999) and *Wonder Boys*, the quiet, illegible smile, the taciturnity reminiscent of Dustin Hoffman's Benjamin Braddock, the tendency to perceive the world in a grain of sand (q.v. Wes Bentley's "wonder" w/r/t a flying plastic bag & a dead bird, for chrissakes, in *American Beauty*, 1999) – all of these things are physical equivalents of the mannerisms of American minimalist prose; that stunned sense of epiphany c.f. Raymond Carver, Tobias ("Tobey") Wolff, etc. Tobeyness can therefore be constructed/thought of as teenage alienation for the creative-writing-class era' – Ellen Mulready-Spofford, *We Need to Talk: Modes of Non-Discourse from Dean to Gyllenhaal*. In her 40,000-

word online review of Lost In Translation ['Sophia and Scarlett: Attack of the Tobey Chicks' – www.salon.com], Mulready-Spofford refined her definition – 'Johansson's gazing upon Tokyo, a gaze wherein wonder and bullshit are perfectly conjoined, is the quintessentially tobey image of the new millennium.'] In general, however, from *American Beauty*, sense **(2)** predominated: tobey increasingly signified either 'strangely compelling' trenchcoat-wearing misfits of the standard freak/creep type ['Tobey Sophomore Sees Donnie Darko, Kills Self, Neighbour's Rabbit' – headline, *Seattle Tribune*] or a more faux-naïf geek/dweeb childhood-worshipping 'kooky' Salinger type along the lines of Jason Schwartzman in *Rushmore* ['From the pathetic tobey way my friends have been talking about this tobey movie, I knew I was going to hate it' – Julie Burchill, *Daily Mail*] – ostensibly opposed definitions which nonetheless connote a general sense of negativity. Many usage purists, however, insist, in the teeth of opposition, on the original and true meaning **(1)** of tobey, closer to Maguire himself: genuinely hyper-receptive and curious with an unfaked stillness and willingness to let the gazes of others simply fall upon him, the time on the ball that the true movie star, like the true sportsman, always has and a bubbling hilarity which carbonates his seeming tranquillity ['He's so *funny*, and I love his duck-bill overbite' – Antonia Quirke, *Madame Depardieu and the Beautiful Strangers*]. The thrust of the usage hardliners' argument being that the corruption of Maguire's seminal, sensational charisma by the lesser actors who followed him should not be matched by an inversion in the usage of tobey. Unfortunately, since the two uses of the term are mutually exclusive, a satisfactory definition of tobey has proved impossible and the word has fallen out of use. Indeed one seldom hears it, even as Maguire gets better and better and better.

3

Jonathan Marr lives in a second-floor flat in a dilapidated Georgian square in Whitechapel, the kind where Bangladeshi boys bum cigarettes off you and women dispense their favours in doorways. Standing barefoot on his stoop he refuses to let Ilana and me borrow London for a trip to the beach – there is a dog show on that afternoon round the corner 'and it's about time the dog earned some fucking cash'.

'How much can you win?' Ilana asks.

'Only twenty-five quid. But if she does win, I can probably flog her for two hundred.'

For five years, so I've been told, he's been writing a novel whose plot nobody seems to be able to describe. In the window of the flat above him London is plaintively silhouetted.

'Look at the size of her,' Jonathan says. 'She looks like a Shetland pony. And giving you this *ears* business, I can't take it. And I don't know why she's looking so fucking heartbroken. She's just scoffed a whole jar of fucking mayonnaise. She looks like the French Lieutenant's Woman's Dog.'

'Don't be such a tight-ass killjoy, Jonathan,' says Ilana, who is clearly in his good books and unafraid of him. 'Let us have the dog and I'll *give* you twenty-five quid. We'll rent her.'

'I don't pimp my dog out to childless women,' Jonathan says. But goes inside and reappears with the dog, carrying his sub-plastic shoes. 'If you really want to take her, I might as well come along. We can have one of our arty chats,' he says to me, a statement which hangs in the air like a threat all the way to Essex while London stands up on the back seat, her head protruding from the 2CV like a periscope.

'It's got to be something left over from the war, that,' Jonathan says of a sign at the beach with a red line through a silhouette of what looks specifically like a black German Shepherd. 'That dog looks nothing like London anyway.'

'Dogs die in hot cars,' I say.

'Do they? Let's leave her, then. Look at the sign.'

He releases the dog and she rushes into the Estuary and laps at it. Crazed on salt water she gives a John Belushi gross-out performance along the shore, trailed by an apologising Jonathan who restores to confused children the frisbees and tennis balls she has run off with while the dog, behind his back, runs off with more frisbees and balls. They make a kind of pairing against the horizon, Little Miss Nitwit and the man smoothing her wake, picking up her pieces. I watch them at the end of my lens, as it were, where the eye begins to wobble like a camera does at the fullest reach of its zoom, where the image grows grainy and flattened. After a while I lose them, and then all at once from the other side Jonathan and his seaweed-draped dog are beside me spraying droplets, with his customary aura that reminds me of school, as if he might laugh at my satchel or steal my diary and read it out.

'What's it about, this book of yours?' I say, pre-emptively. He has London's lead around his ankle and his foot planted deep in the sand. The dog periodically twangs at his blithe shin like a temper held in check. He takes his time to answer.

'It's about a civilisation much freer than our own. More democratic, less surveillance and so on. Set in 1984.'

'Really? Ilana once said it was about someone building a theme park in the jungle.'

'No it fucking isn't.'

'Well then tell me. Or is it hard to say, hard to put literally?'

Jonathan says something like: 'the allowable, permissible

taciturnity, the sanctioned *it's impossible to say what it's about* has always struck me as straightforwardly bad-mannered in that no matter who's asking the question, they're possibly the same sort of person who you claim to be urgently wanting to communicate with by writing the thing in the first place. That's the whole point. A writer is someone who wants to get across what he does. But nonetheless it's just fucking tricky to say.'

'So *what is it about?*'

'Oh, *fucking hell*. Alright. It's about an Arnold Palmer-era golfer, now a course-designer, building a course for a South American cocaine baron on the skids, who inadvertently murders an already-over-the-hill twelve-year-old ex-football prodigy – and the effect this all has on the man who's ghosting his fifth autobiography. Tell me about Marcus,' he says, unexpectedly. 'If you'd like to, that is. And if you don't, then don't.'

This throws me completely. I never talk about Marcus, I just use him as a crucifix to ward people off.

'Well, you know,' I say automatically, 'he broke my heart, what's to tell?'

Jonathan shuts up for a moment and then says, 'Ye-ah. It happens to everyone, you know. But you don't really get your heart broken in your twenties. It takes more than one person to break your heart. It takes a life.'

I spend much of the next hour, until a warden on a quad-bike eventually zooms over to eject us, wondering whether this statement contains a put-down or not. It is possibly the tobiest thing anyone has ever said to me.

'Yeah, I know,' Jonathan says to the warden. London is so matted in sand she looks like a humpless camel. 'I know, I know, you're right, yeah, I'm sorry. Jesus, this fucking dog. How can it *not know* to drink seawater? That's like *Rule One* of being an animal. Come on, Lunds.'

In Whitechapel, Jonathan coughs up the ten-pound entry fee to the dog show resentfully glowering at the dog. 'That's me fucking cleared out now,' he says, and refuses to hand over the pretty-much-mandatory contribution to a dog-related charity that the officials are expecting.

'The thing is,' he says somewhat self-righteously, 'I've got about eight quid fifty in the bank, and this is the big rip-off about cashpoints isn't it? Why the hell can't they let you get two quid out, or a fiver, instead of making you starve over the weekend? Isn't that a *pain in the fucking arse*? Why can't they put some change in the machines?'

'Most people,' one of the officials smirks, 'have got more than ten pounds in their accounts. So I don't think they really mind.'

At which point Jonathan does something that one hardly ever sees outside childhood and even less in films, where actors cry, get drunk and die, but not this – he blushes. And witnessing this minor humiliation, which, being self-inflicted and rather daft, holds the implication that Jonathan is more careless of himself than of others, witnessing this, I feel something like a tap on my heart. *Tok.* Like the tap of a spoon on an egg, where you never quite know what the pattern of the crack will be.

4

Like that – *tok.* How thin the shell is! You forget how love can rush at you and make you want to bend your lover back with kisses, like Diane Keaton does to Warren Beatty in Reds. He's in a chair and she's standing up and she nearly breaks his neck pressing down. Kisses are rare things, I think. Real kisses are much rarer than real sex in this life (they tend to slip your mind) and oh, how I love that kiss! The excess in it! The way it has nothing to do with mouths. As if she might kiss him right through the chair and then right through the floor all the way to China. Not a bullying kiss, though, or a thoughtlessly manic one. She looks like a hummingbird poised over a flower. And though the camera keeps a tactful distance you can see how the kiss multiplies within them like cells. My favourite kiss. I've never really expected to be able to give anything more than that kiss.

Jonathan comes out of the gents with his hair combed back and his shirt tucked in, transformed into an almost credible dog-owning type, and pats London on the tail to make her sit down. Seated she looks somehow even bigger, her chest like the chest of a thrush, like Brian Dennehy's.

'Actually,' he says, handing me the lead, 'why don't you just take care of it? See what you can do.'

As I trot London around the circuit, she swishes her tail like a Flamenco dancer, no longer the dog who shits on windsurfers or sticks her head out of the car window begging strangers for their Magnums. She is as black and shiny as Michelle Pfeiffer as Catwoman. She smiles. She wins! Best Large Youngster. On the prize money Jonathan takes us to the pub and we get slightly high on London's unlikely triumph, taking it in turns to wear her red rosette. His great head of dark hair he manifestly cuts himself, untalentedly, so that he looks like Paul McCartney having been savaged by one of those early scissor-wielding crowds of Beatlemaniacs. 'What do you think of Lisa Simpson?' I ask him, shyly. I can see Ilana a long way off down the pavement on her phone. Already at that time, I think, her marriage was beginning to turn against her, and only afterwards did I see that for her this was a time of calls.

'Why do you say that? I rather fancy Lisa Simpson.' There is no flicker of recognition in his face.

'Oh, no reason. But would you fancy her if she wasn't brainy?'

'A bit less, maybe,' he says. 'But you know she's a fucking sex bomb underneath. Or she will be. Repressed: look at Marge. Looks a bit like *you* actually. Or maybe you look a bit like Kate Winslet, viewed in the wrong aspect ratio.'

'Well, thanks! That's very kind. What's an aspect ratio?'

'It's when a film gets all squashed to fit the screen. You know, 16:9, 4:3, all that. An ever so slightly concertinaed Kate – no, fuck it, you look like Lisa Simpson. You've never heard of an aspect ratio? Shit, I've got to find out the cricket score.'

I flinch silently at the distance I may have to go, at the long cold campaign ahead, at the possibility of failure. All the many lies that being unrequited makes you tell. Oh, god ... and having to project brightness across twenty-five yards of party, and hoping to transmit good reviews of yourself across ten miles of London, and for the twenty minutes you do get every three months, having to talk about the fucking *films* you've seen. My trouble is, though I never expect to give, or receive, more than that kiss in Reds, I do expect it, faithfully. Don't you? Do you? Does it go with age? Is it the movies or just life that makes you so certain that all you have to do is trust to luck, and love will come? I do hope it's not a naïve or even insane principle, because whenever I rummage through my head I find to my alarm that it is the only principle I have. For instance, I'm definitely opposed to genocide, but stick Hitler on a podium and give me a free lollipop and I'm not sure you could trust me. You know what I mean? And it suddenly seems like a very fragile principle indeed – trust to luck and love will come: the movies are telling the truth. Not a lot of philosophical protection is it, it occurs, a life-plan based entirely around things that happen to Kate Hudson. What have I done? Abruptly I have a feeling like I've left the gas on somewhere twenty years ago. At exactly this point Jonathan says 'watch this', and kisses me very very gently indeed. This kiss is an incredibly simple kiss. It is also the right kiss. A kiss like a crucial cog, which makes his whole personality fall into place. It carries a great deal of candour in it, and weight, and when it stops the traffic comes on twice as loud.

'Antonia,' he says, humbly. 'Won't you come back to mine? Come and raise the tone. We could do with a golden girl.'

Above his left elbow, I notice, that night, is a small, perfectly heart-shaped mole. *This is how the heart is . . .* It makes me think how strange we are, us humans, how long it takes us to unwind from a blow, how slow the heart is, for all everyone talks it up, to give up its precious Gwyneth Paltrow pain. The stupidity of hiding out from being hurt by being hurt. In bed, against my cheekbone, Jonathan's breastbone feels cool under his body heat, the quickening cool of September, that feels like a new year.

The next day I find a note on my door:

Dear Antonia

Words are obviously not my strong point but I'm writing to thank you for the best day of my life. It's not all that exciting in Whitechapel. So thanks for the trip to the seaside, the ice creams, and for showing me that I am beautiful. That I should be happy with my beauty, proud of it. You know I was, like, bulimic? Like, I'd just scoff a whole jar of mayonnaise and throw it up? But you have shown me I am not fat. I am a large youngster and proud of it, like Kate Winslet.

London x

P.S. In pub by tube.

5

Tom Ha— oh, who cares? We could just not do him, couldn't we? Yes. Let's not. Good!

6

How can I make you see Jonathan as he was at twenty-eight? One of the first things I learned about him was that his clothes weren't affected. He wore things until they literally fell off him – he just didn't *have* an alternative outfit. Ilana told me that at college he'd sat his exams in a subfusc made partly from cereal packets. There was this one lovely coat he had which London had torn right up the side. The temporary repairs he'd made with sellotape had become permanent repairs. But the thing is, he was very handsome so he could get away with this kind of thing. He looked like Peter Coyote – although not quite. I've heard people tell me that Coyote's not all that handsome but I once saw him walking down Carnaby Street looking, in the flesh, like something out of Scott Fitzgerald. Jonathan didn't have Coyote's hard angles, but he did have that slender, slender body, a body that ought to have tailors going round it with pins in their mouths making suits to embrace it, and a way of standing with one foot poised on its toe like a colt.

He lived off the dribs and drabs of development money he earned for the bits and pieces he wrote outside the book. The flat in Whitechapel he shared with his friends Andy and John – three clever northern boys who had been to Oxford and come to London, done a little comedy and a little acting and not enough work and too much drinking, and were just beginning to fold away their youths – was a tip, carpeted in ash and black hair shed by London, who wouldn't so much insert herself between us in bed as simply lie on top of us. It was a mess, and Jonathan wasn't in great shape either, I could see. His mother had recently died of cancer and underneath his happy shambles there was an unhappy shambles. I'd watch him walk around the room feeling his heart through his chest, checking for an irregular beat, or lighting and re-lighting his roll-ups even when it wasn't necessary, like some crack-addict at their pipe. Or the way that he hadn't realised that he shouldn't unashamedly use my shoe as an ashtray. I'd sit there thinking: *Just look at that, just look at him do that.* I borrowed a collection of Updike stories off him, one of which was called My Lover Has Dirty Fingernails. I'll sort that out, I thought, shaking the ash from my boot. We watched Titanic, which I'd perhaps incautiously told him was *great*, on video one night and Jonathan sat forward in front of me so I couldn't see his face and thought he was riveted when really he was hiding his winces and flinches so as not to spoil it for me – he wasn't easy to *type*. He knew fucking everything, but he cried at Tin Cup. He thought he was right all the time but he knew he was wrong. He moved everywhere with grace, but he was the guy on the tube floor scrabbling for his dropped change. He could cook, properly, but was once offended when I objected to a Bloody Mary made with an old tin of tomatoes and soy sauce. What I cherished him for was his certitude – he was never ambiguous about things. It was almost a flaw that for Jonathan there was too little middle ground. He could flip. He was an old Don DeLillo fan, but when Underworld came out and he didn't like it he went around in a homemade T-shirt that said 'DELILLO SUCKS'.

It was a habit of his to write in little notebooks when people were talking to him while simultaneously apologising for doing so. Also on bus tickets, in the backs of books, and (a rich seam) the inside of the flaps of Rizla packets. We were very close but he had this secret hinterland of the book which he had never invited me to and I was too nervous to trespass on. So whenever his back was turned, I devoured his notes, looking for clues, trying to hunt him out.

Boy avoids homework by saying his father has died. His father
    HAS died. Variations on this
The beautiful cold sand – feet/teeth
Alarms of dead in the luggage scattered from the hold.

Did he always remember what these notes actually meant? Or was it like when I looked back at things I'd written on my press notes – like *Travolta gammon* or *Planet of the Afflecks, do joke* – and I would think: you what? But then something like *Borg speedboat: Odysseus* on a one-day travel card of his would be underlined and have two asterisks next to it, and I'd think, he knows what he's doing.

Being of the city and, we felt, the only city in the world since we barely left it after that day in Essex and certainly not to go abroad – money frittered, passports lost somewhere – we'd walk for miles with London around Camden and Chalk Farm looking for an imaginary flat together, and Queens Park and Kensal Rise and Kilburn, which I liked because the love scenes in Betrayal are set there.

'Do you know that all the films you find most romantic are about adultery?' Jonathan said.

'That's because lovers have drama and soul,' I said. 'Husbands are just ridiculous.'

In Highgate Cemetery, Jonathan looked at the monolithic bust of Marx and said it was the only memorial in the place which seemed to be in denial about Death. The inscription around its base he dismissed as 'boastful crap'.

'You've got to hand it to him, though,' he said. 'They were trying to take the furniture from under him and he was still getting two thousand words a day out. Fucking Jenny shouting at the kids and a bailiff repossessing his ink pot.'

I felt a bit guilty to be associated with this lack of reverence for the great German head in front of us. What would Eric or *Jim* have thought if they'd known I'd come here and failed to lay any flowers? I preferred George Eliot's monument because it was covered in ivy and a little neglected. And I could think about Rufus Sewell as Will Ladislaw in his long crimson coat as we ate our petrol-station picnic. Jonathan shared my love of sugary things – chews, KitKats, sherbert dippers, and those kind of gluey, bright orange, mango-flavoured drinks. Our tongues were raw.

'I'm so glad you're not really a communist,' he said.

'Not *yet*. I'm thinking of taking a course,' I said, to annoy him.

Jonathan hated communists and socialists because he thought they were just there to take your money away from you. Even though he never had any money and was always flogging his books to a secondhand shop in Stoke Newington, he would come over all paranoid about socialists like he was Nabokov about to be dispossessed of his country estate by the Bolsheviks.

'Husbands aren't ridiculous,' said Jonathan. '*We're* ridiculous, spending the whole of our twenties triple-testing each other then collapsing into marriage. I mean, we as a generation, not *us*.'

'Yeah, not *us*,' I agreed vehemently. 'We're not going to do that.' All around us were the records of unions. *Beloved and Adored. Nothing Can Replace.* You didn't tend to make it into stone on your own was the message.

'... we're not going to what precisely?' said Jonathan, unsure, like me, whether a proposal had just been made.

'What do you think of him?' I asked my mother when she came down.

'Dishy,' she said, and quoted Pride and Prejudice at me: '"If he had ten thousand a year, he'd be a fine match."' She was harbouring hopes that Jonathan might turn out to own Pemberley, which she could then divide into a social revolutionaries' commune. When I told him about this, it put Jonathan in a black mood:

'Ten thousand a fucking year. It's two hundred and eighty years later and I still can't manage ten thousand a year. I'm sorry, darling. Once I've finished this book, I'll buy you an animatronic platinum dolphin.'

I liked that my mother had called him dishy. Against all her better instincts her ideal of male beauty was Ralph Fiennes in The English Patient. Always exclusively passionate about my father, she had stunned the family one night by bursting into tears at the sight of the Count striding across the sands. (Deep in my memory Marlon Brando called Stella.) That weekend I overheard her discussing the movie with Jonathan, who was on his best behaviour and being nice about it.

'Of course,' she said, 'I spotted him years ago in Prime Suspect wearing that black leather jacket, and I just *knew*.'

'Well, he's a handsome man. Best Nazi I've seen.'

Jonathan's real position on The English Patient, I knew, was that it was second-home porn.

'If the Second World War hadn't taken place in some of the most beautiful parts of Europe, half these writers would be screwed,' he drawled. 'Take Ian McEwan. Black Dogs. What that book's really about is picking up a farmhouse in the Massif Central for a fiver.'

'Really? Is it a bit like A Year in Provence?'

'Sunshine,' said Jonathan, getting down on his knees. 'My grown-up Lisa Simpson. Where have you been all my life? You are a critic of genius.'

7

You know how I knew I loved him? It's those sequences in films of men getting up, getting dressed, going across the road to buy groceries, putting the kettle on – but *on their own* – those little private dances of the everyday. My favourite sequences. Michael Caine, David Hemmings, Clint Eastwood, Steve McQueen, Elliott Gould, brown paper bags, catfood, coffee pots, keys, the sorting of post, the handling of money, the pace at which the stairs are taken, the crossing of the road, yawns, toothbrushings, fingers and wrists, fingers and wrists. Well, when Jonathan did that – which of course I never saw – I loved the way he did it.

8

Not my type, though. My type – and allow me to say this with contempt for the idea of the *type* as a conscious selection rather than something imposed upon you by life, and which in any case is something one should perhaps strive against – my type, with many exceptions and caveats, the type towards whom I feel a, how do you put it, a genetic tug, . . . oh, get on with it, it's Kris Kristofferson in Pat Garrett and Billy the Kid. Like, gubluhbuhuglguzhffffffffffffuuuuzzh . . .

There is, first of all, the heedlessness of his flesh. The memory of fat in it, and the destiny of fat. The foalish sense of a body not quite cohered, its weight. It's the sense of an organism happy to over-ripen. Smiles spill out of him like seeds. The absence of the exquisite, the absence of grace, the acceptance of the thousand natural shocks that flesh is heir to. A body full of time – puppy-fat, double-chin, growth-spurt limbs, untoned muscle. Big, easy, nearly slobbish, thick-haired, big-headed, and ever so slightly out of shape. That's my type. A muscled torso above the age of twenty-seven is nothing more than a fear of nakedness. The contemporary male body is a flinch from the contemporary female eye.

Three years after Pat Garrett, in A Star is Born (1976, when he was thirty-nine), Kristofferson had condensed into that long-faced, rangy, distinguished personage one always pictures him as. But as Billy the Kid his body incarnates freedom. James Coburn as Garrett, hunting him down, is upright and endomorphic, a withdrawing thing, an inhalation. Kristofferson is unfenced like weed, bovine in pace, an exhalation. One goes in, the other goes out. One is the bar of a jail cell, the other is as unimprisonable as air. The whole mysteriously marvellous film *is* their two bodies. Liberty. That is why my type is Kris Kristofferson as The Kid, and Depardieu, and the young John Lennon before Yoko got on to him with her beansprouts, and Rufus Sewell untyrannised by personal trainers, and Michael Madsen (of course), and Tom Sizemore, and all the rest of them.

Liberty!

9

Jonathan looks up from the Independent on Sunday and says: 'You're always fucking flirting.'

'I'm not *flirting!*'

' "Plunkett and Macleane is blah blah blah blah . . . the *extraterrestrially beautiful* Jonny Lee Miller isn't so much looking at the camera as offering himself to it, like someone with peace on the tip of his tongue." What on earth does that mean, anyway? It's just flirting. They're not going to let you get away with this.'

'Oh, come *on*. He *is* extraterrestrially beautiful.'

'And people will think you're not getting any sex. It just reflects badly on me.'

I don't believe that Jonathan really minds about my flirting. It only annoys him because he thinks it's corrupt. He knows that all reviewers harbour the faint hope that an intensely complimentary review might lead to a relationship with an actor, that I hope to pick up the phone one day and hear a voice on the other end saying, 'Allo . . . ees, uh, Vincent Cassell eer. Everysink you said about me in your piece on La Haine was *SO RIGHT!*'

(It never happens, of course. No actor has ever gone out with a critic in the history of the world. That's my book knackered, then. I hate actors.)

'Are you saying,' Jonathan asks me, 'that you fancy *everyone* in cinema? What about John Goodman?'

'Of course I fancy John Goodman!'

'Oh, yeah, yeah, yeah, I see what you mean. Sydney Greenstreet?'

'A certain exotic dignity and charm.'

'Uhm . . . Buscemi, no forget that, uhm, uhm . . .' He lapses into silence.

Don't blame me, blame *him*. Isn't it the case that when you're at your happiest with someone, you don't only have eyes for them? When you're discovering somebody, you're not jealous, you're generous, because other people's beauty and happiness has suddenly stopped hurting you: it's the opposite of possessiveness. And I couldn't stop taking pleasure in other people. Why should you? Love is about knowledge. *Knowing, being known . . . having that is being rich. You can be generous about what's shared – she walks, she talks, she laughs, she lends a sympathetic ear, she kicks off her shoes and dances on the tables, she's everybody's and it don't mean a thing, let them eat cake; and while knowledge is held, it makes you free and easy and nice to know, and when it's gone everything is pain.* Tom Stoppard – The Real Thing (and isn't *he* gorgeous – Christ, they never stop coming, do they?) in which Stephen Dillane (oh, God, him too!) gave such a magnificent performance on the London stage in the role Roger Rees created (remember *him*? Cor!) that the foyer was thronged with reconciling couples and men holding their wives' hands saying, 'I'll change.' And who knows why it's never made it on to a screen?

I offer the following list in a spirit of mildly defiant humility. But I don't believe there are any factual errors involved.

The Fellowship of the Ring: 'Sean Bean plays Boromir, one of the last in the book's line of noble men. He is *hot to trot*.'

Fact.

U571: 'It's hard to be honestly enthusiastic about McConaughey. But as a Southern boy-man, and with his murmurous "Y'all"s and solid head and natural leading man physique which could speak of any era or place, he is well, plainly, *peel me off the floor . . .*'

You simply cannot argue with statistics.

Gone in 60 Seconds: 'Nicolas Cage has a kind of stupidity that passes so beautifully for sincerity, transmitted by a voice that keeps hitting those same three muffled sax-notes. *God,* the way he calls you "sweetie" like you just might be at any minute . . .'

Y Tu Mama También: 'Gael García Bernal smokes like someone playing the pan pipes. It's one of his picture-stealing gestures I can't get enough of. I can't get enough of *him*.'

Thirteen Days: 'The one good thing (or rather gobsmacking thing) about this otherwise ordinary film is Steven Culp. The guy is a shoo-in for Bobby Kennedy (the curly lip, the tanned forehead, the prominent eyes) and has already played him before in the NBO movie Norma Jean and Marilyn. He's HOT.'

28 Days: 'As a sex- and cocaine-addicted baseball player Viggo Mortensen looks inappropriately healthy, as though he

mistakenly went to Portugal on a fruit fast in preparation for the role. Even his name sounds like some Swedish pro-biotic. But he is *gorgeous*.'

Pola X: '. . . stars Guillaume Depardieu as a young novelist who quits his luxurious life to love and stink in Paris. Depardieu has his father Gérard's nose, sitting in Julian Sands's face. It's an odd combination. The lorry driver's nose, the gilded, classically beautiful rest of him. Give me the nose. Give me, *give me*.'

The Long Goodbye: 'The film of the week is the re-release of Robert Altman's The Long Goodbye. I just want to add that as Marlowe, Elliot Gould is the sexiest thing that has ever sloped across the screen and I mean it. He's sexier than Dennis Quaid in The Big Easy, sexier than Laurence Fishburne in Boyz N the Hood, sexier than Jeff Bridges in Thunderbolt and Lightfoot. Clear? Now pass us a smoke.'

'Alan Rickman gets the Sex on a Stick award this week as Snape . . . but there is Denzel to ogle – the vertical descent of his top lip is so sexy . . . Carrey is so *handsome* . . . there's something so sexily furtive about Philip Seymour Hoffman and his belly. I have a crush on him . . . the delicious Tom Hollander . . . the adorable Jon Favreau . . . Giovanni Ribisi has a face so perfectly heart-shaped it's cartoonish and my heart is his . . . Jake Gyllenhaal is so ridiculously touched by *it*, the thing itself, that I kept having to turn and examine him from different angles, through one eye, then the other. He has a smile as though all the happy youth in the world got together and drew it . . . the heart-flutteringly wrecked-looking Kevin McKidd . . . the irresistible sex clown Steve Zahn . . . Owen Wilson's nose resembles Mount Triglav, the three-peaked national symbol of Slovenia, in its complexity, its beauty and its *endless* attraction . . . I want to go out with Julian Rhind-Tutt . . .'

I'm sorry. Please do forgive my banging on, although the simple truth is that I need to write this book for the sake of my marriage. There is no pride in repeating the above. I'm amazed I was allowed to get away with it. Occasionally the editor at the Independent on Sunday would comment, but it was quite dreamy down there, and I could always commit my worst offences in the Journal anyway – Eric didn't mind, although he did once ask me to stop mentioning Alan Rickman. ('But he's *local*, Eric! He lives in Paddington!' 'Does he? Ah, well then, that's alright.') And after that I just carried on writing about Rickman but adding ' . . . who lives in W2' and 'who lives down the road from the Journal'.

And on the radio, to which you're sure nobody is actually listening, I'm afraid it really did get a bit out of control. Sometimes I would look through the glass to see the producer chatting away to the technician in their own world, just letting me jabber on unstoppably in mine: '. . . Matthau never stretched himself but because his joke was about intransigence, the joke just got *better*. I love the way his lips are always wet as if he's been sucking a mint that's just dissolved. And I love the way he wears hats. He's always in hats to make him look more rumpled. He's very attractive, really. He's *incredibly* attractive. Don't you think?' and more, just jawing on until a friend rang me up one day and told me that I was on some website called 'Daniel Craig: Essence of Talent' and I should check it out. The site – set up, incidentally, by a woman *who used to work for the CIA* I later found out – comes up all pink and blue and sort of ambiently mystical, with lots of pictures of Craig in jeans looking stern. It's obviously the work of some fanatical maniac who's going to show up at Craig's wedding and knife the bride, and there's me, floating across the screen in enormous letters: *'CRAIG IS REALLY SOMETHING – ANTONIA QUIRKE.*

CRAIG'S MASCULINITY IS COMPREHENSIVE NOT DEFENSIVE – ANTONIA QUIRKE. HE IS EASILY THE BEST YOUNG ACTOR OF HIS TYPE IN THE COUNTRY – ANTONIA QUIRKE. IN A NATIONAL CINEMA HEAVY WITH EITHER FALSE MALE HEROICS OR MEN WITH HEADS OF CURLS AND DELICATE FINGERS, CRAIG REMINDS YOU WHAT A MAN CAN BE – ANTONIA QUIRKE.' And so on, and on, directing people to log on to a further site called 'Dedicated to Daniel' and another called 'Discuss Daniel' (I mean, this chick is *serious*) and then back to me for some more (*'THERE IS NOTHING DECORATIVE ABOUT CRAIG – ANTONIA QUIRKE'*), making me come over frankly as some kind of weirdo who has nothing better to do than, like, think about how great Daniel Craig would look in one of those button-down 1950s shirts reading Kerouac to me while I sit in the bath. And I'm not, alright? *I'm not.*

10

Oh, oh, oh, oh! Matt Damon! What's the consensus on Matt Damon? What do you think? Because I reckon that of all the lunk-headed, wooden, gym-bulked, Westpoint cadet-faced, inexpressive hunks of Yankee multiplex tedium, he takes the biscuit, just kidding! The kid is it. I bloody love Matt Damon. There are boys and there are men – and it has nothing to do with age. Charlie Sheen will never not be a boy. Mickey Rooney will die a boy. Jean-Pierre Léaud started off as a boy and stayed there. Javier Bardem has never been a boy. Harrison Ford was never a boy. Robert Vaughn is a man with a boyhoodectomy. And when someone makes the transition (which is rare – that nitwit Penn managed it, and Dennis Quaid), it's shockingly intimate to observe. And this is Damon's generosity to us, as he turns from boy to man: he lets us in. He's like his face – you can't but wonder where it's going. Is it going to keep lengthening and become the face of a guilty, hollow man, the face of appalled self-disillusionment? Or is it going to cloud over completely and conceal all its monsters? I don't know, and he doesn't have a clue either, and that's why he's thrilling to watch.

What happens to boys is: the growing shame of self-knowledge slowly forces them closed. Damon is open like a desert flower in a rainstorm – wide open. Leonardo DiCaprio and Jude Law, two quintessential boys, are closing in front of our eyes, but Damon retains that ingenuousness which means he'll still be responding to the world, he'll still be making himself, in fifteen years' time when he's fifty. Relish how complex he might be in all the standard divorced cop, lawyer who accidentally runs someone over, punished-adulterer parts! And that's why, as Jason Bourne, the amnesiac assassin of The Bourne Identity to whom the whole world is new and possibly not brave, he (I'm afraid there's no other word for it) *rocked*. Because he was a man putting himself together in front of us, vulnerable, and uncontaminated by secrets, queasy, uneasy, but fresh. He doesn't have the pane of glass over him that other human beings seem to come fitted with as standard. It's the naturalness of his delivery whenever he's called on to shout: 'I don't know who I am!' It's those nimble fingers sorting through the dead Clive Owen's things so deftly his tempo hits you with the force of a special effect. Damon is taking his youth into manhood, too youthful to end up as one of the *boys*.

11

Well, you shouldn't tell your dreams, should you? But of course, I dream about actors all the time. Russell Crowe, for instance, I once taught, painstakingly, to say the word *mnemonic*. Another time I found Ian McKellen curled up like a goblin in a plastic bag in a supermarket. He was woundingly rude to me for no reason. I was in an airport one night when the message came over the tannoy: 'Would Signora Javier Bardem please proceed to checkout where her husband is waiting . . .' and I made my way, very slowly and proudly, through the whispering tourists. But only Al Pacino haunts my dreams. Soon after I see Any Given Sunday I gain a private audience with Pacino. He is sitting papally in the pose he adopts on the posters for Godfather III, his fingers dripping like wax over the arms of the chair. The Grand Inquisitor. He has just caught a pike, which lies across his lap. I bend to press my lips to his forehead and wake up with the thrill of his warm skull still on my mouth. *Please come back* I find myself saying. *Please come back.*

'Come back? Who come back? I'm here,' Jonathan says in a sellotapey voice, ''s OK, 's OK, it's just a nightmare.'

'I was kissing Al Pacino and he had a pike. It was so weird. His head was hot.'

Jonathan says nothing for a while.

'Wake me up when you have a proper nightmare.'

'He was in Rome in his what-do-you-call-it chair.'

'It's a Catholic sex dream. The pike is Ted Hughes. Lethal and phallic. Now shut the fuck up and go back to sleep.'

There used to be a shop on the Clerkenwell Road that sold

bad seventies furniture on purpose. By the window was a framed and autographed photograph of Pacino, a head-shot taken around the time of Dog Day Afternoon (1975). The point about this picture was that the shop (which really did sell terrible things, ugly orange retro sofas) used the photograph as bait. And at least half the people who entered the shop went in there to buy the photo. Jonathan went in to buy the photo. I had been in to buy the photo. Everyone knew the photo. It was like the major point of reference in Clerkenwell. They would have put a 'Not For Sale' sign underneath it but that would have ruined the photo's weird magnetism – and it was only the sort of picture you could have bought off the internet for fifty quid. But people wanted to possess it. It was like something out of an M. R. James ghost story. The Face on the Wall.

Will we ever break his spell? Will we, fifty years down the line, still think of Michael Corleone as the greatest performance in the history of cinema in the same way we'll still think of The Beatles as the greatest band? *Yes*, is the answer, not that we'll necessarily be right. I'll say one thing about Michael Corleone. Because Michael is hypnotic and magnetic and powerful and ought to dominate every room he's in, it's easy to confuse your appreciation of the performance with the tractor-beam of the character. So of course you're awed. But isn't Robert Duvall acting as well as Al? Isn't Brando? Yes, they are. Pacino is mysterious because you cannot quantify charisma. You cannot definitively say why someone is *the best*. You cannot put into words why Michael dancing at his wedding to Apollonia looks like the most beautiful man you have ever seen full stop. He just does. Look at any pavement spread with posters or café decorated with movie stills and who do you see? Jude Law? Tom Cruise? Robert de Niro? You see The Face on the Wall. Who do they like best in Lithuania, in Sierra Leone, in Uruguay? It's Al (or Tony or Michael or Frank). For what it's worth, I think a lot of it is to do with his chameleonic ethnicity. To Greeks he looks Greek. To Argentinians he looks Argentinian. To Russians he looks Russian. And Italian and Mexican and Israeli and Arabic. And there's his breathing. Sinatra used to swim underwater in order to improve his lung-capacity so that he could sing longer phrases without taking a breath. Pacino has that same capacity. I said that his Michael sounded like an oboe – but he also breathes across phrases like no one else. *Do you expect me. To let you go?* He's got an upper register – his New York likeable-scamp, Panic in Needle Park register – which nobody else has. He's a *musician*, and musicians, let's face it, are more popular than actors. That's why it's a bit unkind to be harsh about Shouty Al. Because he took his greatest pleasure in finding melodies and cadences in language. And now he's found them all, he's like a guy boredly taking a tour round the museum of his old discoveries – see, say, Carlito's Way, or most depressingly, Devil's Advocate, in which he cannot get through ten consecutive words without howling, as if he were a narcoleptic continually being woken up. But the early long speeches are so full of structure, of hooks and fills and middle eights, they're hummable. He's more than a musician, he's a *songwriter*. A great songwriter. And on top of that, in the 1970s he had a more neutronium-dense presence than any other actor has ever had. Oh, how mealy-mouthed of me, how timid, how diplomatic! He had more presence than anyone else, ever. Now *that's* film criticism. That's why he's the best, and that's why when I say I am obsessed with Al Pacino, you might shrug and say: *So what? Everybody's obsessed with Al Pacino.* But I love him, I love him, *I love him.*

12

Sometimes, when pushed, Jonathan says that his book is actually narrated by a foetus not sure whether it's going to be aborted or allowed to live. Once, at a drinks party, I hear him tell someone it is called Daughter of the Steppes and is 'set against the turbulent backdrop of the Russian Revolution'. In other moods he says it's called Love All and concerns a pair of transsexuals winning the mixed doubles at Wimbledon. He's always trying to fob me off when I press him on exactly what it's about.

'But what about the golfer? It's definitely got golf in it.'

'Yes. Golf, and leisure, and tamed nature, and Arcadian landscapes, all that sort of thing.'

Which is definitely fobbing me off. I have heard Jonathan himself say that that kind of statement is really scraping the bottom of the barrel and how he hates it when writers answer with a deftly bullshittery abstract noun: 'It's about identity loss. It's about redemption and the acceleration of society. It's about trust.'

He never looks at me when he's talking like this, which means I can really look at his neck and shoulders and admire how his clavicle bone is uniquely elaborate, and that he has a way of playing with the end of his nose, wiggling it, as though it's only recently fitted and he isn't convinced of the quality. And his genuinely olive skin, which seems to be somehow self-cleaning because he never smells bad even though he rarely washes or cleans his teeth or anything. In fact when he did clean his teeth once before a party and the gums bled, he literally staggered back in horror at this evidence of his mortality. I generally think that Jonathan is insufficiently aware of his own mortality. He gets into fights in pubs like he thinks he has nine lives, he threads through the traffic like he thinks cars are made of silk. Death is scheduled to start once he has finished the book. This conversation is taking place as he recovers on my bed having fallen off the front of my building fifteen feet into the basement well, floppy with booze, after a fight we've had about a fight he's had.

'What's it called?' I ask.

A pause and a frown. I have a photo of him, taken when he was five or six, in a field of red and yellow weeds and feathery grass, looking into the distance with that same frown, the frown all six-year-olds have, which he's retained. There's an innocence to the way he hates things.

'You know, you've stopped sneezing,' he says.

'Yes, three months ago, Jon. What are you going to call the book?'

'News, Sport, Weather,' he says, carefully.

'Right, er . . . big book,' I say. 'Sounds kind of . . . that's a lot of information.'

'Yeah, yeah, yeah . . . it's not Anita fucking Brookner.'

'And this golfer who's designing the course, what's his name?'

Jonathan is trying to think of something else to point out other than my non-sneezing.

'Pro Bandersatz,' he finally says.

'Why d'you call him that?'

'Dunno. Just did it for a laugh,' he says, and then, 'Oh, *all fucking right*. *Pro* is an acronym of his first three names – Patrick blah blah. And it's got *ersatz* hidden in it. But it's really from the Bandersnatch from Jabberwocky, you know, which itself hints at child murder: Bander-snatch, see? *Beware the Jubjub bird, and shun the frumious Bandersnatch!*'

Which sounds reasonable enough to me, so I drop it. Although when I do inquire why it's taken five years to write, he simply says, 'It's just a really bloody long kind of story.'

13

So even Jonathan – who would leap back in alarm should anything he had ever written even vaguely scout round the edges of banality – was not immune to the use of an American golfer as a symbol of the enemy. It sometimes seemed that the European relationship with America was like a love affair that had grown increasingly polite and silent and full of unspoken resentments – like we were from Venus and they were from Mars – until some time in the late 1990s when the strain of keeping up the pretence finally became too much to bear and we stopped sitting silently across the breakfast table from each other and started to row. So someone like Kevin Costner – perceived as a Republican, not cool, not complex, not smart, not *dark* – was always going to be finding all his past work slung in the stocks next to Waterworld and The Postman. People dislike Costner in the same sniggering, slightly triumphalist way they dislike America. The same way you hate John Wayne or George W. Bush – big dumb creatures too slow to realise they're being mocked by us lithe types. Lithe types, like that hollow cacophonous bird made of beaten tin painted gold (and failed actress) who sticks a finger down her throat after meeting Costner In Bed with Madonna, blind to the non-synthetic idiosyncrasies that unspun blandness might contain.

Two words about Costner: Tom Hanks. Cast Costner in

your mind in The Green Mile or Cast Away and then tell me those films haven't suddenly become twice as good. Tell me that you really think You've Got Mail mightn't have stood a better chance of not making you throw up with Costner in it. Costner is dull alright, but do you remember the old Chinese curse: *May you live in interesting times*? In his best movies, like Bull Durham or Tin Cup or Field of Dreams or No Way Out, Costner's dullness is the exercise of freedom – the freedom to be uninteresting.

But he's not stolid like Hanks. Costner has a beautiful vein of sadness running through everything he does, like when the light begins to strain at the end of a summer's day. His sadness lives in his mouth, in the initial reluctance of his smile, in the heart-breaking precision of the outline of his lips. It's the sadness of sports – games like golf or baseball, which are the two sports which most humble their players, the two sports where even the best are continually brought low. Another famous quotation: *America is a vast conspiracy to make you happy.* Costner knows the conspiracy won't work on him. He's cool. And it's why he's such a humane, defeated comedian, much more subtle than 'wry', much more touching than 'bittersweet' – those corporate qualities of HanksLand. He's complex. That's why Dances with Wolves, which should have been awful, came off, because of Costner's undemonstrative sadness. He wasn't going to hector you with his narration. Instead he droned it, pre-defeatedly, and squashed all the melodrama right out of the story. That's smart. And *dark* – well, dark is just a word we use to kid ourselves that there is artistic merit per se in the sour and sad, the most self-congratulatory of all contemporary critical terms. Costner's too good to be bothered with dark. His gaze, that's the heart of him. A great gazer with lucent green eyes. I like Kevin Costner, and *so do you.*

14

Jonathan gets dressed, apart from his shoes, and goes with me down the stairs and the hallway. At the door he suddenly puts his hand to my back and pushes me out.

'Go on, get out of here! And don't come round bothering me again, yeah?'

He stands on the stoop, gesturing. I'm smiling so wide words can't form and staring at him, amazed.

'Go on, clear off!'

He can't ever have seen me smile so wide. I am making steps like someone hit on the head, and staring at him amazedly.

With a kind of drop in pressure or loss of light, he says:

'OK, don't get lost. You can't get lost, it's easy.'

'Alright then.'

My smile and my amazed look have both faded. I smile at him and stretch on my toes. 'Alright then,' I say, 'better go. See you!' I remain stretching on my toes by the gate.

'Come on,' he says. 'C'mon, c'mon, c'mon, come here, give me a kiss, come on.'

I have to come back from the gate to the stoop to be kissed. He kisses me and says loudly into my ear: 'Now fuck off out of it!' and goes back inside without looking.

Oh God, but that's a happy moment!

We are arguing about Jonathan's face, which is an open book. His thoughts are legible there in 50-point bold. He could have been a silent movie heroine, salvaging a puppy from a cruel policeman, having his bonnet knocked off by ragamuffins, or realising that what he feared was a debt collector is in fact his great-aunt's solicitor bequeathing him a million bucks. He's incapable of lying, I tell him, everybody says so, and his face clouds over. 'Really?' *'Da!'* 'That's rubbish,' he says. 'It's just a technique to put everyone off the scent. I'm lying away quite happily inside here.' 'No you're not, you've gone red.' 'There you go. I've even got you fooled now.' 'Do you love me?' 'Yes.'

Once you're totally secure in someone the best is over, he says, another time, quoting something. All his wisdom comes from books. 'Shut up and kiss me,' I say. All my wisdom comes from films.

15

He reaches down into the sunlit grass and slides his left hand around his child's wrist, pinning it to her chest, and picks her up, twisting the little body round his elbow in mid-air so that it flips about and can be slung over his shoulder like a sack of wheat. That could have been Jonathan in the radiant grass, aged six. Harder to picture him as the lifter. *That* was Nikita Mikhalkov, the movie is Burnt by the Sun (1994) and the child is Mikhalkov's own daughter, Nadia. A king of an actor: six one and a half, barrel-chested like a Victorian swimming champion, twinkly-eyed, eight-time winner of Moustache and Moustache Wearer Magazine's Moustache of the Year, a moustache that looks like he's grown it to exhibit it in Moscow's prestigious Hall of Moustaches – I mean, this is a *moustache* – a pillar of a man, sentimental, full of joy, ridiculously romantic, love-drenched, life-brimming, stoic, all those qualities we like to call Russian, unfrightened, unstoppable, the father of four children, the son of two famous poets, and himself the most famous and respected (though opinions polarise) writer-director in Russia, who made the quiet but incredibly beautiful An Unfinished Piece for Mechanical Piano (1977) and Urga (1990), and who was, for a time at least, a serious aspirant to the Russian presidency. He is also *very good*.

We have no figure analogous to Mikhalkov. Imagine Olivier trying to win the 1950 general election. Imagine Schwarzenegger with talent. Imagine a Norman Mailer that wasn't a joke. In Burnt by the Sun he plays a Red Army hero, Colonel Kotov, enjoying summer with his family at his country dacha in 1936. One long hot day an old colleague comes, villainously, to arrest him. To his neighbours and friends Kotov is a born silverback around whom an entire community organises itself. To Stalin he is nothing. One of the movie's ironies is that Kotov actually *is* the benign paterfamilias Stalin presented himself as. To me Mikhalkov was the kind of man I had never met, had never even *seen*, and I couldn't resist the impression that Kotov was merely autobiography, that the writer-director-star fulfilled the same role in reality, a sheltering presence in whose lee others' lives could clarify.

I really fancied him. I mean to say, *really*. I even went, I suspect, a little over the top. Nothing too serious, nothing requiring medical intervention. ('The medulla oblongata has a screening mechanism which prevents unrealistic love-objects from penetrating into the central cortex, and yours, Miss Quirke, after a lifetime of lusting after stars, has become perforated.') I'm not mad, as I believe I have proved beyond a shadow of a doubt. But I did get hold of a tape of him being interviewed from the Russian Embassy press office, buy a stone of books on Russia, several pages of which I read, and become an irregular attendant at Mass at the Russian Orthodox Church in Ennismore Gardens in Knightsbridge, where the sermons were cerebral and the incense was thick. And got Mr Young's to do a private screening of the film for me in celebration of Jonathan's twenty-ninth birthday. And then put it on the video when we got back to mine. Perhaps I did go on about it rather. 'One: we're not going to Russia because we can't afford it,' said Jonathan. 'Two: how fucking old are you, anyway? D'you think Pauline Kael had a Warren Beatty duvet cover?' (It's a possibility.) 'A fixation on a movie star is an attempt to convert impotence into omnipotence. Textbook narcissism. Freud could rip you to bits in ten seconds, kid. Robin *Williams* could rip you to bits in ten seconds. Just shut up about it and please, please stop trying to talk in Russian.' I think Jonathan, not unfairly, resented the rebuke implicit in my Mikhalkov crush, which was that he was not solid, that we could never plan anything substantial because his life was so up in the air, that as a couple we were fatally provisional and were not upheld by a Chekhovian network of uncles, aunts and grass-stained guests returning from picking mushrooms in the birchwood. That Mikhalkov was the opposite of shambolic. In truth it was just a fever, as crushes are. Just a fever and just a movie star.

But that *just* – a real man recorded walking and talking and gesturing: where, precisely, does the *just* come into it? Justify that *just*. *Debate me*, as Steve Buscemi would say. *Qu'est que c'est ce mot* 'just'? *Ce n'est pas 'le mot juste'*, as Depardieu might say. Oh, Gérard, you're so witty. Did I mention I wasn't mad? Picture the art forms parading like Olympic teams around a stadium each preceded by a cautionary placard saying 'JUST'. 'Ladies and gentleman ... Just a poem! ... Just a book!' But the movies, being the most mimetic form, the one easiest to confuse with reality and therefore the most threatening to it, have a placard a hundred feet high. Stewards precede them,

enjoining us through megaphones to remember that *just*.
Safety regulations. Disregard that *just*! That *just* has caused me
a lot of trouble in my life. And this book is a *just*-free zone. Just
Bogart and just Bacall? 'Just put your lips together and blow.'
Just Citizen Kane? 'Just a piece of a jigsaw puzzle, a missing
piece.' Just Billy Wilder? 'Just us and the cameras and those
wonderful people out there in the dark . . . alright, Mr DeMille,
I'm ready for my close-up.'

When you see a god the punishment is, conventionally,
blinding or death. Actaeon would have known the score when
he saw Diana bathing, would have felt those antlers growing
on his head and the fangs of the hounds ripping into him
as a fair cop. And is there not an aspect of the mercy killing
to Actaeon's death? We moderns have a million Dianas and
Adonises dancing under our eyelids, and coping with it is part
of our condition. So we carry our *justs*. But having seen Nikita
Mikhalkov, I couldn't quite blink away the after-image of
this solar man from my retina. He had gone in deep. I had a
perforated screening mechanism!

16

*Love, which begins and ends in acting: at first self-projection, in
the end dissimulation.*

Sh. St. in form of a dedication, called Dedication

Borg speedboat: Odysseus

One day I go over to Whitechapel to persuade him out to the cinema and find him so fast asleep on his mattress it's like he's been buried. I couldn't have phoned him because his phone is always out of juice or on the blink or in a field. The decay in the flat has gained another magnitude, has attained seediness. The computer is on, so I sit down and scroll about, not really snooping, just browsing, you understand, slightly nervous that all it will say on the screen is 'All work and no play makes Jonathan a dull boy' over and over. London snuffles around the encrusted sauces on old Styrofoam cartons, failing to raise the alarm.

You had to get along with words. Certainly they were useful, but they weren't quite us; were greedy for influence and territory, too, and maybe even (the implication was) a little opposed to the human. Like any of our good creations, potential parricides.

OK. I'll come back to that one.

In the air, slightly over-dressed, a boy, he feels himself guessed at and ungettable, one to follow; fit for opening credits to pass the time with.

Film reference! Autobiographical?

In the photographs that were to break up his text you saw Bandersatz strewn across the several landscape, often with his arms half-outstretched as if asking whatever's behind to come forward and share his bow, his palm next-guestily out for a half-constructed course, for some kids whose day he's made, for a Lear jet like a pet, facetiously for rain; with the brand he smokes, the clothes he wears; with a flow-chart, an easel, a racket, a bat, a steer, a stag, a staring tuna, a crooner, a president; and flourish-

ing all the time the extra variousness of a century which itself is in the habit of taking admiring looks back at all the different ground it's covered. It all meant: here is a life that has overflowed the banks of a single career. It has brimmed, burst from the linear and flooded a plane. So Marley was working across Pro Bandersatz, not through him, and Time, the A to B device, was going nowhere. The book wasn't a history so much as a taxonomy, a bland tarot for a ghost to lay down in an auspicious pattern. The Champ ... The Businessman ... The Breeder ... The Architect ... The Ambassador ... The Old Guy. It could be read sideways; it couldn't be read forwards.

I get that. That's about a golfer, right? Jonathan wakes up noisily, not catching me. But from this point onwards I stop snooping. Or at least I cut down. Or ration myself just to checking for other girls' names (who is this 'Lolita' he keeps saying is so brilliant?). Because I think – what if he finishes his book and I read it ten times and it's still a mystery? Because I don't have a clue what *this* is about. What if, in the end, people just get more and more mysterious, so that all you ever really know of them is *Borg speedboat: Odysseus*? Secrets, perhaps, are nothing to be paranoid about. Some men, like Marcus, love theirs. Other men, like Jonathan, who don't relish having a hinterland, nonetheless have the same number of secrets as the Marcuses. It is *just fucking tricky to say* what you were about, that's all. You have to have a little faith in people, as Mariel Hemingway says at the end of Manhattan.

'Listen to this, Jon,' I say, reading out from the Sun: 'Nick Fisher – "Although in the past few years Woody Allen movies have been a bit hit and miss, *Small Time Crooks* is a definite return to his old-style comedy form!"'

'Bit of a risk,' says Jonathan.

17

I wrote an 800-word column on something like nine films a week, starting with 300 words or so on the main film, and then sort of talking faster and faster and faster as you got down the pecking order until you ended up with the last one getting about three. So you'd get these reviews of Angolan or Afghanistani films saying things like 'Sorab's Camel (cert 12) is no good'. Or 'Masukki Jaaskelin (Finland, PG) is tender and precise'. Or even 'Dreams of the Manta Ray (cert 18) is out'.

But it happened that I was sharing the page with two of the best film writers in the world, Gilbert Adair and David Thomson, author of the Biographical Dictionary of Film, which every film critic reaches for when they don't know what they think about something (you can always tell in articles when it says 'David Thomson says that Cagney . . .' that the writer has been sucking his biro wishing the words would come until eventually lurching over to the bookcase). Gilbert wrote the main film review, and David a piece in which he considered a particular topic or actor. It was a coup to have them both. And there I was, like a decorative putto beneath the gaze of two Titans. The then arts editor at the paper told me that he'd sent Thomson an unsolicited fax requesting a piece on Robert de Niro, not expecting a reply, and an hour later got a fax back with five hundred words. Thomson just happened to be sitting around in the mood. He's English but after years in America his voice has a transatlantic lilt and his giggle is high up and reckless. It's a blood-deep thing with David. You'd send him an email asking whether any movie stars had ever killed anybody and you'd get something like this back: 'Jimmy Stewart in the war. Audie Murphy. Clark Gable in a driving accident but it was hushed up. What a great movie it would make – a serial killer who's an actor. Yes. He kills whenever a role is over. And the film buff detective gets him by *realising that link*. (I reserve all rights to this.)' He's like Pauline Kael in that you wish he'd been allowed to make just *one* movie. Gilbert Adair, on the other hand, is a rude European intellectual, a postmodern novelist whose real love is mathematics. A man of great talent and range and an enigma to other people. At a Christmas lunch I remember people talking for hours in his absence about how an editor had called him and heard the voice of a young man in the other room at the end of the line (Gilbert is gay). Nobody at that lunch would admit how much they envied and admired Adair's chilly, competent attitude to his own life. *What does he do all day? What does he talk about?* We were gossips, stymied by the ostensible absence of some human imperfection. Gilbert couldn't abide horror movies, which meant I got to write about films like The Blair Witch Project. Occasionally he would call me up and ask if I would see this film or that instead of him, as though the prospect of seeing them was causing him actual pain. Once he rang me to ask if I would review the main film that week because he was worried about his eyes: he was at a station somewhere and they were paining him, and I think his father had some trouble with his eyes – but there was a suggestion that he feared he might go blind with all of this. Or that he would rather go blind than watch Matthew Perry in Two to Tango. Then later, just before he gave up the page, he called to say his scalp was falling off with the stress of all the crap on screen.

Thomson is all heart, Adair all brains. But they both love cinema. I mean *love*. Or they did then. Adair has branched out. Thomson seems more interested in the Industry than the product these days. But as critics they have been immensely useful to movies. And *actors* . . . ooh, they're so bloody oppositional. I was always shocked when, in The Year of the King, Antony Sher would stop woozily reminiscing about his colleagues and turn his gaze on the critics. He wouldn't even give them Christian names: 'Billington. Coveney. Wardle. Tinker.' Like they were swear words. The sort of swear words that Garrick might have used. I once had a one-night stand with an actor who was lovely and friendly when we met, and we had a nice time together, but when we woke up and I said that I'd be going to see Dog Soldiers at 10.30 because I was a film critic, he jumped out of bed looking completely horrified and asked me if I had any idea what kind of grief 'people like me' caused.

'But I told you what I did last night!'

'No, you didn't.'

'I *did*! You said you were in Dirty Pretty Things and I said wow that's great because it's a really good film and that I had said so in the Journal. Then you told me the story about the cab.'

(He'd been so drunk, with the great Tom Hollander, I'd been thrilled to learn, that he'd kept calling for a cab to take him back to his hotel even though he was actually in it.)

'What journal?'

'The Camden New Journal.'

He stood naked in the threshold of the room, the night sweat still on his pale stomach.

'I must have thought you meant your sodding *diary*. Oh, Christ, d'you think anyone saw us leave together?'

One of the reasons actors hate critics more than, say, writers hate critics is that their profession is such a mystery to themselves. Because of the lack of concreteness in the whole process (you don't get to look back over your first drafts as an actor), actors are often in awe at the inexplicability of what they're doing, so why the hell should anyone else claim to know what they're up to? But the them-and-us fallacy always ends up as a pallid unwillingness to offend – especially in the theatre ('The good members of the cast will go from strength to strength and the weaker ones, well, they can only get better' – Hilary Finch, The Times). And it's not helpful. It's a shame that film-makers don't really write about film much any more. They used to. Truffaut's famous 1954 essay 'A Certain Tendency in Cinema', basically went: French movies are rubbish so I'm going to go out and make some better ones, which of course he did. These days film-makers sound like footballers or tennis starlets they're so fearful of knocking anyone. When criticism is just for the know-nothing bogeymen on the other side of the fence, the only valid critic becomes Mr Weinstein or the domestic gross.

Critics are *lovers*. Because they can only be great when there's something to love. Their best work comes from an excess of love. You can only get Ken Tynan and Lester Bangs and Clive James and Pauline Kael and Robert Hughes during periods of high explosive burn. You just cannot be a great critic when there isn't great art. Look at someone like Brian Sewell, up there on the ramparts with his barrels of boiling oil. He loves art but he hardly gets to do any *writing*, because negativity doesn't stretch you. Sewell has longevity, but the mark of the great lover-critic is that he burns out. All the people on that list above started to whine at some point towards the end because their love had been disappointed: the kind of love you need can only have a short lifespan. Coming out of a screening in the early 1980s, Kael said, or should I say, *whined*: 'It's no fun any more.' And that's critics. They want it so much. They want The Masterpiece *so much*. They are *die Hungerkünstler*. The hunger-artists.

18

'Dear oh dear oh dear oh dear oh dear oh dear,' said Jonathan as we came out of the press screening of The Phantom Menace, and I said, well, it was crap, for sure, but possibly, you know, *possibly* it was a bit like listening to Be Here Now – it only *appeared* terrible, but they might secretly know what they're doing, which is precisely the kind of diplomatic response you learn on Breakfast Television where you're essentially a cheer-leader and discouraged from saying, 'To be frank, Lorraine, having wasted two hours of my life, I want revenge, I want *blood*.'

Naturally, like the rest of the planet, the producers at GMTV were in a froth about the film and had been running competitions and special features all week, and even a trailer for the review slot which went: 'We've gone Space Crazy!' On Friday morning, I arrived at the studio to find things changed. As the Head of Programming had promised, they had built a darling little film set on wheels with red velvet cinema seats and flock walls and a screen. You could have wheeled it into the Black Forest or the Nevada Desert and watched Ivan the Terrible in your own portable movie paradise. But today it was gone and the studio had been tarted up with not Star Wars creatures exactly, just lots of non-specific extraterrestrials hanging around like the drinkers in the space-port bar at Mos Eisley. I think they'd even managed to get hold of one of those vulture things from The Dark Crystal. It was space-related, anyway. The walls looked like a collage off Take Hart with lots of glitter and silver paper used for the rings round planets.

Somebody plonked an alien in the seat next to me, as if it

were shortly to be asked for its perspective ('Mmyeah . . . there are *certain* inaccuracies,' you could have imagined it beginning), and Lorraine and I switched on the two lightsabres that had been handed to us moments before. She looked, as she always did, warm-hearted and optimistic, with her customary ambience of knitwear and sheep-in-the-glen. She had such a lovely Scottish voice, reminded me of the innkeeper's wife in The Thirty-Nine Steps.

'So Antonia! It's been fifteen years and the wait is over at last! I can hardly believe I'm finally sitting here about to find out once and for all how it all began! So. *How was it?*'

Well, everyone knows the answer to that. (I particularly treasured Lucas's infuriating quote in the press release: 'Acting is acting whether it's a human being or computer generated.')

'It's a disaster, Lorraine. A total disaster.'

Lorraine's lightsabre sagged.

'A disaster? But this is just awful! What about Ewan? Surely he peps things up a wee bit?'

'Ask *him* what he thinks about it.'

And so it went.

'How many buckets of popcorn would you award it? One to ten.'

'None. Zero.'

'*Antonia*, surely a two? Or a one?'

'No, I'm afraid it has to be zero. No buckets.'

Lorraine switched off her sabre. No buckets. We went to the adverts.

And I'm only telling you this because there's this pernicious thing about big expensive movies that makes people feel like they can shed all their civility, that they can be irresponsibly vicious because it's only a big corporation on the receiving end. And if you're not careful, you can get quite hooked on trashing things and think of yourself as a lone crusader for truth, coming down from the hill with your sword of justice and your self-righteous anger. To be honest, I prefer those geek sites which always find something good in the lousiest blockbuster. It's better for the soul.

In fact, I once had to dictate my review of The Matrix Reloaded over the phone when I was on a train. 'Understand that I loved The Matrix comma . . .' I began. (Remember there was that same excitement in the air about Keanu's return as there had been with Star Wars?) Anyway, I couldn't help, *I really couldn't help*, but be overheard, and I could sense the carriage pricking up its ears to eavesdrop on the first news of the sequel. Oh, this is a shameful story. I simply couldn't stop myself from relishing my role as Ringer of the Leper Bell.

'. . . and then trust that I am not displaying the bitterness of the disappointed lover in saying that The Matrix Reloaded isn't flawed comma or sporadically entertaining comma or an heroic failure comma but a catastrophically incoherent comma boring comma uncool comma inert film full stop. It isn't a loveable mess comma it's an unloveable mess full stop. It isn't any good italics at all close italics full stop end para.'

Me and my sword of justice, displaying all the bitterness of the disappointed lover. Because that's all it is. Your love gone sour. The viciousness you only allow yourself over something you once loved. And why would you want to crow about that?

19

And now we have arrived at the point in this book where Keanu Reeves must be praised. Keanu is better than Johnny Depp. Imagine you're going to see your son in a school play, or your daughter's band, or your boyfriend play for his Sunday league team. Your response is peculiarly distorted, is it not, by your connection to them, by your desire for them to do well. Am I not right? Because of your protective nervousness, it's impossible to tell how good they actually are. Keanu is like that for the whole planet. You could call it the Monroe Effect. Like Marilyn, Keanu introduces an electric tension into everything he does because of the combination of uncontrollable charisma and technical incompetence. And this is one of the hilarious mysteries of cinema – it works. The experience of watching Keanu teetering on his highwire, or Marilyn finally managing to say 'Where's the bourbon' on the fifty-seventh take, is closer to the heart of the movies than watching, say, that nincompoop Sean Penn. Keanu and Marilyn *don't know what they're doing.* So Keanu, who is butt-of-the-joke sexy like Monroe, is a bit of a laughing stock. Whereas Depp is cool, clever, arty. The numbskull versus the authenticator.

And yet as much as I love Johnny Depp, what has he left us with other than, on the one hand, his whimsical collection of beautiful losers and on the other, respectable but hardly searing middleweight leads in things like Blow and Donnie Brasco? (Only on his day off – Jack Sparrow – did the longed-for Johnny come sparkling out.) The answer is: he's been a mascot. A kitemark of the correct indie impulses. A badge of cool whom movies as a whole are rightly grateful for. Thank Christ he's in *our* gang, you can hear Hollywood saying. But there's something so suffocating about that miasma of reverence surrounding Depp that I want to puke. Cool is all about control. And if there's one thing I know about this life it's that control is overrated.

Keanu has no control. Unlike Johnny, he has the correct response to his own world-historical beauty – utter bewilderment. He acts like he has no memory of what has occurred five seconds ago, his brain, like his face, a palimpsest forever wiping itself clean. He exists in the present alone, that condition to which dancers and singers aspire. And in The Matrix, a film all about befuddlement and the disgrace of human stupidity, Keanu gave the *greatest movie star performance of our lifetimes.* It's the Monroe Effect. His palpable concentration on trying to get things right actually works to draw you further into him, and, as I've said, to raise the tension. But unlike Monroe, he is wholly passive because he has nothing to project. Like your son in the school play concentrating on his lines, he has no time for us. Had The Matrix been a reality TV show prank on Keanu, you feel that he would have given precisely the same performance, with the same scarcely concealed joy at getting to swish a long leather coat about his ankles, and the same anxious desire not to let the other humans down, and the same temple-clutching confusion at the shifting of realities. Because he doesn't have the equipment as an actor to control the experience and make it happen to us, it all happens to him instead. And this is why Keanu is, kind of, the greatest of them all. He has the quality nobody else has, the absolutely unfakeable secret weapon. Innocence. While Johnny painstakingly constructs his many man-children like Edward Scissorhands, J. M. Barrie, Willie Wonka, Ed Wood, etc., you get a whiff of the faux-naïvety of a kid's drawing on the cover of an Eels album.

Innocence is what's being craved here. But only Keanu actually has it. He makes the rest look like just a bunch of actors.

20

Take M40 to Birmingham, then M6 north at Junction 7. Stare aghast at the traffic, the sovereignty of the car. Take M61 to Horwich. Get out of the fucking middle lane, you're driving too slowly. Come off at the Reebok Stadium exit. Ree Bok. In Inuit it means 'the place which has flowers'. Turn left at Crown pub, turn right up Stonefield Lane, park outside house, check your hair in the rear-view mirror and come and give me a kiss.

I did all this, and then kissed him on the neck, and then kissed him on the cheek. The marvellous smoothness. It had been three weeks since I'd seen him, three weeks since he'd gone up north with London to see his father and try to nail his golfer. I held his head.

'How's everything going?'

London bounded around us, trying to get in on our embrace.

'Nothing happens. It's great. The only way I'm sure I'm alive is that the thermo-sensitive burglar light goes on when I pass.'

The two men seemed to subsist exclusively on Leibniz biscuits, so I offered to cook lamb chops for them and a biscuit dragon, chocolate chip cookies dunked in brandy stuck together with cream, which we ate while Michael Marr berated Jonathan for not writing Shakespeare in Love.

'It's bloody easy, you should have written that. Would have taken you a couple of hours . . .'

Michael had faith in Jonathan. As the evening wore on, he would suggest a series of increasingly brilliant works of art that Jonathan could have knocked off. Shakespeare in Love. Some Richard Ford or other. Ulysses. Jonathan didn't blow a fuse, though I thought he might. He just looked at me out of the corner of his eye and rolled us cigarettes while I wondered when we were going to get to go to bed together. When we did I thought he looked very thin, like he'd been feeding bits of himself to the book. His room was a mass of papers and notes and golfing manuals and books on cocaine and ecology, a chaos which he was supposed to be compressing into a neat little brick of a hundred thousand words. I nervously flicked through Snowfields: War on Cocaine in the Andes, taken aback by the extent of the disorder. 'What's this one about?' 'It's about the old days, the early eighties in Bolivia and Peru, though obviously I'm not using a specific country.' 'Why obviously?' 'Because I know fuck all about Bolivia and Peru. It's interesting, though, the manufacturing process, the coca-pits, the laboratories. Basically you need a lot of toilet paper. The DEA are always looking for people importing lots of toilet paper –' 'It's a *motif* is it, then, toilet paper?' '. . . Yes it *is*, actually. Waste paper. It's a theme. A bit of a stand-ard Dickens/Pynchon money-shit-waste-product thing – *litter*, that's the point. And the insane wealth in general; it's like Howard Hughes, waking up and saying, "Let's have a Cézanne in the zoo" . . . this militantly happy golfer . . . formalised romantic relations between hyper-wealthy twelve-year-olds done in the second person . . . I just like the colours in it . . . section about biodiversity isn't coming off . . . *better* than Ballard . . . penultimate bridging passage is in the wrong tense . . . writes this book called Guilt and How to Get Over It, a confessional, a sort of self-help manual for murderers, but that's in the background anyway. That's just hinted at.'

It was getting away from him and he knew it. I had always been aware that the book wasn't wholly naturalistic, that it had slips and slides into something more poetic, but it just seemed to be getting wilder and wilder and had now hardened into something massive, like he was trying to cover the whole world with an only apparently Conradian plot. Not actually Conradian. That would have been too easy. It was always 'the fascination of what's difficult' with Jonathan. From Bolton he had been sending me long insistent letters in his delicate spidery hand with many PS's and footnotes, beautiful letters which were nonetheless symptoms of his book's unravelling. After a day spent not getting things right, it was pleasant for him to chivvy me, to be effortlessly right about films and criticism. I never could rid myself of the feeling that Jonathan could stroll, a *flâneur* with a cane, down all the paths I was paid to negotiate with ice-axe, rope and sweat. *Otto e Mezzo*. But in the arrows which mapped his digressions, in the turmoil of his marginalia, I could detect signs of perfectionist woe. And then coming on to me down the phone like André Bazin when all I wanted to do was to watch Dead Poets' Society. 'Don't do it to yourself! Switch it off.' 'I don't want to switch it off. I'm quite enjoying it actually. It's not like you've ever seen it.' 'I will never fucking see that film, ever. If you have to see it to be sure that it's crap, you're already too stupid to be allowed to have an opinion on it. It's evil.' 'Well, I like Ethan Hawke's mouth. He always looks like he's just drunk a cup of Ribena.' 'Fuck him. Read some Montaigne. Read a dead poet. *Robin Williams?* You know what his ideal role would be? Josef Mengele …' And then he was off on the relationship between comedy and denial and camp – his pet hate – and Robin Williams in the voice booth for Aladdin with the technicians in stitches every time he said *houmous*. 'Just get off my back, Jonathan, will you? There's lots of nice shots of trees.' And then another letter the next day: 'I'm not on your back. Please don't picture Charles Foster Kane with Susan Alexander, or the ex-KGB lesbian gymnastics coach, herself abused as a child, with her checklist, stick, and secret shrine to Stalin. I was only trying to be your little helper, Tom Hagen to your Michael Corleone, the Chinese kid in Indiana Jones and the Temple of Doom, your caddy, your cornerman, your Ariel . . .'

'When are you coming back?' I said.

'A month,' he said, shuffling papers into right-angled stacks. He was so thin, and the world was so big . . .

'But I'm going to Cannes in a month,' I said. 'I was hoping you could come out and see me afterwards. We could go fishing. Catch a trout in the Rhône.' It was very quiet in his room and when we made love Jonathan put his hand over my mouth. We were officially in separate bedrooms, you see.

First thing in the morning, London impatiently decanted an unharmed duck on to the kitchen floor, so Michael and I took her out for a long walk in the snow around Rivington Pike, a breast-shaped hill with a nipple of a folly on its summit which maternally presided over the surrounding countryside, while Jonathan worked. We quizzed each other about him, his blue-eyed son, my darling young one, but we were like two people going through their pockets saying to each other, 'I thought *you* had the keys.'

In the car on the way back, he told me about Leslie Halliwell, author of the Halliwell's Film Guides, who had been in his class at school. Halliwell was the very first movie anorak – the first person to turn being a movie-buff into a job. 'He was the most boring man I have ever met,' said Michael. I liked Michael very much. He played the Rolling Stones on the car stereo, and yelled 'Beat that!' at the end of Sweet Virginia while London drooled on my shoulder. The rest of the day she spent with me on Jonathan's bed, sombrely watching him drink his seven daily cans of Tango Tropical and nurse his cigarette butts, which he paranoiacally hoarded in case of emergency. It was there that he said that afternoon, not wholly out of the blue, gravely, as if speaking of something long considered, that he was going to give News, Sport, Weather a rest. You could see that these were very, very hard words for him to say. Throatstickers.

'I'm going to put it on the back-burner for a while.'

We could hear Michael watching a rugby match downstairs, occasionally calling out the score in accents of resignation or hope.

'But what about Pro?' was all I could manage.

'Pro'll be there. He'll wait. He's had a valve replacement, he can go and design another course.'

'I thought you said you were nearly finished –'

'It's not going to be a month, sweetheart,' Jonathan interrupted me. 'It's going to be a year.'

He had broken his bad news like a policeman on a doorstep with that uninflected voice which tries to minimise the surface area of pain, I thought, taking refuge in the downstairs loo, a little room like a kaleidoscope. I was surrounded by a collage that Jonathan's mother had put together. And there she was, next to a picture of Michael chomping down on a cigar and holding up a newspaper with the headline THIS MANIAC WILL KILL, on a canal boat in a Dylan cap and flares sometime in the irrecoverable 1970s. By the disappearance of everything red in the photos and postcards, you could see how old the collage was – it had been done before such things became ubiquitous. There was Nureyev next to Frank Worthington, there was La Maja Desnuda checking out Michelangelo's David, there were Chagall angels flying over toddlers at pianos and families lined up in order of height like pan-pipes, people lagged like boilers in all their Christmas-present clothes, glasses raised, glasses removed, women awkward at games in their cocktail dresses, children on shoulders on summits. There was Jonathan's brother who worked for the Foreign Office gunned down in a cowboy hat, there was Jonathan seven and naked except for a pair of wellingtons, playing cricket.

Like all of our corkboards, the room was trying to say that our ideal world is a whirligig of bright fragments like the recollection of a film is – so all-coloured it is hard not to wish yourself into it. I did. I do. I always do. I want to set all the pictures going, see the glasses go down or back on and the awkward women hitch up their skirts and run, all the lives begin to turn each other, like cogs in an infinitely intricate machine capable of generating plots so head-swimmingly more various than the elementary scripts you project for yourself which end, always, in standing ovations, and a wise old mentor slipping tearfully away from the auditorium. Perhaps, after all, Jonathan wasn't Prince Hamlet, nor was meant to be. He had veered from my script. But fuck the script. It is a very, very straightforward concept indeed that life is not like a movie, but one I have amazing difficulty in grasping. Maybe I am just thick. It simply *will not stick* in my ivory dome – as Robert Donat calls Madeleine Carroll's head in The Thirty-Nine Steps (great film!). And things like those collages help remind me, for a while at least, that life is broader and wider and *better* than my mental movieland where Dustin Hoffman always gets the job at twenty to five on Christmas Eve. Jonathan and I could go on, could maybe see more of each other, could roll with whatever happened. Could have guests around to pick mushrooms in our birchwood. He could take some other job and earn a little money, get back out in the world.

'Twenty-one eigh*teen!*' shouted Michael as I made my way back upstairs, lighter-hearted, to the chaotic room, where Jonathan outlined his plans to me.

'Before I do anything else, I need to do this one thing,' he said amid his Manhattan of notes. 'Something quite small but very saleable. A sharp little book. Half of it's in verse.'

'What do you mean?'

'You know how Vikram Seth imitates the Eugene Onegin stanza?'

'No.' (What?)

'Well, it's like a piss-take of The Golden Gate. The form, I mean. A kind of tribute to and undercutting of the sort of rich-tapestry-of-life, middlebrow urban-idyll thing. Tetrameter sonnets. You'll like it. It's about someone who wants to kill himself.'

Time did whatever time does for a while. *Do you expect me. To let you go.*

'But isn't that going to be incredibly difficult, Jonathan?'

'It'll be a fucking doddle. A long novella.'

'You're nuts! Listen, the last "saleable, sharp little book in verse" was written in 1840, or something. And what about *us*? What about the trout? What's this one called? Borg Speedboat Odysseus?'

'. . . *what*? No.'

'So what is the title?'

'I was thinking about a quote from Bellow actually,' he said, fiddling with the end of his nose. 'It's called The Slow Artist.'

Turn right out of house down Stonefield Lane, turn left at Crown pub, pull over, bang steering wheel for a while, pull self together, take M61 to M6, swear at everybody who ventures an opinion on the radio, rejoin M40, come off at Paddington. The empty orange city, getting its early night. Turn right into Bayswater, find a space, go inside, put Gérard on the video: Le Colonel Chabert. Don't cry.

21

The Love Song of Michael J. Fox

Let us go then, Marty McFly,
When the evening is spread out against the sky
Like a patient when the meds are taking hold,
Let us go through time to 1985,
When I am twenty-four years old
And the most famous teenager alive . . .

In the room the women come and go
Talking of Ralph Macchio

In sleeveless puffas, stonewashed jeans,
We glide through suburban summer scenes
And suffer the indignity
Of being asked to show ID
Whenever we go to a bar,
Goddammit. Life is sweet. So far
This year, *Teen Wolf* and *Back* have grossed
300 mill, and *Family Ties*
Is still enormous. Marty flies
Around on skateboards, having fun

With that revolving, stumbling run
Of his, and slays Hill Valley High's
Girls with his husky voice. I satirise
My own height – *I feel four foot tall*
I say, of my success, and all
Adore it. This amazing year –
Let's stay, I say, *let's both stay here*
In this extraordinary time.
Junk the DeLorean, Marty, we're
Not going to need it again. I'm
Going nowhere. We turn our thoughts
To the Huey Lewis album *Sports*,
Drink Moosehead Ale and think upon
Van Halen's fate now Dave has gone.
We glide. The sun shines. What *glasnost*
Actually means we don't quite understand
But it appears to mean we've won.
The news is beautifully bland.
The News are Huey Lewis' band.
There's nothing wrong with Marty's hand
But mine won't do what it's supposed . . .
He can stay here. I must go on.

In the room the women come and go
Talking of Vincent d'Onofrio

＊　＊　＊　＊

I think time-travel really takes it out of you.

Everyone travels through time, I try to say –
We travel at our daily rate.
But I cannot move. I am stranded here
While time flows past on its way

Elsewhere. Without my dopamine
It is impossible to say just what I mean!

I grow old . . . I grow old . . .
I shall wear the sleeves of my jackets rolled.

The mermaids call to me but my face is numb.
I shake. I cannot communicate
Until the Sinemet hits eighty-eight
Miles an hour and shoots me
With tyre-tracks incandescent
Through the space-time continuum
Back into the present.

I will sing to you at Enchantment under the sea
And the mermaids will dance to a fast blues in B
Called Johnny B. Goode. I can hear them calling me
Because I was good. They say:

You were good, you were good, you were good.

22

For three years I had been happily gadding about at the
Independent on Sunday, and since my editor had left after
Christmas to write a novel, I had a new one, a young man
called Alex Haslam. He arranged to meet me for drinks in a
gastropub on Abbey Road.

'This thing about the animation,' he said, scrutinising a
photocopy of one of my reviews, '*We see Visa-like barcodes
glowing above the crust. We see wake-angles shimmering along-*

side spaceships; we hear the sob of an ice-planet . . . Are you sure? How can a planet sob? And this stuff about *the uncomfortable tinkle as stalactites fall, and the stars stretching out like some mighty sky-snake, twisting its way north.* I'm just going to say this, Antonia. It's purple.'

'It's not purple. It's reasonably colourful prose! Purple means over-ripe.'

'OK, here's one. *Adrian Grenier in Drive Me Crazy is not a coiffured ponce. He is romantically handsome in a cunning way and I fancy him like mad.*'

'Yes, he *is*, he's very good-looking.'

'Well of course he is, he's in the movies. There's just this sense that it's all a bit indiscriminate.'

'No way! It's not indiscriminate. It's very *personal*, that's the whole point.'

'And here's another.' Alex had a whole stack of photocopies. '*The film also features David Caruso, who you might remember from NYPD Blue. Caruso left that series some six years ago to try and make it in the movies, but his career didn't really take off – this is a shame because he is a live-wire, articulate, a real turn-on.* You know what, Antonia? This is sexist. If you were a man writing about actresses like this it wouldn't wash.'

'But I'm *not* a man. So it's different.'

'How is it different?'

'*It just is.* Stop being so repressed! I don't like *everyone*. I don't like David Duchovny.'

Alex's scooter had broken down on the way from Canary Wharf and in the ninety minutes I'd been waiting I'd had a few. I was feeling great.

'Generally I've noticed that you're hardly ever rude about actors and you're hardly ever kind about actresses. It just makes you look less objective.'

'But I'm always saying actresses are gorgeous.'

'No, you're kidding yourself. Almost never. This is something I've marked in particular . . . about Eileen Walsh . . . *She is supposedly, by turns, daffy, moony, dippy, fluffy, kooky and feisty. In fact, she is gloopy, dreary, hammy, corny, wishy-washy, lousy and about as fresh and innocent as a divorcee wearing a skinnyrib T-shirt which reads "Groovy Chick" in un-joined-up writing.* It's just abuse.'

Oh, the idiot sword of justice!

'I didn't mean *her*, I meant the part.'

'You're over-nice about actors and horrible about actresses. Now, *this* is the one I wanted to talk to you about, from The Driver. Have a look at this.'

Highlighted in pink, it said: *Even when Ryan O'Neal is driving like a maniac around an underground car park, Isabelle Adjani holds her handbag under her arm like someone waiting at a bus stop. She looks bored to death. Ludicrously French. But Ryan! You can smash through my shop display any time!*

'You've got to be kidding! That was a *joke*! Don't be such a killjoy. Last week I said that Kelly Macdonald had perfect skin.'

'You said Catherine Zeta-Jones looks like a catalogue model who likes to wear slacks.'

'She does!'

'She does not. You are *wrong*. She *never* wears trousers.'

'She does in that house.'

We sat quietly.

'*And* when she plays golf.'

The one that had really got Alex's goat was about Winona Ryder, which said that she was the kind of girl who would cry angry tears at the thought of Nixon *lying like that* (I really couldn't stick Winona Ryder) – *but could this girl ever have really been into The Grateful Dead?*

'What on earth have The Grateful Dead got to do with Winona Ryder? Look, just tone down the actor stuff and try and take a look at the bigger picture a bit more. At the industry. At the context. And don't keep getting bogged down with all this personal stuff. Be a bit more authoritative.'

I didn't want to be authoritative about the industry. It made me nervous.

'OK, OK, I'll tone it down.'

Bunch of squares. Nobody read the Independent on Sunday anyway.

23

I don't really want to see movies in a silent screening-room. I don't really want to watch them with 3,000 others in a sea of dodecaphonic sound on a Saturday night. I don't want to know about them two years beforehand, or to have been looking forward to them. I don't want to get them out on DVD or video. I don't want to watch them with a lover. This is what I want:

I want to miss the first five minutes of a film on television around midnight and have no idea what the hell it is. I want there to be advert breaks, definitely. I want not to have a paper so that even when I find out the title I won't be sure what it is. I want to have to get up very early in the morning so that it'll stretch on way past my bedtime. I want to get the feeling that only twelve other people are watching it. I want there to be an annoyingly insufficient half-glass of wine left in the fridge door only. And the film – the film would look like a 6 at first and turn out to be an 8 out of 10.

An 8. Something just a little better than it need be. A thing which would have been a 6 or a 7 but for the unnecessary love, the voluntary art which saved it. That extra point or two, which, coming unasked like alms, makes the difference between a pigsty and a culture. Between The Bourne Supremacy and The Bourne Identity, between Insomnia with Al and Insomnia with Stellan. The sort of films that fill you with gratitude that the machine is working as it should. That stuttering, incompetent machine of which we ask so goddamn little except that it can do things like briefly cheer you up after you've had a potentially fatal row with your boyfriend about his coming to France with you or not.

Le Rayon Vert, Bringing up Baby, Tootsie, Persona – those are the 9's and the 10's. Those are the bonuses. But Jagged Edge, Tampopo, Crossing Delancey, Belle Epoque, Gorky Park, Body Heat, Shoot the Moon, Midnight Run, Hear My Song, Breaking Away, The Last Seduction, The Edge are the 8's. None of them films which could be called great, except in the sense that you'd call all of them *great*. I like them better than the 9's and 10's. I prefer them. I . . . *love them*.

24

The director of the BBC Knowledge documentary Cannes 2001 was an unstoppably enthusiastic Scot called Sally whose conversation was like a bus map, continually looping past the street you want.

'Have you ever seen The Girl on the Bridge? With Vanessa

Paradis? It's black and white, or more black and silver in a way, black and pewter, metallic, shiny, well, whatever, that's the look I'm going for. All shot at Magic Hour with the lights coming at you and exploding like blobs of glass, and you sitting there all mysterious and pondering . . .'

This was my big chance. By almost unimaginable persistence and effort (watching films and living in London), I had ascended from my orphanage in the Mississippi Delta to the apex of my profession. I was hot! They wanted me to go on the Late Review, which meant I was an Intellectual. I had also become one of those people who were forever popping up on Top 100 countdowns sitting in an empty cinema saying something incisive like 'it's just really, really good' or 'for Coppola the filming process actually *was* like his *own* Vietnam', while the viewer (incensed, perhaps, by the strapline of *movie expert*) thinks: *Who the fuck is that?* In fact I was doing an awful lot of little gobbets of digital telly film stuff by now. You always had to put your hands in your jeans pockets to project that student bar air of never using directors' Christian names, like some girl who spends all evening telling you that Cronenberg is the best director of the last thirty years (which they do).

'Vanessa Paradis is awfully thin, Sally,' I said. 'She's a Chanel model.'

'Yes, and her hair is cropped. Perhaps you could crop yours. Just to see what it would be like?'

She took me to an expensive shop on Marylebone High Street and picked out a couple of dresses for me.

'I'm thinking more sort of 1950s couture now,' she said. 'Jayne Mansfield on the nightclub circuit. With your hair in a chignon. Kind of up but down at the same time, falling over your eyes, bleached to candyfloss, like Monroe just before she died. False eyelashes. We're going to shoot in cafés at Magic

Hour with people smoking heavily all around you and laughing.'

'What's magic hour?'

'Tea time. Oooh, no no no, no, absolutely not. How about something more nautical? High-necked stripy sleeveless tops and 1940s slacks. I *wish* you'd cut your hair.'

'I'd really rather not.'

'It's more *nautical* if it's short.'

'The thing is, Sally – what am I actually going to be *doing*? What will I be talking about exactly?'

'Oh, God, *everything*. The whole *festival*, the different *themes*, the his*tory*, Scott Fitz*gerald*, the *at*mosphere, the *jury*, the de*bates*, Coco Cha*nel*, the way things *strike* you, who's here and who *isn't*, what the place *feels* like, what it *looks* like, what's being said behind closed *doors*, what happens at the *parties*, the *future* of the festival, the future of *cinema*, the future of *art*. And how in a *weird* way it all always leads back to *Coppola*. So it's just you walking about and talking off the top of your head about that kind of thing, all very dreamy, and then there's a panel discussion on the final night which is going to be very hand-held, very edgy, very *Dogme*.'

'A panel discussion? Who with?'

'Oooh, that's *splendid*.'

I was wearing a deeply scoop-necked, midnight-blue, cinch-waisted, knee-length gown bedewed with crystals, filthy as all get-out, like one of those dirty girls Marcello Mastroianni's always cheating on his wife with. I wanted to just go out and have it off with, like, a hundred Italians at the same time. With Rocco e Tutti Sui Fratelli.

'With Godard, hopefully.'

'*Jean-Luc* Godard?'

'Yes. Or Bergman. But don't worry. They'll do all the talking. It's not really all that *nautical* is it?'

It was the first time I had been to the South of France. I bought Tender is the Night, and The Rock Pool by Cyril Connolly and got fitted out in a Breton top and spotty nautical scarf that Nicole Diver might have worn during the good times with Dick. A double booking meant that Sally and I had been bumped up to a marble penthouse on the Croisette next to the Carlton, with cushions fat as spinsters' cats and bolsters like pig-swallowing snakes, and valanced chaises longues which looked out of the floor-to-ceiling windows on to the Golfe du Lion where superyachts lazed with the threatening indolence of star-destroyers. I lay on all the beds listening to the clink of cutlery ascending from the parasoled terraces below and turned on the taps in our four en-suite bathrooms to see whether the hot water would come on in all of them at the same time. There was a friend of mine, a Northern Irish film-maker called Dudi, who was also in Cannes trying to get his adaptation of a Peter Ackroyd novel out of development hell into development purgatory, and he would sometimes come over to help me practise my lines.

'OK. So, I'm standing here looking at the camera, and I say this: *We're right above the centre of Cannes and over across the bay is the Cap d'Antibes,* and I point down and –'

'It's good if you stumble a bit or repeat yourself. Looks more live.'

'More Dogme!' Sally shouted from another room.

'Sorry. Right. *And over across the, uh, bay is the is the Cap d'Antibes, where the whole, the whole, uh, notion of the Riviera was kind of . . . dreamed up by expatriate Americans in the . . . in the 1920s –*'

To supplement my nautical look, I would sunbathe most mornings, idly casting Dick Diver in Tender is the Night.

25

(Edward Norton? The Cusack/Broderick problem again, and metallic, meticulous, *marrowless*. Kevin Kline? What *is* the matter with Kevin Kline? He's just too damn happy, that's what he is. Viggo Mortensen. Too damn sad. Jonathan. Too chaotic. Crowe, of course. But you'd keep waiting for him to break Nicole's jaw. Mind you, Dick does hit that policeman, doesn't he? God, Crowe. *He'd be brilliant.* He's just the best. Oh, Christ. Get a grip of yourself. Crowe, Crowe, Crowe . . . in a minute Diego Luna's going to come out and sit on this lounger beside me. 'Oh, no, of course it's not taken. Actually, señor, I've got a light . . .' – Penn. Bloody *Penn*. Who else has that tragic, haunted glamour? Who else could cover both golden boy and whiner so realistically? Well, Crowe, obviously. But Penn has that twenties elegance. Up at the Villa with Kristin Scott Thomas, remember? Better posture. More Celtically melancholy. Wouldn't be as good as a doctor as Crowe . . . but I don't know . . . 'This book? You like Fitzgerald? Oh, careful! Your cigarette! Oh, oh, up in flames! You have a copy in your room?' No, unrealistic, try again. But *Christ*, what a movie! Penn as Diver! Penn as Monroe Stahr in The Last Tycoon! Penn as Gatsby – 'An elegant young roughneck, a year or two over thirty.' Could he do the smile? A test of Penn's range, whether his tight-fisted little slot mouth could ever frame Gatsby's smile with its 'quality of eternal reassurance'. Does he have enough to give to do the smile? How annoying that Robert Redford screwed it up so badly that we'll never see Sean Penn as Jay Gatsby!)

26

and worrying about Bergman and Godard.

'Godard's out,' said Sally. 'I'm *so* annoyed. He's only giving one interview, to some tennis magazine, which is *typical*. And Bergman's staying on his island. We're going for Polanski instead.'

But Polanski couldn't make it.

'What we want are people with opinions. *Bons viveurs*. Hal Ashby, Dennis Hopper, people like that.'

Hal Ashby was dead. But Todd Solondz, who was there promoting Storytelling, agreed to an interview. And Hal Hartley! Solondz had just become famous with Happiness, the sort of depressing misanthropy which people were too frightened of not to praise as *dark*. He wasn't exactly Peter Ustinov. Sally told me to wear lots of kohl to give my eyes a *noir* look.

'I want you to look junked on a metaphysical movieland. Keep it chatty and smoke.'

We set up in the garden of a smart hotel and when Solondz arrived, looking low, Sally mouthed *bon viveur* at me across the lawn. I was wearing the nautical top and a polka-dotted scarf tied coquettishly around my neck.

'Welcome, Todd,' I said. 'You know, in the 1970s, which you could describe as the great era of Cannes, you've got Altman and Scorsese and . . . Hal Ashby . . . and Coppola, and there seemed to be this great oppor*tunity* for all sorts of dialogue between film-makers, for film-makers to get together and share ideas! Has that been your experience of Cannes at all?'

'I haven't met any film-makers,' said Solondz in a clinically depressed whine. 'I've just met interviewers and publicists.'

That was the best bit.

'Oh, fuck him,' said Sally. 'Some people want to talk and others don't. Let's go for lunch and discuss . . .'

We ate langoustines and *dorade* in a restaurant up a steep street opposite a church, while Sally cajoled me to be a little more northern, a little more bolshie on camera. *Like Café Rouge*, I thought, charmed by the little ramekins of unsalted butter. 'Champagne hangover, that's the look,' said Sally. Afterwards I went into the cool of the church and lit a candle for Jonathan, and one for Wilson, and one for poor old Zelda Fitzgerald, who had grown older and unhappier and crazier not twenty miles away under this same blue sky while her husband failed to finish his book.

I'd always had a bit of a crush on Hal Hartley, who was so tall and dark and carried this sexy aura of circles of friends around with him – someone who stuck with his rep of actors, capable of inspiring loyalty, the glue that all groups of mates need.

'Welcome, Hal,' I said, in our hotel garden, while Sally mouthed *northern* at me across the lawn. I was talking to Hal Hartley. *Hal Hartley!* 'In the 1970s, which you could describe as the great era of Cannes, you've got Bogdanovich and Schrader and . . . Hal Ashby . . . and Coppola, and there seemed to be this great oppor*tunity* for film-makers to get together and share ideas! Has that been your experience of Cannes at all?'

'Listen,' Hartley said, 'I just got off a flight. I can't do this. I'm sorry.' His eyes looked like they might fall out of his head. I imagined them splatting on the grass like cowpats. 'So sorry to have wasted your time.'

Sally was rattled. She had an idea that the 'Japanese New Wave' might supply us with an angle. I didn't even know there was a Japanese New Wave, but that's what you did, you attempted to subdivide the Niagara of film into pithily captioned movements as if cinema weren't swimming in circles at the start of the new century but in schools of thought (how we crave it, the idea of progress implied in our taxonomising! How we *miss* it!). We managed to entice a Japanese director into our garden. He had a suitcase handcuffed to his wrist and talked, through his interpreter, quite wide-rangingly, about the strangeness of French cuisine. I wasn't going to ask him about Hal Ashby.

'What's in the suitcase?'

'No suitcase questions, please.'

'What's your favourite film?'

He mulled this over for a minute or so.

'Smokey and the Bandit.'

'It's OK,' Sally said. 'In fact it's a good thing, because the panel discussion is going to be shot like a feature *in itself*, really off-the-cuff, like the end of a very in*tense* dinner party, lots of empty *gla*sses on the table, *very* Dogme.'

I went for a long walk around Cannes and ended up blowing my entire presenter's fee on an old poster of Buster Keaton in a shop behind the train station. I wandered for miles out to the rocks past the Hôtel du Cap and poked around with a shrimping net for tiny crabs in the tidal pools, trying to contemplate the future of art. The anemones retracted when I touched them. Because we hadn't managed to snare anybody famous for the discussion, Nick James, the editor of Sight and Sound, and Dudi had agreed to fill the breach. That night, as Sally's Dogme camera craned its neck and randomly zoomed in and out, Dudi suggested that it was possibly an insane idea of mine that people in the 1970s were all sitting around sharing ideas and lending each other scripts. Sally signalled him to keep smoking with the same gesture my old headmistress had used at the convent to exhort us to say the Hail Mary louder in assembly. There were so many empty wine glasses on the table it looked like we'd all drunk our way into a deeply unwell sobriety, an impression abetted by the sozzled refocusings of the camera.

'They were much more generous, much more! They shared everything!'

'They shared their *girlfriends*,' Dudi said.

I persisted. 'They were just *much more generous*! They just *were*!' (They were!) I waved us off in front of an open-air screening of Apocalypse Now Redux, just as the air-strike was called in.

27

Several days later, in the little town of Biot in the hills behind Juan-les-Pins, I worried to Dudi that I hadn't been *northern* enough.

'What does that *mean* anyway, northern? In TV-speak it just means kind of sarky and unimpressed. Why should I wander around being unimpressed by things?'

'It's like Jonathan, isn't it? He's northern,' said Dudi. 'It means Peace and Love or I'll knock your teeth in with a brick.'

'Jonathan is about as northern as Princess Margaret.'

Using the present tense felt dishonest. I wasn't sure whether or not I should have said 'was'. The past tense we employ for the dead and exes both. Dudi drowsed in his chair, wrecked by meetings and tough parties, coming down in the sunlight. On the cobbles of the square where we sat, swooped over by swifts, Buster Keaton lay unfolded, eight feet by twelve. If the mark of an artist is survival into posterity without dating, then you're already the greatest artist in the history of cinema, I thought. The poster, a French one for Steamboat Bill Jnr (1928), was simply your face, eyes lowered with a Madonna's modesty. I couldn't look you in the eye. Just like an angel. Your skin made me cry. It wasn't that you never smiled, it was that you were more silent than anyone else in the silent era. More silent than Arletty, or Marcel Marceau, or Garbo – infinitely more silent than Chaplin. 'The perfect organism would be silent,' as Professor Godbole says in A Passage to India, would be unmoved by the unending destruction and creation of the physical world. In Steamboat Bill Jnr there's the famous tornado sequence where a town is demolished around you, hospitals, libraries, prisons, theatres, as if all civilisation were just an illusion. Funny to think that the greatest comedy is essentially Buddhism. You don't care if it hurts. You just want to have control. You have a perfect body. You seem to have a perfect soul. 'The Little Boy Who Can't Be Damaged', you were first billed as, touring the vaudeville circuit with Houdini, an act which consisted of your alcoholic father punishing your 'misdeeds' by throwing you about the theatre as hard as he could while you ignored the pain. Everything an illusion – pain (that broken neck which you can *actually see happen* in Sherlock Junior), speech, civilisation. And why aren't you here now? How we could do with you! At the cashpoint, on the freeway, on a mobile, in our stadia and skyscrapers and air-ports, now that the cocky world thinks of itself as so much more immoveable and we need constant reminders of how ephemeral it is. Only you could remind us. Because your films have one value. Love. It's always and only all for love. And they have one message. That *you*, that is to say love, are tougher than the world, as trees topple and boats sink and trains fall off bridges and armies clash irrelevantly. You cannot be damaged. You're so amazing. You float like a feather in an unbeautiful world. What the hell are you doing here? You don't belong here. You're so fucking special.

And I was thinking that perhaps Jonathan hadn't been right when he said that it took more than one person to break your heart. You never, whatever happens, you never suffer again like the first time. It's not as if you never mend, it's just that your body remembers it for you, the unforgettable shock, and has its antibodies stationed in the right places. Even should something worse happen – your marriage shattered, your career ruined by alcohol – it's not the same. The heart has to be broken, like a horse. The unbroken heart will throw you, break your neck.

28

Who are the people on the end of the line when actors talk down the phone? Is there somebody there, reading in at the other end? Or do the actors relish the silence that they can act around, which they can spar with and interrupt? I suppose that some of the time there has to be a voice there, but mostly there must be nothing, and what you are seeing are actors talking with nobody, fighting and flirting with no-people, blown into shapes like sails by the breath of no-ones.

I didn't get in touch with Jonathan and he didn't call me back. Who are the people on the end of the line when actors talk down the phone?

29

Back from Cannes, GMTV were in a complete tizz about Charlie's Angels. Matthew Wright and I had to stand behind a screen waiting for our cue (he with a golden plastic gun, me with a golden plastic gun and a catsuit) and then prance unerotically towards the sofa while drawing a bead on the camera lens and pouting. *The cheesiness isn't real, Antonia. The films are.* It's not that I had anything against dressing up as Drew Barrymore per se, or even Anne Boleyn. In fact I approved of the GMTV look – the look of the Get To Know You Ball at the start of a singles' cruise – but you did want to go home from that sort of thing into the arms of Sam Neill. Good old Sam. Good old reliable, husbandly, decent, sane Sam. Who, unlike my EX-boyfriend, found time after fending off Billy Zane to bring Nicole Kidman the most marvellously thoughtful breakfast at the end of Dead Calm. Let's see. Coffee, freshly squeezed orange juice, wholemeal toast, I think, some fruit definitely, and I seem to remember a perfectly soft-boiled egg. A starched white linen napkin. Surely not a rose in the middle of the ocean? But it seems somehow to be there. The Tray of Life! Because Nicole is struggling with the handsome smart-alec nutcase Zane, Sam – who has deseeded her mango and pre-dipped a soldier in her yolk, like a proper husband – drops the Tray! Utterly ruined! It always upsets me enormously. I never feel like the film has a proper happy ending. I mean, they survive and everything, but I for one would be pleased if the film lasted another five minutes detailing the preparation of a second Tray of Life. The *love* that had gone into that breakfast. It made me want to go out and shoot

Jonathan through the head with a flare gun and watch him drown in the Pacific in flames. Not Jonathan, I mean Zane.

How can you not be grateful for Sam Neill and his ability to confer complexity upon stoogily steady guys? Without Sam the black-and-white schematics, the sense of agenda, in The Piano would lie exposed like a lecture. A lot of people other than Keitel could play Baines (Nolte?). But not a lot of people could have your sympathies switchbacking around for Mr Stewart like Sam Neill does. So that you feel *fear* of Holly Hunter as well as identification with her. They're not so bad, these reliable fellows like Sam, you end up thinking. Of the three of them in The Piano, isn't he the most human? (In fact, when the nuns at school showed us My Brilliant Career in which Judy Davis opts for a literary destiny over the husbandly Sam, meaning to encourage us to work harder for our upcoming GCSEs, it backfired horribly. You got the impression that the nuns had sort of misremembered the film. Confused themselves, they were unable to supply any credible rationale for what seemed to have been the inexplicable error of a madwoman. *She's just crazy, isn't she, Sister Eileen?*) Or if not Sam then Ciaran Hinds as Captain Wentworth in Persuasion (1995), the single best Jane Austen adaptation ever, by dint of its cinematography alone. Or the best actor in America, the never-to-be-famous Liev Schreiber in A Walk on the Moon (1998). Nice reliable husband types.

There is the cliché, isn't there – the actor described as a 'reassuring presence'? I have a big thing for reassuring presences. Three-quarters of the pleasure of movie-going lies in the reassurance of catching up with your big, comforting family. And Sam Neill, I always hoped, would be cast in a government-financed movie (to be released in times of crisis) called It's Alright, Calm Down, an ensemble piece co-starring

Anthony LaPaglia as the dog-loving family doctor taking care of Sam's collie while he's away in Washington, George Dzundza as the high school ice-hockey coach who accidentally runs it over, Forest Whitaker as the owner of the dog pound where LaPaglia picks up an initially unpromising replacement, Jim Carter as the exasperated parent of the teenage girl who wants the dog LaPaglia has picked back, Judd Hirsch as the girl's English teacher (and, later, as his own ghost), Don Cheadle as the blocked writer who helps Sam's (still-keen) ex, Bonnie Hunt, try to save the whale which has beached itself by Sydney Pollack's jetty during Charles Durning and Teri Garr's annual Thanksgiving cook-out/chamber music evening, Alan Arkin as that amusing psychiatrist, Brendan Gleeson as Carter's divorced alcoholic buddy whom Carter inadvertently causes to drown while bass-fishing, David Morse as the duck-whittling local cop who discovers that the bass-fishing accident wasn't Carter's fault but the result of a heart attack brought on by what Denis Lawson as Morse's ne'er-do-well investigative journalist elder brother (his best work in years) finds out was medication which Gleeson's doctor – *LaPaglia!* – had incorrectly prescribed in the period of turmoil after the collie's death, Bernard Hill as the publisher Cheadle punches in that great scene on the racket-ball court, and Mary-Louise Parker as the creatively overshadowed daughter of Durning and Garr whose troublesome junk-sculpture memorial to the dead whale Sam's new dog knocks over and accidentally perfects, with William Hurt (doing his Children of a Lesser God thing, with those intonations that suggest he is speaking in a foreign language, and that small smile of his – the world's smallest – which says *yes, well, that is pleasing, that is a small, good thing*) as the philosopher-tramp whose recipes for soup punctuate the narrative. That would be *money well spent*. That would get us through some dark days indeed. And I pledge, if elected, to make good on this promise.

30

On the bright May morning Ross set me up with an academic he described as 'ultra-sensible and super-sane', I remember Ilana was wearing her Anti-Seasonal Affective Disorder helmet. The light beaming down from its visor was trying its best to save her marriage. She had the Trout Quintet on repeat to keep her serotonin levels up, and the Schubert contending with Ross's Art Blakey records pained the back gardens. 'He's not *entirely* unlike Sam Neill, I guess,' said Ross, having fulfilled the specifications of my order.

In retrospect, I think the time I spent with my academic was an attempt to cheat at love. To stage an impersonation effective enough to fool myself, him, and God. I had an image from a film in mind, a man and a woman peaceably reading at either side of a mote-filled room, but I couldn't remember where I'd seen it or even if. Alun had a beautiful stark pallor like the photos of the Endurance flash-lit at night while the shards of ice-field crushed its ribs. He had the sort of skin that was the most beautiful white skin can be. And he was kind, and un-bemused by things. But in truth I was trying to embezzle his reliability and sanity, as one might fiddle the housekeeping money. I wanted to nick his well-lived life. After all, what was the alternative to the well-lived life? The badly-lived life, that's what, with rennet on soggy Frosties and a suspiciously fizzy yoghurt on the Tray, eh, Jonathan? Plus, whenever we went to see a film (Alexander Walker: 'After a disappointing run of Allen comedies, The Curse of the Jade Scorpion is him in prime form again') – well, when the credits come up, one is always faced with a fanned deck of choices. There's the question of when to break your silence – whether to just come straight in as soon as it says *Written and Directed by Guy Ritchie* or to leave it for a minute or two or to sit there throughout the whole Aerosmith ballad hoping to find out whether it was filmed in Nevada or Cornwall and eventually muttering, 'I just thought they were going to *say*.' And then there are the people who do their analysis publicly, in the foyer. Or the ones who remain silently tranced for so long you really have forgotten about the film by the time they own up. Or those who have a talent for dipping their toe in the waters so that a disagreement isn't going to turn into a divorce. Oh, there are a million ways to get it wrong when the credits come up. It's a very intimate moment, that reawakening. It's like sex. Too fast, too slow, too much, too little, too reverential, too brash. It's like life!

Well, whenever my academic and I finished watching a film, he would say *Oh, well, you know, I thought it was pretty good* like he was commenting on a salad dressing. Now, I think I'm fair in saying that I'm not being a Nick Hornby obsessive about this – though I am a bit, I guess – but wouldn't that drive *you* mad? Someone who comes out of Citizen Kane and Cannibal Holocaust alike saying *Mmm, not bad, I suppose*? They're nuts, people like that! Nuts! They sound like school kids coerced into a museum, asked what they make of Les Demoiselles d'Avignon (*S'alright*). And where are all these 'sane' guys anyway? While equably synopsising the flaws in Keynes's own demolition of J. B. Say's Law of Markets in the Kew Gardens tearooms, my academic was sustaining himself on an Andes of cocaine. It wasn't the drugs that I minded. It was the eerie way he just got more and more sensible on them. Like Sherlock Holmes. And Sam Neill's nuts, did you know that? He's supposed to be a right bastard. William Hurt? At least three people have told me he's the most peculiar man they'd ever met. Liev Schreiber was brought up by fruitcake acid casualties on an ashram. Alan Arkin – straightforward? You must be kidding! And actors ought to be nuts, anyway. We need *more* mad actors. The decline of cinema is in large part the history of an increase in movie-star sanity. You know the truth of this in the grief you feel at the disappearance of Daniel Day Lewis, that delirious actor. Give us more actors who cannot handle it, more James Foxes and Vivien Leighs, more Brandos and Nicol Williamsons. Viva burn-out! Our intuition tells us, does it not, that acting ought to injure your reality? And especially movie acting, which doesn't mean being somebody else for two hours a night and twice on Saturdays so much as every second of a three-month shoot. In Mexico, probably. Movies are *the* delirious form. And frankly who cares about sane and reliable anyway? Nobody comments on these virtues if they're complemented by something else. I don't believe that's a contradiction or an unreasonable statement. It's not *me* that's being unreasonable. In fact it's *you* that's being unreasonable in bringing all that stuff back up! I don't care what I said about sane guys! That was in the past, OK? Let's move on shall we? And not keeping *bringing the academic up*, like you seem, *for some reason*, to be so keen on doing! Men are nuts. We're not talking about *my* sanity. And take your hand off my arm, I'm perfectly calm. Rape! Officer! Offi . . . oh, shit it's a traffic-warden. Anyway, listen, I've got a perforated screening mechanism. It's a *condition*.

31

'It's such a comforting film, Antonia, such a heart warmer!' said Lorraine.

'Isn't it! I think the kid is brilliant. The way he dances is great!'

'And isn't Julie Walters brilliant too? But she's always brilliant. I love her.'

'So do I, Lorraine. I love the bit when she says, "I've been thinking about the Royal Ballet School," and the kid says, "Aren't you a bit too old, Miss?"'

'I laughed so much, and I *cried*. *Oh*, I cried. This film has got it all. And the dancing!'

'Well, that's what makes it so special. When he taps down that hill it's . . . it's like West Side Story meets Brigadoon!'

'I just loved it so much.'

'So did I.'

'Isn't it just the best?'

'Well, I just *adored* it.'

'Do you think it's the best British movie *ever*?'

And I thought, I'm not Pauline Kael nor ever will be, and I know I'm supposed to join in with the ***** *A Masterpiece!* but I hadn't seen a masterpiece in two years and when Patrick Malahide (Patrick Malahide!) calls back Billy's dad softly to wish him *Good luck with the strike* reminding us that posh folk are decent sorts too, you frankly want to go out and join the Young Conservatives. Not to mention that awful casual PC way in which Billy's gay mate is shown, in the last minute, to have a black boyfriend as if the last bastion of our prejudices has finally been courageously stormed, and I was anyway feeling somewhat grand, since having reviewed films for seven years now I was finally *hot* – a star of brainy digital TV shows about film festivals and people like Man Ray, and a voice on a broadsheet Sunday so controversial my editor was trying to *gag* me, and was furthermore going on the Late Review in a couple of weeks – so I just said:

'Lor*raine*. It's not exactly Kes, is it?'

They sacked me very nicely.

32

'A very warm welcome to everyone here tonight at another of our rather special Cinephiles' Evenings on board this beautiful cruise ship, and may I say how lovely it is to see that so many of you who came to our rather successful screening of The English Patient on Wednesday are back again tonight for a film which, well, I think is perhaps even more prestigious: American Beauty, directed by our very own Sam Mendes. I'm sure, like me (and the Academy Award voters!), you think that everything about the film is marvellous, a really intelligent movie with lots to chew on and no car chases! But if I may strike a personal note in my introduction tonight, for me American Beauty's magic can be summed up in two words: Kevin Spacey. I can see that that rather puts me in the majority! Well, *how does he do it*? I think a few of us here may have strutted the boards in our time (and I'm sure I speak for us all when I say we're champing at the bit for Anthony and Felicity's Speed the Plough once we're through the Corinth Canal!) and we all know how much depends on *good technique*. Isn't it breathtaking how Spacey manages to convey Lester Burnham's liberation? He just can't get that smile off his face, can he? In the first half of the film you can see how false Lester's smile is – there's a wonderful bit when he's making a business call and as soon as he puts the phone down that smile just snaps right off! I'm sure a lot of you have felt like that sometimes. I know I have! But when Lester finds himself, we can really *see* his inner life because the Master, shall I call him, has always got this rather wonderful, curious, ironic smile playing around his lips. Ooh, I can just see it, even talking about it! Spacey even keeps that smile on his lips when Lester's been shot!! That's *technique*. I suppose that's the thing about the Master, is how much *quicker* he is than everyone else. There's that bit where he's working in Mr Smiley's (a really waspish mickey-take of American burger chains!) and he catches Annette Bening cheating on him. Does he rant and rave or go to pieces like I'm pretty sure most of us here would? Not a bit of it. "You," he says to her, with those droll pauses he does so well, "don't get to tell me. What to do. Ever again," and he gives that clever little Spacey waggle of his head as if he can see right through how silly everyone is being, and you know he's really picking up on the irony of holding out a couple of bags with "Mr Smiley" written on them at such a moment. I suppose that's why he garnered the Oscar, because being so cerebral is very rare among actors. But he does *everything* so well! When he's lusting after that young cheerleader, you can really see it in the way he lets his mouth hang open and gets that tearlight twinkling in his eye! And, when he's stoned on a marijuana joint, how he keeps giggling and forgetting his lines just like you imagine potheads do! (Though I never knew they liked to smoke drugs at the same time as lifting weights! Is that normal? Fascinating!) But most of all it's that inner peace he captures.

We used to live next door to a lovely couple who were tremendously spiritual – *they'd* downsized too and were running this homeopathic therapy business right out of the farmhouse – and they had those wonderful peaceful smiles all the time too, just like Lester. I could tell they had inner peace because they always had those smiles on. And that's just the way Spacey lets you know that Lester has found inner peace. Well, he must have, because he always has that smile on, telling you exactly what he's feeling! And that's what's so good about the Master – he always lets you know *exactly what his characters are feeling.*

Anyway, enough chatter. There's oodles of ham and cheese on the waitress-trolley if anybody's feeling peckish. Oh, and I must remind you all that on Sunday we have another treat for the connoisseur in Farewell My Concubine, an intelligent, sweeping epic which won the Palme d'Or. But now, let's just sit back, if I can manage to get this thing working, and drink in that marvellously clever and subtle artist, Mr Kevin Spacey. I give you American Psycho. What? Oh, sorry.'

33

'The thing is, Antonia, what I really want is to be with someone I can feel in every part of me. Right in the roots of my back teeth,' said my academic the last time I saw him.

I knew how he felt. Wherever Jonathan was, he was with some French girlfriend or other about whose endearing Anna Karina-esque impulsiveness I kept hearing ominous hints. You don't feel it in your teeth when you're with someone, I thought. You feel it in your blood, in your eyes, in your mouth, in the patterns of your speech. It's when they're gone you feel it in your bones, neuralgically.

Yet it so happened that that very night I met a 'new genera-tion' science-fiction writer, celebrated for the serious non-Star Trek social commentary of his novels, whose modus scribendi was to dictate his work on to tapes which I pleaded with him to play for me while he undressed and, with those exquisite manners that physically very powerful men so often have, took me to bed, struck both by his courtesy and the fact that his book seemed to consist wholly of stuff like *'Reinforcements!' screamed Zartek to his co-pilot, gazing horrorstruck at the laser battle below* which thrilled rather than disappointed me so that I started the next day full of good intentions and finally took my phone into the Carphone Warehouse to be sorted out and ended up in bed that afternoon with the guy who fixed it, whose right leg, after a motorcycle accident, had been rebuilt in metal, which you could feel underneath the skin grafts as if he were an early British prototype for the Terminator (and which was just about the most exciting thing I've ever touched in my life), after which, rather feeling in need of old company, and thinking *this reminds me of being twenty-five, I've been here before*, I went for a drink among the cosy wooden casks of Gordon's sherry bar on the Embankment with a gay friend who sold gossip to the Peterborough column on the Tele-graph and who was so unstoppably charming in a louche Amontillado-swirling, smoking-jacketed way that I allowed him to seduce me entirely unhomosexually in the cab back to his house, which, funnily enough, was only a fifteen-minute walk from Ilana's place of work, thus enabling me to go and have breakfast with her during her lunch hour the next day – a breakfast whose accompanying Bloody Marys shored up my umbrage at Ross's infidelities to such an extent that I could not but insist on accompanying Ilana to a divorce-lawyer's chambers 'for support', at which chambers I was, perhaps not all that perspicaciously of me, astonished to find myself heavily attracted to a barrister who had himself been taken to the cleaners by his ex-wife whom he had walked out on three years before, leaving a note which read, simply, 'There is so much *disorder*', but who had nonetheless managed to cling on through the bitter alimony battles to his one true love, a country pub in Hertfordshire called the Bowler – as in cricket, not hats – to which he drove us that evening under the spirals of reintroduced red kites hanging on the day's last thermals and beneath whose Tudor beams I awoke the next morning feeling great love for, oh, time and life and people and what seemed to be turning out to be an uncriticisably beautiful summer, and all those sorts of feelings you have when you're younger, so much so that when I got out of the barrister's car the next afternoon, already picturing that final, crystalline, super-dry single perfect glass of gentle yet sharpening white wine which I would drink alone at an umbrella'd trestle-table while reading the Jules Verne anthology which the non-non-Star Trek science-fiction writer had lent me, I was feeling so crisp, quick-thinking, distinct and calm that I couldn't help perceiving the underlying beauty – nobility even – of the Cuban barman whose attention had been attracted by the giant squid on the cover of my paperback and who later, at the end, as they say, of a perfect day, kept grasping my jumping-jack shoulders in his bed and saying things like *hey, whoah, baby, cool it down lovely lady*, causing me to raise my hands up to his mouth to try and catch such hilariously sexy words as they left his lips, catch them so that I could turn them over at my leisure while he slept and I listened to the static of the suburb thinking: *So this is Dollis Hill. Well I never. Why don't people do this sort of thing more often?* So I started to do that sort of thing more often.

34

Arts Diary
Aug. 20. To the Athens of the North with the Festival in riotous swing to do *Late Review* for Beeb!

We had to review Fury by Salman Rushdie, a not entirely terrible film about a transsexual rock star's search for respect called Hedwig and the Angry Inch and an internationally acclaimed Merce Cunningham dance piece which I thought was at least twice as bad as the worst film I'd ever seen. I'd vaguely met Tom Paulin, poet and pundit, before, so when I arrived at the hotel and saw him sitting at the bar I went over.

'Hello, Tom. Is that Cinzano you're drinking?'

'Yes, it is. Have some?'

'Oooh yes, please. This is so exciting! I've never been to Edinburgh. It really does feel very high up, don't you think?'

I thought he might be able to give me some pointers on the Rushdie novel, which seemed either beyond me or beneath me, I couldn't tell. I wasn't going to be able to get away with saying *Philip Seymour Hoffman's cameo is the best thing in it* and I needed help.

'The Rushdie? It's written in a kind of *menu* speak. It's Lego prose. *Uniquely* terrible. Everyone has "radiant smiles". Buildings have "majestic panelling". Cliché after cliché . . .'

'I didn't like it much either.'

'It's *so* bad. It's *so* awful, you cannot *describe* it.'

Tom had a way of speaking, hard to render, which meant that every single word he said was italicised.

'He's been *murdering* the English *language* all his writing *life*. He's *destroying* it! It's a kind of metafictional post-magical realism which the English voice is almost *comically* inept in its handling of. Of American syntactical energy.'

'Yeah, I know. Can I have some more of your drink?'

'Oh, of course, let's have some more. What would you like? Champagne, vodka, one of those *nov*elty drinks?'

Tom Paulin's voice reminded me of a teacher's or a barrister's. While speaking, he rocked back and forth rhythmically, hypnotically, with a great reserve of patience. Actors never seem to capture lawyers or teachers very well, possibly because they think they would make great lawyers or great teachers. Great orators. But they're too musical, too fearful of monotony. That's why they can never read poetry. None of them. Why your toes are always curling throughout Radio 4's Poetry Week. No, there is one: the magnificent Stephen Dillane, whom I once saw play Hamlet as if he were a guy disappearing into the words, delivering the lines like he was reading a railway timetable, as Eliot recommends a poet should read poetry. The artlessness of Dillane's voice! You listen to Eliot or Auden or Larkin doing so little with their own stuff – or Bob Dylan singing, or even Tennyson captured on a wax cylinder in 1890 chanting The Charge of the Light Brigade – and you realise how the purpose of the reciting voice is to make the reciter disappear, to abolish everything but *ear*. Actors are never quite happy being all words.

'*. . . and only God could love you for yourself alone and not your yellow hair,*' said Tom, settling into a Yeatsathon five hours later in a bar by the cinema where we'd watched Hedwig. The producer had gone home to prepare for the broadcast the next day and we were drinking Kir Royale. Also lager – like going downhill on a bike slowly, not at all the fizzy chore I'd remembered it as being. It's a declining art, the technique of the reciter-deliverers (Cagney, Mitchum, Cary Grant, Steve McQueen even, and all their fast-talking dames) – the great flat art of just saying the lines and not bumping into the intonational furniture. In fact, the dominant voice in contemporary acting is its antithesis, the miked whisper, which overfreights everything. Ah, lager – the colour of a nice dog. 'But did he love you as much as his work, this Jonathan?' Tom said. *'All things can tempt me from this craft of verse / One time it was a woman's face . . .'* And Tia Maria, which turns out to be every bit as mysterious, sophisticated and alluring as the adverts always claimed. Gérard Depardieu was a true poet, like Richard Burton had been. Because Gérard understood the endlessness of poetry he didn't overcook it, just as a great Shakespearean must be immersed in the whole ocean of Shakespeare in order not to be fazed by the smaller-scale brilliancies. You have to understand that poetry is being constantly transmitted in a casual voice to us by the universe 24/7, 24/7, in order to speak it properly. You *have* to understand this. You have to! Gérard does. The taxi-driver didn't. (Who else but Gérard could play Shakespeare – the fanciable, ear-ringed, foaming tankard-swilling Shakespeare of the Chandos portrait? Eh? Who else? Nobody could give me a satisfactory reply.) I switched to mojitos in tribute to my beautiful Cuban from Dollis Hill. And Guinness, naturally, since we were in Ireland, after all. 'I thought that fillum tonight was *unique*. A very very serious fillum. *Huge* historical and political themes. What it's doing with trash *culture*. The cloacal nature of *all* culture – see

Swift – aggravated by a disposable aesthetic. I mean that whole *Portaloo* theme . . .' Dentine too, hot on your teeth, and Pastis, so refreshing after a period of blackout. Such friendly people, the Irish! On these very streets were Ulysses and Trainspotting set. And perhaps this surprising ineptitude at reciting poetry was telling you, once again, that actors were more dancers than singers. They owned their bodies in a way they didn't own their lines. They were freer even in their bodies than dancers, who are subject to the laws of the dance. And so that's where they put their real poetry. They were the poets of walking, running, kissing, everything. Actors were everything to the cinema – because the human body was everything to the cinema. It was the ghost that animated all the machines, kept them imitating our walks, our eyes, our height, our flinches, our pulses; kept them human. 'Actors are cattle,' said Hitchcock. In which case, Hitch, you're just a fucking farmer. That was my critical epistemology in a nutshell. I was a genius. Thank you and goodnight. 'It doesn't *sound* like he hates you,' said Tom, paternally propping me up against the toilet bowl, ever the gentleman. 'He may even miss you. *But, dear, cling close to me; since you were gone / My barren thoughts have chilled me to the bone.* Reconciliation. From The Green Helmet. Yeats would have liked that dance piece tonight, I think. The almost uniquely *communitarian* aspect behind it. Elitist yet democratic – a very Yeatsian opposition, that.'

'Fabulous piano man. He's the one.'

'Who?'

'*Jeff!*'

'Geoffrey Rush?'

'Jeff *Sbridge*. He cares. Not like *some people*.'

Reader, I like my drinks like I like my men – all over the bathroom floor when I get home.

Late the next evening the BBC got a doctor round to my hotel room to inject me in the bum with some kind of – I don't know, a Bloody Mary or something, some kind of new-fangled intravenous hangover cure anyway. The producer was there with a dead look in her eyes. I was conscious of being mantled in some massive disgrace but was too shy to ask her what I really wanted to know, which was could I not just be put in an ambulance and dropped off at the Edinburgh Royal? She said nothing – we were live in ninety minutes. And I, a rough beast, my hour come round at last, slouched towards the bathroom to be sick.

(Yeats: *Stephen Dillane.*)

35

Paddy Considine. Best actor in the world right now. Born Burton-on-Trent, 1974. First movie A Room for Romeo Brass (2000, Shane Meadows) and five minutes in – *tok*. The thrill was coming off him. The full De Nironic thrill. Considine plays Morell, a loveable simpleton who is in truth a viper-pit of hurts, a misfit in his mid-twenties who makes friends with a couple of twelve-year-old boys (there's nothing sexual going on here, by the way). But even this relationship he cannot control – the kids tease him as they would a mate, Morell disintegrates still further, and comes out snarling like a whipped dog. Considine basically improvised it all, in a hilariously bizarre accent nicked off a gypsy boxing champ from Uttoxeter. It's his first go. It's all his own work. It's totally *tok*.

Morell is like the old description of poetry – something the heart never knew it knew, but instantly recognises. He's the guy who you wish would stop talking to you on a National Express journey. He's the guy you were mates with for a week at college, though it turned out he had nothing to do with college. He's the guy you spent an afternoon smoking grass with at his house when you were sixteen and it all started getting toxically paranoid, heavy waters rising up in the front room, with a wicked undertow. His limbs have the gangly surprise of a school victim who has just gained six inches and become belatedly hard. Considine gives these limbs the over-eagerness that made Morell a victim in the first place: his arms blurt. He looks like a clown, with a dishonourable discharge from the Territorials. He has the face, you can't help but think, of his own grandfather, who would have died in the trenches and whom you feel sure he loves too much, having never known him. The teeth are perfect, like a survivalist's always are, but sad and equine, a glimpse of cold bone. I can't look at him without thinking of bones and dead regiments. Considine *plays* him bonily, as a white knuckle. And as a portrait of the effects of abuse Morell is a bullseye among a million rim-shots. How many, many times we get shown how the damaged come to be, so many undershirted, sofa-bound fathers and stinging slaps in the TV glimmer, so many mums with suitcases giving a final guilty roadside kiss, so many blank-faced looming uncles! How many times they tell us this is why and this is how – how a terrorist is made, how Aileen Wournos, how Hitler, and when does it ever amount to anything more than a dutiful gesture towards 'motivation'? It always feels like being told. But Considine's every gesture understands how Morell has happened. How the abused-beyond-repair worship innocence, and how because they always end up hurting that innocence themselves they are compelled to seek ever weaker, ever smaller and younger things to worship and to smash. He shows you, painstakingly, how the absence of love ends with a sledge-hammer through a skull. I only know this because of Paddy Considine.

So I was down the pictures with my woolly Paddy hat and Paddy scarf, cheering him on. He was clinchingly brilliant in The Last Resort (2000), reassuring you that he wasn't just some nutter Meadows had found on a tip somewhere. He was hysterically funny in 24 Hour Party People (2002), and heartbreaking in In America (2003). Go Paddy! Your Oscar-winning paraplegic is just around the corner! *6-7-8-9! Give it up for Considine! Oh m'darlin', oh m'darlin', oh m'daaaarlin' Considine! / He's our hero / The new De Niro / Sign him up, Weinfuckinstein!* And then I thought – oh, who gives a toss? Look at yourself, Quirke, it's not *sports*. Can you not resist, for once in your life, that delusional urge to impose a hierarchy? Leave that to the suits. Let *them* think of it as a matter of ranking points. Now grow up and dump that woolly hat.

Nonetheless, right now, in my humble opinion, Paddy Considine might well be the best screen actor in the world. *6-7-8-9 . . .*

36

In loyal anticipation of my imminent celebrity, Eric had added to the little box which adorned my column in the Journal. After 'Antonia Quirke writes on film for the Independent on Sunday', it now said: 'She can also regularly be seen on tele-vision as a presenter on BBC Knowledge and a contributor to GMTV and the Late Review. Her book on Jaws will be published by the BFI next year.' Given half a chance he would have put in that I'd won Best Large Youngster at a dog show once, and was hoping to do a bit for the Samaritans if I could find the time. I dreaded having to ring him up and tell him to remove the bits about television – like ripping the medals off a disgraced old pensioner's chest. But it had to be done. To my *chagrin*, the last I ever heard about presenting arty documentaries for cineastes was a Post-it note biked over at great expense from the producers of Cannes 2001 which read: 'CUT HAIR OFF'. My career resembled one of those villages you get at the start of Conan the Barbarian – a gently smoking wreck through which I made long mournful tracking shots.

'It's good to come back to the written word,' said Eric, enfolding me in his kindness like Burt Reynolds embracing the prodigal Mark Wahlberg at the end of Boogie Nights. 'Television makes people unhappy. Television brought down the Soviet Union.'

Right on. I'd always felt a bit out of time on television, like someone from the 1950s. I never could stop *smiling*, as if I were being continually introduced at a cocktail party. (I had a second mode: serious. Isabelle Huppert carrying a kitchen knife in her handbag in The Piano Teacher.) In short, I suppose, I just wasn't very good at acting. This made my little book on Jaws ('A slackly narrated and sometimes flatly handled thriller with an over-abundance of dialogue' – Halliwell's Film Guide) all the more important.

My old Anabaptist-commune flatmate Susie had a holiday cottage on the Llyn Peninsula near Caernarvon and after finding out that the bank wouldn't give me any more money I begged some time off work and fled up there in the 2CV one day in October. The blackberries were still glossy on their bushes, scratching the sides of the car down the lane which led to the clifftop where the cottage looked out over the grey Menai Straits. I wanted to feel like Quint, Robert Shaw's sea-dog, suffused with ozone and brine. I'd write in the mornings, futilely attempting to pick one of Dreyfuss, Scheider and Shaw over the others, and then go down, lonely as a cloud, to the pub which actually sat on the beach like an award-winningly brilliant sandcastle for some crab and chips. Then I might go to the village shop to buy Orange Matchmakers. Maybe go for a walk along the golf course, or drive up the coast to Caernarvon hoping to get a little tour around a castle or at the very least pick up an interesting leaflet about fortifications. I was following the Hemingway model: work in the mornings, live life to its fullest in the afternoons. I was managing to analyse about a frame a day. Since Jaws was 125 minutes long, and therefore about 180,000 frames, it was going to take me four hundred and ninety-three years. Which was fine. I wanted to do a good job. This was going to be the definitive book, done with love. Half buried in the sand of the beach were dozens of leathery mermaid's purses, each one containing an embryonic shark waiting for the right tide. In a melancholy slate mine I bought a bushel of pencils and bookmarks and marbled notebooks – the sort of literary paraphernalia that gift shops offset your fudge-guilt with. Feeling a responsibility towards the dumb wealth of the brambles, I filled bowls with them to pick at and squashed them on to toast.

Things were going OK, and then again not OK. I was going to be thirty in three months and everything I owned was in the back of the 2CV. But that was only money, and stuff. I felt light, as if knowledge just banked up and banked up like vapour within me and never condensed and fell as wisdom. What could you say about men except that they thought of themselves as dwellers of steep-sided islands who would come running out when a ship hove to, ready to trade? Wasn't that the same as saying you knew nothing at all?

One afternoon on the golf course I saw a fast-moving disturbance on the surface of the sea a hundred yards out. It was about a dozen feet long, and flashed greyly in the unstable sunlight. There was a long thin fin at its end. It was a shark! It really was a shark. Maybe a basking shark in a hurry. Or possibly a blue shark. Or perhaps the fin was a tail, and it was a thresher. A goddam *shark*, a fearless fish, a mackerel-hunter, a slash of muscle, an Atlantic-cold shiver of life! Unless it was a basking shark, in which case it was just a big fat lump – the Garfield of the seas. And honestly, I'd just about had it with Jonathan Marr. But there was no one in the world I could call to tell about this shark other than him, who loved me for myself alone, *I knew it*, and not my yellow hair. Slim and steel-minded like a shark. Even when we were arguing we could never tear ourselves away, so we'd always end up ordering eighteen glasses of wine instead of a couple of bottles – because we really would have to be going in ten minutes. Non-Sam Neill Jonathan, with his inexcusable French girlfriend. I thought, *Christ, what if he saw me on the telly looking like Ruth Ellis about to be executed?* Sitting there laughing with Juliet Binoche. But he never would, that was the thing. He wouldn't harbour anything. He knew we were all guilty, all comic, all crap on telly. Who, not to put too fine a point on it, which I may not have mentioned before, *had a perfect arse.*

There, I've said it. Dennis Quaid, obviously. James Dean, Jim Carrey, Richard Gere in a pair of hideous tartan teddy-boy trousers in Breathless. (He's not walking in that cruelly underrated film, he's *dancing* – and when it came out everyone was so *snooty* about it, all the Americanaphobic critics sneering at the Yankee Imperialists' attempt to possess the great French work À Bout de Souffle: you could almost hear them spluttering *You don't make Pierrot the Mad with Matthew McConaughey!* as though an American remaking À Bout de Souffle was such a nuts idea when it is an intensely American film that happens to be French in the first place. Besides, it's Gere's best performance outside of American Gigolo: that glassy shallowness, that brittleness as if he's about to cry or snap at you, that cock-of-the-walk gait, that *arse*.) The French, funnily enough, don't *do* arses. Too humourlessly masculine for them. Gael García Bernal. David Hemmings. Peter Cook. Brendan Fraser. Dustin Hoffman, no question. Sam Rockwell. Terence Stamp in Poor Cow. Eddie Murphy. *Yes*. Oh, yes. Clint Eastwood has a *terrible* arse. And so does Sam Shepard. I think the erotic component of arses is centred in the owner's comical unconsciousness of them. It's behind you. To remove the undignified element of the arse is to remove its sexual essence – you can't *force* a male arse into beauty. You can't make it pump iron (Sylvester Stallone in the shower in The Specialist). It's the most feminine part of a man. Between the four compass points – a Gene Kelly gluteal muscle and a Keith Richards scrawn, a slovenly acre of sexless John Wayne flesh and a priapically preening Antonio Banderas baboon backside – lies the ideal arse, lolling like a pampered Edwardian schoolgirl in a hammock: innocent, delicate, unconsciously dirty-minded. Anyway – goodness me! – Jonathan's was awfully nice.

37

By the time I get back to the cottage I've calmed down a little. I am also fearful of calling him up and finding him in the Maldives with Juliet (*ee cannot talk now becoz ee is taking ze speedboat to ze awards ceremony. À bientôt!*). And maybe it had just been a basking shark. Or a dead windsurfer. Plus he ashed in my shoes, still hadn't worked out that a two-hundred-page novella written in tetrameters was not going to be 'a doddle', and reminded me of a kid called Wormold from a Quentin Blake children's book – the Boy with the Worst Table Manners in the World (Lancastrian mothers would tell their children to *stop Wormolding*). I call his number, a number which I have always found beautiful in itself – rich in red sixes and gold eights – and am told that it is no longer available. *Typical.* I have to track his new mobile down via friends whose deadpan cadences fail to conceal a scintilla of raised eyebrow. He is in Clapton.

'I just saw a twelve-foot shark and it made me think of you.'

'Where are you – at the aquarium? You know they magnify the glass? It's probably a fucking sardine. They got their "giant squid" from Billingsgate market.'

'I'm not at the aquarium, I'm in Wales. In a house by a golf course overlooking the sea.'

'You're on a golfing break?'

'I'm rather a good golfer actually, Jonathan, I just never told you. I tour the local slate mines and watch Pobol-Y-Cwm. I'm writing a little book, you know. This is my rural retreat.'

'Christ, how accomplished. No, seriously ... that's really impressive.'

I had thought almost that Jonathan might take that as a blow – that since he'd started out, there seemed to be nobody who wasn't now writing a book, crowding his patch.

'It's just a little thing on Jaws. That's why I was thinking about sharks.'

'Nice choice. And this shark – is it in the bathroom? Do you want me to come and kill it? Can't your professor deal with it?'

I am disgracefully gratified by this. It is the first trace of jealousy Jonathan has ever shown other than at international screen icons. If the shark *had* been in the bathroom, Jonathan would have tried to get it out with a glass and an envelope, for underneath his belligerence he's the least bloodthirsty of men. He would mutter violent threats at moths and spiders, but only as he gently cupped them to the door.

'Has he been out-thought by a fish?' Jonathan is asking me.

'No. I mean, he's not here. I haven't seen him in ages.'

'Uh-huh. So, what's the matter? Who's been degrading you and posting it on the internet?'

'Oh, nobody in particular.'

'Who not in particular?'

'Bloody *dozens* not in particular, if you're asking.'

'Right. What?'

'How's this French girl of yours?'

'Er, I'm actually in bed with her at the moment. She's on the extension. Small packet of – *dozens?* – small packet of Amber Leaf, please, and this Dime Bar. Yeah, sorry, no, she's *histoire*. I couldn't afford her, to be frank. Also she dumped me. *J'ai gâché des semaines de ma vie pour une femme qui n'était pas mon genre.*'

'Ah, Proust,' I say, covering my glee with a show-stopping flourish of literary connoisseurship. By pure luck I know it from Jeremy Irons's turn as Swann in Volker Schlondorff's adaptation. (Underrated movie.)

'Fucking hell, have you been *reading*? What are you doing this weekend? No, no, forget it. Sorry . . . I didn't mean –'

'There's a pub actually *on the beach*. You could come up. Just a well-earned autumn break.'

'Two old friends enjoying an ichthyologically themed getaway sort of thing. Like people do in the Observer?' says Jonathan, cautiously. 'It doesn't necessarily mean . . .'

'Look, I've missed you. OK? If you want to come, come. And if you don't, then don't.'

I have never laid my cards on the table before quite as baldly as this. I feel quite adult. I am Meryl Streep.

38

'*Scheider's skin, like a loved and creased handbag, makes the viewer's fingertips tingle with desire to caress it smooth again,*' quotes Jonathan from my first draft. 'It never fucking stops does it?'

'Are you kidding? Have you seen his body in Marathon Man? In the white shorts doing press-ups in the hotel room? I *love* Roy Scheider, he's so *warm*. Like a ski-instructor who wouldn't let you seduce him because he's too nice.'

'Jesus.'

'And what about Dreyfuss? Wouldn't you just love to get stuck with him at a party and let him bang on at you and try to pick you up for five hours?' (This is definitely one of my top ten fantasies, knowing that it's in the bag but making Dreyfuss go on talking really well, occasionally bustling off to get more drinks or a volume of poetry which he's been quoting from.)

'No,' says Jonathan, 'he's the guy you meet at a party who's supposed to surprise you by being unexpectedly ardent in bed.'

'I think he'd be really great in bed. The best of the lot, probably.'

'What you mean is that he'd be surprisingly good in bed. But he wouldn't be. Because he's supposed to be surprisingly good in bed.'

While I mull this over Jonathan reads on, only partly visible behind a tower of tangentially Jaws-related research – a two-volume hardback edition of Moby Dick, the complete works of Ibsen, Shark! Shark!: Unpredictable Killer of the Sea and Close Encounters of the Quiz Kind: So You Think You Know Stephen Spielberg? 'You know,' he says gently, 'I think you may be a little dyslexic. Either that or I'm just a fuck of a lot drunker than I think I am. It's very good, darling. It's just . . . *unbelievably* badly spelled. Bruce Willis –' (who I'd manage to squeeze in somehow) '– it's not a *moo* like a cow that he does, it's a *moue*, m-o-u-e. It's French for *pout*.'

'Well, it could be *moo*. It looks like he's saying *moo*. Maybe that's why cows are supposed to say *moo*.'

'Look, Dreyfuss has got an *e*, Spielberg is *e-r-g*, Yeast is not an Irish poet, it's not the *Red* With *and Blue*, "et cetera" is two words and it doesn't end in an *h*.'

It occurs to me that maybe he is right – maybe I'm dyslexic and nobody has had the nous or the niceness to point it out before. In fact, this book is actually *about* my struggle against dyslexia. I can see Emma Thompson triumphing over the odds in the adaptation. Or maybe Sophie Okonedo. Writing 'Fredom' in the sand on a beach while Jeff Sbridge blinks away tears of pride. Humiliating to say, but it's always galled me the number of times I have written out the words 'Antonia Depardieu' and been unable to get even the spelling right. But Jonathan is delighted by this. 'I'm going out with a disabled person. Do you realise how cool this makes me look?' I let the *going out with* pass, and we drive down the peninsula in search of a Catholic church for me and, finding none, wash up at a bedraggled petting zoo where Jonathan gets into an argument with the owner while I surreptitiously feed his mongrel a choc-ice.

'Seven pounds fifty is just too much to look at a sheep in Wales,' Jonathan says.

Back in the car I upbraid him. 'How can you be so *rude*?'

'We're nature lovers, not nature addicts, for fuck's sake. And you shouldn't feed ice cream to a dog.'

'He wanted it! You give cigarettes to schoolchildren.'

'But that's not dangerous. It's *dangerous* to feed a dog ice cream. Their stomachs freeze, or something.'

'And it's not dangerous to encourage twelve-year-olds to smoke? I've seen you. You used to be like a *dealer*.'

'But they *want* the cigarettes, it's their *choice*. Plus it's not necessarily true that cigarettes are dangerous. Give a dog a Feast, it's like giving it its last supper.'

'If you stopped this car and asked someone what was more dangerous, a cigarette or a choc-ice, what do you think they'd say?'

'They'd say you were fucking nuts.'

Things are going better than I could possibly have hoped. I've missed him so much. I've missed the feeling Jonathan always gives me, of being in cahoots, and perhaps more than I know, the reassurance of having his brains on my side. You get superstitious about *going back* but is it really so weak, such a throwing away of good money after bad? To think so is to credit some deterministic Love Power which knows you better than yourself, which tells you that you can never change, you can never grow, you can never take control. If you're so down on going back to someone, you ought to be equally down on the possibility of ever landing somebody better. You're just down. You're cynical.

And as we drive past the scooped and carved mountainsides, through the grey glitter of the grass, the granite, the sea, I watch him at the wheel and let my taxonomising Terminator eye flip through its menus, thinking that the heart misses the wood for the trees sometimes, that it sulks long after you've stopped, longer than seems humanly possible, *that it takes things too much to heart*, and all the time my Terminator eye is scrolling up the information that Jonathan's hair has grown so that he now resembles Tom Conti in The Duellists, that he looks a little like Jean-Pierre Léaud only less earnest, more sardonic, like James Woods in a way and snippy like him too, yet at the same time as loveably ingenuous as John Savage in The Deer Hunter, a face as unprotectedly open as Stan Laurel's, or as incapable of dissimulation as Jack Lemmon is stuck in The Apartment with a tennis racket for a spaghetti strainer, with that same febrile clownishness running through his arms and legs that you see in footage of Bob Dylan except more sort of elegant in a Jonathan Rhys Meyers kind of fashion but not effete, just unstoppable, like Spike Lee telling his stories and amusing himself in She's Gotta Have It, internally furnaced, with a thrilling lack of consideration for himself like Klaus Kinski ranting his way to the Gulag in Dr Zhivago, a vulnerability which is by now already curdling into a faint trace of that fatalism you can read in every wrinkle of John Hurt's face, spiced with a genuine dash of latent lecher and lout as if Oliver Reed is downing doubles inside him, and still my Terminator eye is shuffling through these near-matches because with all this Jonathan is *kind* and makes me think of Rupert Graves's sensitivity as his master King George shivers on his haunches in the wet grass at dawn, or, no, Kevin Bacon in the unsettling Murder in the First (1995), stealing food for his little sister in the Depression and making a balls of it.

'What are you smiling about?' Jonathan says.

'I'm thinking you're almost as sexy as Kurt Russell in Silkwood.'

'Christ, *thanks.*'

39

I remember a conversation we had that weekend, on the Sunday, on the beach, down by the tideline, where all the wrack collects. We had our catching up to do: a number of young men had just murdered 3,000 New Yorkers and nobody could get over how much like a movie it had been. And Ilana and Ross had failed to reconcile their irreconcilable differences.

'If she'd been English she wouldn't have got married in the first place. They'd just be a pair of college sweethearts splitting up after eight years like everybody else,' I said, thinking of Highgate Cemetery. I was panicked by the word irreconcilable. Nothing in this world should be irreconcilable. We talked about whether people changed or not. I remember I mentioned The Edge – that prototypical 8 about Anthony Hopkins fighting a killer bear – to which I always referred back on this subject (Alec Baldwin says *Nobody ever changes* and Hopkins says wryly, three-quarters meaning it, *Well, I'll be the first*). It was something that Jonathan disliked, he replied, the self-congratulatory wisdom implicit in being so sure that we don't change. The showily unfoolable way in which people said it: 'Nobody changes, really.' And these same people, he pointed out, spent their entire lives terrorised by the thought that their husband or wife or lover *was* changing. 'You know, it's like, "People don't change. Oh, you've changed! You've *changed*." All they mean is they think people don't change for the better. They're perfectly happy, philosophically, with the idea that we get worse.' People change. They change like hour hands. We sneered at Moulin Rouge and raved about Ben Kingsley in Sexy Beast and wrangled about who'd dumped who. And Jonathan *had* changed a little. He was a bit humbler, I thought, a smidgen more solid. My sockless love who fell off houses and disdained toothbrushes. The Slow Artist was crawling on and he was getting commissions to write other things. He was bottoming out. I worried to him about myself – my faith in my own judgement had been a little shaken by my failure to turn Alun into Sam Neill. 'And it's completely ruined Sam Neill for me now, too. I was watching Jurassic Park and I had to switch it off. Which was kind of a mercy, anyway.'

We picked our way through the minefield of mermaid's purses, trying not to crush the tiny sharks within them; every so often a bigger wave would rush over the tideline like a young radical breaching a cordon.

'Poor old Sam,' Jonathan said. 'Another one down. You and your ideal men. *Love is not love / Which alters when it alteration finds / Oh no! It is an ever-fixed Marcus.* You build them up. Like you did with me.' He said something about worshipping and over-idealising people, something like, 'It's not that you truly love those qualities; their solvency and their handsomeness, that they're faithful, that they're good at everything. It's that you end up worshipping all this stuff because it means you're not going to have to get *involved*. In the human mire. And when they let you down, you hate them because you're suddenly faced with all this fucking *life* you thought they were going to spare you from. It stops you from living.'

'You're just saying that because you didn't finish your book and you don't have any money.'

'Well, probably. But everyone does it. You do it. Typical fucking Catholic. That's what Original Sin is. God's perfect, you're not and it's just nice and simple all round. But it still means you're supposed to think *life* is bad. You and your perfect bloody Gérards and your Jeffs and your Jim Hewsons and your ever-fixed Marcuses – we're just all so brilliant, aren't we? It's anti-life. Shit, I am only saying this because I didn't finish my book and I don't have any money.'

We'd reached that end of the beach where there was a small village of jumbled houses half constructed out of bits of old wrecks and salvage. I was dubious.

'But you're just saying "lower your expectations", really, aren't you? It gets on my nerves. I *hate* that.'

Jonathan laughed. 'Yeah, I know, I know. People talk about setting your sights too high. But it's not *you* that set them, is it? Your DNA does that. And in your case, that fat French fool. That's why we're all buggered. So listen, kid, do you want to go out with me or not?'

40

We drive back from the beach to the house on the clifftop. In the afternoon light I can make out the true dimensions of the building silhouetted against the sparkling waters of the tempestuous ocean below. The blackberry bushes are better tended than I had previously thought, bent under the weight of their luscious, burstingly ripe fruit.

'I see you are admiring the grounds of the hacienda,' the chauffeur observes. 'The master has transformed the estate ever since he got back from filming in Cuba. If you wait in the drawing room, I'm sure he will attend to you presently,' he adds as we sweep across the expanse of gravel that gives on to the hacienda's elegant façade.

'I . . . I didn't know that he was expecting me,' I stammer, flusteredly, hoping that the chauffeur will not notice the tremor in my voice.

'On the contrary,' the chauffeur rejoins, 'the master has been eagerly anticipating your arrival.'

What can he mean? I had assumed that whatever there had been between us had been over since that quarrel on the casino terrace. As I step into the drawing room, bedecked with Old Masters and the most sumptuous of objets d'art, my pulse is racing.

'I sometimes think,' declares a low, husky voice from behind me, 'that the back of a woman's neck is the most sensual part of her.'

Javier. *Him.* I spin round, my cheeks colouring with anger . . . and something else, something I dare not admit that I am feeling contending with that anger within me. He is wearing hand-stitched Italian loafers, attractive designer trousers, an expensive sports shirt embossed with his initials 'JB', and a navy jumper casually draped over his shoulders. My heart gives a fevered lurch. That divine rugby player's face, bronzed from film shoots in exotic locations, a face which seems to contain ghosts of both George Clooney's and Robert Downey Jnr's! Javier's face has all that mischief and dimples in it but also more profound sensibilities – it had never been easy to buy him as a testosterone-sullen stud in his early Bigas Luna movies. His face has so much *information* in it, so many characters, that you know Javier's dedication to the Method isn't merely an artistic choice but his fate. With an epic of a face like that he could be anyone – a middle-aged policeman (The Dancer Upstairs), an old man wanting to die (The Sea Inside), a Brando-esque peacock (Jamón, Jamón), a homosexual writer (Before Night Falls), Che Guevara. *The next Marlon Brando.*

'The back of your neck,' Javier growls softly across the evening air, 'was the last thing I saw of you.' He looks me up and down with a ravenous gaze which makes me shiver from my head to my Christian Louboutin pumps. I affect a nonchalance which I do not feel.

'How could I stay?' I riposte witheringly. 'You were gaining two stone in order to give the requisite dignity to your un-employed shipbuilder in Fernando León de Aranoa's excellent Mondays in the Sun! I'd scarcely *seen* you since you'd returned from that precociously self-effacing performance – and it showed genuine hunger for reality that you should embrace such an unshowy part at that period in your career – as the cop in Malkovich's The Dancer Upstairs, dammit! Was *that,*' I conclude acerbically, 'the behaviour of a *gentleman*?'

Javier stiffens, pale beneath his tan. 'And is *this* the behaviour of a gentleman?' he murmurs, grasping my arm. I can feel his hands through the expensive fabric of my designer suit. God, when I think about the magic those hands are capable of arousing . . . In one swift movement Javier's hand had deftly slipped itself under my lapel and begun expertly to caress my peaking breast. Before I can react, his lips come cruelly down on mine.

'Javier,' I beg weakly, forcing us apart, but I can say no more, drunk on anticipation, remembering that he is still only thirty-seven and has potentially a more golden future than any other male actor on the planet. He is hard-working and dedicated to the discovery of the characters he plays. He takes great pains in the choices he makes, zig-zagging wildly from old to young, from lithe to bulky and back again, chameleonic in a way that ought to astound anyone who thinks that De Niro getting fat for Jake LaMotta is the acme of Method transformation. He has hunger, longevity, talent to burn, and will be playing Pablo Escobar in 2007 and the lead in Love in the Time of Cholera in 2008, I think through the forest fires of pleasure which rage in my heart. I feel no disloyalty towards Gérard as Javier's other hand deftly seeks the zipper of my crimson Stella McCartney gown. I can feel the hardness of his arousal against my abdomen, can see an expression of such intensity in his dark eyes that my doubts fall away as easily as my limited edition Citizens of Humanity jeans.

'*Más que amor, frenesí! Dio mio!*' he whispers, roughly pushing me back among the cushions of the chaise longue.

'*Dio mio, Javier?*' I gasp. 'I thought, as you once said to Julian Schnabel, director of Before Night Falls, for which you were the first Spanish actor to be nominated for an Oscar, that your god was not the heavenly father but *Al Pacino*. But, for the love of whichever god is yours, ravish me now!' His finely-tapering fingers are already ripping apart the silk ties on my coral and cream Princesse Tam-Tam panties with bestial avidity.

'Actually,' I somehow manage to moan, '*do it for Pacino.*'

A wave of indescribable pleasure rips through me like a flash of hot lightning and Javier mutters something as he stares down at me, our bodies as one. If he manages to shed just a little more of the Spanish accent from his English, I think, in an ecstasy of joy and fulfilment, then he may just be the first true great of the twenty-first century. With methodical thrusts, raising my hips to his, he brings me to a place where there is no time, no fear, nothing but this unutterable completion. My body threatens to shake itself apart, racked with bliss, as Javier, chanting, 'I love you, I love you, Antonia,' masterfully rides his own desires to a climax like a galaxy exploding, showering billion-coloured fragments of stars through the universe as planets collapse and space-time folds in on itself and I swim to the far shores of eternity where nebulas glow opalescent in the wind of the solar flares and then ebb back, spent on my own wreckage, to the hacienda on the clifftop above the sea, which seems to have lost some of the scale I had attributed to it.

(I mean, Javier Bardem, for *crying out loud*. To quote Emily Lloyd in Wish You Were Here: 'Seeeeeeeeeeeeeeeexxx!')

'Are you OK?' says Jonathan. 'It's just you seemed . . . a little distant.'

'Yeah. That was *great*.'

41

'. . . that's perfectly normal. My mother used to fancy Gregory Peck –'

'God, so do I. The way that man wears slacks.'

'– just shut up for a fucking second. She used to fancy Gregory Peck and Alfred Brendel. That was it. That's like your permissible mental adultery, whereas –' (*. . . mmm, Peck: that flat wide stomach, the way his goodness has forced his left eyebrow permanently up in surprise at the world, those long-reaching cuffs resting on his hands. There are one or two more beautiful than Peck, but no man ever fitted the word* handsome *more . . .*) '– perfectly understandable in a Rothian sense, if you follow. Not this continuous two-dimensional saturnalia.'

'You must fancy *somebody*,' I say.

But Jonathan doesn't. He just doesn't lust after actresses.

'Well, I mean, I don't know, let me think. No, not really. Ornella Muti in Flash Gordon, maybe. Anna Karina, I suppose. But the only person I ever *really* fancied was Connie Booth. Who just had the most amazing tits in the history of the world. And of course, she's so slender. So they're very unusual. They're sort of *miraculous*. There's one episode when Basil thinks everyone in the hotel is having sex and she's, what is it, she's not wearing a bra, or is it that you see her *in* a bra . . . yeah. Jesus. Connie Booth. Christ, John Cleese. What a *lucky bastard*. And she's small too. So she has this *beautiful bum*. Though maybe I'm confusing it with Prunella Scales's. There's a bit when Sybil goes golfing and you think, yeah, not bad. 'Cos Polly's always in a *dress*, isn't she? She has this dress . . . oh, God, you *do* . . . Jesus. Yeah. Yeahhh . . . I mean *yours* are very nice, don't get me wrong, although, it's funny, you think they're bigger than they actually *are*, but hers are just . . . they really are just awe-inspiring. They've got these beautiful nipples. They're sort of . . . yeahhh . . . they're . . . *knockers*, that's what they are, a real pair of –'

'So: Connie Booth. Super. Anybody else?'

'Not really. Er . . . there's the girl from S Club 7. Frances de la Tour, I really fancy her. Franka Potente from Run Lola Run, she's OK. Joanne Whalley. Kate Winslet in Heavenly Creatures in her old-fashioned underwear. *Christ.* Claudia Cardinale in The Leopard, she's *unbelievably* fit. Oh, Rosanna Ar*quette*! Rosanna Arquette in After Hours. *God*, she's so, she's so . . . so *rude*. She's *vulpine*. There's this bit where – *will you for Christ's sake stop changing CDs?*'

This is fair enough. It's a rather incensing habit of mine, but I am becoming a little miffed.

'You say one thing and then it turns out it's completely untrue,' I say. 'You're always doing it.'

'When do I do that?'

'You always used to bang on about how much you hated The Deer Hunter, you kept calling it "average", and then you actually saw it.'

'That's just a venial sin, it's not a big deal. It's a virtue to allow the possibility that you're wrong. At least I've got an attention span.'

'I'm not talking about changing your mind; I'm saying you say one thing and do another.'

'Yeah, but what you're *really* accusing me of is a sort of habituated latent disingenuousness, to which my response is: fuck off. *Just put one record on, and keep it on!* Christ, your attention span. That's the whole trouble. Taking these shallow sips all the time.'

'I'm just changing records, alright?'

'No, you're just making sure you don't grow out of them. By never listening to them. It's a repetition-compulsion. That's what attention deficits are all about, really.'

'Don't be so pompous, Jon. You're just defensive about being all mouth and no trousers. And now I'm getting all this waffle about dyslexia and repetition-compulsions. What the hell does that mean anyway, a latent disingenuous whatever? And *vulpine?*'

'It's not fucking waffle, it's the fucking English fucking language, you fucking idiot.'

'You're such a bloody know-it-all, aren't you?' I say. I am very hurt that Jonathan has called me an idiot. 'What's so smart about setting a book somewhere you've never even *been*? And then you spend all afternoon trying to write about some tree you've never laid *eyes* on. You genius.'

'How long did Shakespeare spend on Barbados? How long did Kafka spend – oh, what the hell do you know about it anyway? Every time we go into a secondhand bookshop, every time, you buy Lady Chatterley because you don't know whether you've got a copy or not. You've got eight copies. Does it not strike you as a sort of addictive thing to do? Something which stops you from getting deeper into things? A fucking *monkey* in a laboratory would at least once in a while buy Sons and fucking Lovers.'

Jonathan starts making gestures that I assume are meant to be an ape self-administering Lawrence by syringe and we descend into a tenth-rate row, there in the kitchen with my rubber shark mascot and my Ffestiniog Railway tea-towel hanging off a beautiful Welsh dresser which is in fact covered in a collage of Susie and her family seemingly forever on holiday in cagoules. All those things that look quadrupally tragic when you're having a bad time of it. We both know that Jonathan has to get the last train back and eventually he stomps off to pack while I sit at the kitchen table looking at my half-reflection in the window. *Lisa Simpson without the brains.*

Except I'm not. I am a doctor's wife living in the Normandy countryside in 1857, reading novels and magazines from Paris. I am deep in debt. I am a consumer of mass culture awed by the fashionable performers of the day. *Madame Bovary, c'est moi.* Emma Bovary. She was the first. The first to thrash around in the space between a packaged wonder and reality, trying to reconcile the two in her enormous, inarticulate heart. *Madame Bovary, c'est toi*, perhaps, dear reader. *Madame Bovary, c'est tout le monde.*

Jonathan breaks the silence on the drive to the station. He says: 'Hey. I'm sorry, sweetheart. I *am* a pompous smartarse.'

'I'm sorry too. Forget it. It's been lovely to see you.'

I can't think of anything more to say. And if you've got a head full of films and you're sitting on a bench in a railway station trying to formulate things to say to someone you've just had a row with, someone who also has a head full of films and is sitting on that same bench failing to come up with anything to say, and both of you are aware of how filmic that bench is, and that undelayable train, then you might just get a little strung out on the whole layering of realities of the situation. On the shadowlife of movies. I don't know. I haven't got a clue. But when the train pulls in and Jonathan gets to his feet and says, so late in the day, 'So, what ... uh ...' I do this terrible thing. And it really is the single stupidest thing in this whole book, a truly idiotic thing which I so wish I hadn't done, and to which Jonathan has no comeback, but I cannot resist it, and it's done now; I cannot resist saying, like a *real* obsessive, which I'm *not*, only somebody with a slightly more than averagely perforated screening mechanism; I cannot resist saying in a light American accent –

'A relationship is like a shark. It has to keep moving to stay alive.'

Annie Hall.

'And what we've got on our hands, Jon, is a dead shark.'

PART THREE

Kinerotiquana

1

Truthfully, on the whole, I don't really want to marry an actor. They're too proud of their cigarettes and treat their iPods like *mirrors*. Yet how is it that Gérard Depardieu manages to slip past my border guards? Every time. Lately I've even begun to suspect my guards are turning a blind eye. Or worse – I have the impression they may be encouraging him. Though I've cancelled all leave and doubled the patrols, I find things in the barracks at odd hours (flowers, empty wine-bottles) and get the sense my officers are lying to me. And every morning a fresh Polaroid insolently pinned to the flagpole.

The strangest thing about Depardieu is that he hums through his performances. He's like Keith Jarrett or Glenn Gould, singing along to an internal melody. And this isn't just Frenchness. He really does give off little bleeps and pops like an orchestra at rest, a cello string brushed here, a stray note on the chimes there. Or no, like a baby in its sleep. Or no, like the guiding key-finding sounds you make before singing. Or no, like the sketch-marks you make before you commit to ink. They increase in frequency the happier he gets as an actor, the more he can hear the story in his head. In Truffaut's rather constipated The Woman Next Door (1981) there's really only one scene where the film begins to roll, in a hotel bedroom with Fanny Ardant, and out come the bleeps and pops. *Buh. Ap. Du. Gh.* In Cyrano he does them all the time. *Hn. Oop. Wuh. Mm.* In things like Buffet Froid (1979), where nobody knows what the hell's going on (Depardieu's twenties must have been like being permanently on acid he was in so many loony Gallic experiments: he is perpetually in danger of being shot for no reason by dark-haired women), there are no bleeps and pops at all, and you know his mood is down.

Depardieu's moods . . . they're not so much bipolar as just too much, too rhapsodic, in every direction. You worry about his tendency to depression but there is nothing clinically manic about it – it's more that he is intensely susceptible to other people's moods, and in turn, intensely contagious. And when he's up, especially when he was young, I think he is – and this, of course, is the thing – the happiest man I have ever seen. When Isabelle Huppert visits him in hospital after he's been stabbed in a street-fight in Loulou (1979), you think he's going to bust his stitches laughing. In Barocco (1976) he hunts down a retreating Isabelle Adjani with the most lyrically hilarious kiss you'll ever see, burlesquing the waltz moves he feels inside. In Bye Bye Monkey (1977) a baby chimp in a cardigan elicits his all-time career-biggest grin, which goes off like burning magnesium. But it's in Loulou that I love him the most, stretching in bed and, seeing his muscles, giggling like a prat. Depardieu has *jouissance.* He has a poet's ecstasy. He has an unmatched ability to vault through the classes, he has probably the widest range of any actor in this book, his far-focused eyes are so full of time you can't help but wonder about reincarnation (he acts like he misses the sixties, and the 1860s, and the 2060s). But above all he's just . . . *daft.*

2

'Y'know, when my cousin David was a kid, he went on this summer Hebrew School outing to a Kosher abattoir where they were all forced to walk through a room of dead chickens and he developed this nervous vomiting tic. My Aunt Estelle *totally* refused to acknowledge that he had a problem. Every weekend she made us go to a restaurant together and every weekend David threw up. And before he did, he always said the same thing. *I smell a smell.* So this one time we're in Friendly's –'

Ilana started to cry, like a man, very ashamed and un-practised at it. Just then, I was about the only person she could stomach. It killed her that I didn't mind her face, her picked fingers, her slept-in shirt. Crawling by, like uncomplaining nine-to-fivers on an endless commute, were scores of slaughtered fish in bubble cars: a sushi bar – the only place in town you could get dead shark. Sushi made Ilana feel less homesick, but the place was such a sterile lab there was nothing for her to wipe her nose on. I found a napkin in my bag with the initials 'HL' stitched into it, which had once been part of the extravagant press pack for Hannibal, and offered it to her and she wiped away her snot with it – the one tiny good thing to come out of that movie. There was no point in talking about Ross and his lover, and all I could manage by way of comfort was: 'You'll find someone. Don't worry. There's always someone about to turn up. You'll find someone,' and the infinite-seeming and various procession of choices looped past us, undecided upon, unchosen.

Yeah, so the odometer of girlfriends who were happily married, which had stuck at one for a while, had clicked back to zero. As a team, so to speak, that was our score after thirty years. Zero. No buckets. But it's always darkest before the dawn. Except at the start of a thirty-month eclipse stranding you on an inhospitable planet with several billion ferocious aliens and an untrustworthy Vin Diesel (Pitch Black – *nearly an 8*).

Plus it's not all that easy sometimes, nine films a week, week in, week out. I had come back from Wales into a London November, and a London December, and a London January, and often the films would come like a succession of rainy days too: 9.30 a.m. at Fox in Soho Square, Bless the Child, two hours of horror bollocks with a little cameo from Ian Holm in a wheelchair as if he'd been just about bothered enough to turn up for his cheque but not bothered enough to get off his arse for it; 1.30 p.m. at Columbia on Wardour Street, Crime + Punishment in Suburbia, an indie kids' Dostoevsky (+ = indie!) so talentless it's going to put you in a foul mood for a *year*; 4 p.m., Mr Young's, LA Without a Map, an off-beat-by-numbers non-movie with un unfledged David Tennant and the worst one of the lot; 6.30 p.m., Mr Young's again, The Trench, an utterly average First World War picture whose general okayness you are by now seeing through a shimmer of tears of gratitude that it's not actively terrible (great ensemble cast in that movie, by the way – Daniel Craig, Julian Rhind-Tutt, Danny Dyer, Paul Nicholls). And then you're standing in the rain on Oxford Street next to the guy with the 'Golf Sale' sign, unable to think *how dare I complain?* because your head is so smeared by editing and explosions and dead language and dead gestures and a general sense of waste, which you, reader, will recognise from those rare terrible days when you accidentally end up watching twelve hours of television. And then you go home and watch Abendland on tape, a long arty German film you've been looking forward to because it sounds pretty serious, and within fifteen minutes you want to ring up the director and whisper death threats down the phone.

Oh, *boo hoo hoo hoo*. This truly is a Dickensian tale! But it was 2002 and it wouldn't be untrue to claim that there was a general anxiety in the movie air. Too many bad films, too much unfulfilled or sidetracked promise, and a nervousness about the immediate futures of all the potential Great Ones. Was Wes Andersen a genius or had he just lucked out with Rushmore? Was Paul Thomas Anderson really going to be the David Foster Wallace of cinema, or was he actually not all that deep? Was Shane Meadows going to blow it like Bogdanovich? Would you forever be standing around at parties saying, 'You've never heard of Lisa Cholodenko? She made this *brilliant* debut film'? Would Todd Haynes deliver? How good was Charlie Kauffman? No one knew. Was Festen going to be the first film of Thomas Vinterberg's brilliant career? Was Harmony Korine a genius or just a pain in the arse? Oh, please, please, please, please, please . . .

3

So it was with a great thirst for good stuff and a sense of bad stuff coming at me like the bits and pieces of instellar piping with which Darth Vader once telekinetically bombarded Luke Skywalker that I went to see The Patriot, about the American War of Independence, with Mel Gibson. I don't know if you've ever seen it, but it's so bad you want to join forces with a renegade NASA scientist and laser-project the message 'Do not, whatever you do, pay eight quid to watch The Patriot' on the moon. Truly crappo. It was also very *typical* in every way: the music, the editing, the cinematography (the American rebels are so hysterically backlit, you think their cause isn't liberty but Readybrek), the lack of interest in history, etc. And after a few hours all I had was a, frankly, depressed review ending: 'This is the popular mainstream and *it's no good.*'(This was one of the long ones I did when Gilbert Adair went off to Paris or something.) So, rather ashamed of my gloominess, I just kept in a hundred words of that, and had a nice long rave about Mel Gibson instead.

And since then, while he has faded from view and disappeared into directing and religion and the occasional turkey, my opinion of Gibson has altered. He was the finest figure of a man in his generation, or the screen thought so, anyway. How tall would you say Gibson is? 5' 10'' – surprised? I was a little. Though you can see it in the first Mad Max (what a movie! what editing!). Because he looks perfect, like a composite of every leading man that ever was, built so perfectly to scale you never notice that he's not 6' 2''. So I used straightforwardly to love Mel. But now I increasingly (and ungratefully) worry that he really might have been the best leading man there ever was and we missed him, or he missed it. He could have been Cary Grant but he wasn't that much more than Harrison Ford.

Look at his eyes. *Look* at his *eyes.* If those aren't the eyes of a born, genius *farceur*, someone around whom a brontosaurus skeleton could happily collapse, then Cary Grant didn't have grey temples. If those aren't the eyes of a force of vengeance such as Leone and Kurosawa could scarcely dream of, then Lee Marvin's voice isn't deep. But in the end he was no funnier than Bruce Willis, no more frightening than Clint Eastwood. Yet surely, taken together, that's a hell of an achievement? Why do I feel this lack? Because Mel *isn't there.* Mel is elsewhere. Mel is made of air. He is the greatest ghost there never was. Stick him on a horse for High Plains Drifter, stick him in a suit for The Sixth Sense, stick him in drag for Rashomon. Imagine him as Banquo: Macbeth wouldn't even have to act, he'd be running out of the theatre with his hair on end. Mel's not *there.* When, in The Bounty, he suddenly erupts and wails, 'I am in hell!' you have no doubt that that's where he actually is. Again, in The Year of Living Dangerously, he plays a journalist trying to live through the revolution in Indonesia unscathed. He's trying to be there and not be there at the same time – the journalism is a metaphor for his attempt to remain separated from the human convulsions around him. The whole film is about Mel's ghosthood, and Sigourney Weaver's attempts to remind him he is flesh and blood. He's perfect. And when he makes his walk across the tarmac to catch the last plane out of Jakarta, saved by the bell, he looks like a man in pain with the new life flooding back into his body, as blood hurts when it flows again down your frozen fingers. That's why he could have been a much greater comedian, because comedy is all about being brought back down to earth. And though you may imagine yourself splitting a few tinnies with rough-faced, wise-cracking Aussie-lad Mel, he wouldn't be there either. Here is the true revelation of my book: think of Meet Joe Black and how Death takes on the form of Brad Pitt (which is just typical of Death, isn't it? Death is stupid and forever doing stupid things). Well, nevertheless, it's an established fact that beings from a different order or galaxy take on the bodies of amazingly beautiful people, right? Look at Mel Gibson. Look at the consternating beauty of the young Mel Gibson. *Look at his eyes.* What would you do if you were an alien? Who would *you* pick? There is no way that Mel Gibson is not some being from another dimension.

Pure. Scientific. Fact.

Quite understandably, Alex Haslam was soon on the phone, saying, 'What's all this about Mel Gibson?' and I said, 'It's not all about Mel Gibson. I've commented on the Industry at the end.'

'Yeah, with about twenty-five words. You'll have to re-do it. And what's all this business about The Creature of Tar?'

'Yes, I haven't quite perfected that yet, Alex. Earth is really not Mel's element, is it?'

Alex sighed. 'I don't think this is going to work out, Antonia.'

4

So by now, having been sacked from the Independent on Sunday, I was in terrible trouble since my career had dwindled to my Journal column (£80) and an intermittent series of actor-profiles on the radio (49p each, or something like that).

I was hiding out from the bank, and living on a freezing wreck of a boat behind Paddington Station. And let me interrupt myself at this point to tell you a little story about Harvey Keitel. In the spring I started seeing a computer animator. He was extraordinarily dedicated to his strange little two-dimensional creatures, things neither properly drawn nor properly filmed but *rendered* somehow, mysteriously. 'Tonight I'll be rendering,' he would say, like some steelworker pulling down his faceguard in a foundry, and then work through the night and come to bed at eleven o'clock in the morning where I would occasionally kiss him hard on the mouth to try and wake him up, which he never did. He was De Niro in The Deer Hunter ('The three-hour running time is taken up with crosscutting of a wedding, a deer hunt and a game of Russian roulette. Presumably the audience has to guess the point, if any' – Halliwell's Film Guide) collapsed in the motel while I stood there forlornly in a towel.

My strongest feeling for Tom was that most mysterious one. Lust. It wasn't simply that I fancied him. Lust, to my surprise, was a wholly different emotion. Lust is given its force by insecurity. We squabbled a lot. Anyway, this is the only short-story-shaped thing that has ever happened to me in my life. In April a colleague of his invited us up to a weekend in a hunting lodge in the Western Highlands. While I desperately paced the gravel on the phone to the bank with one finger in my ear, Tom would be taking delivery of some gold-plated laurel-wreath or plexiglass blob. It was spring, season of awards, and he was being unstoppably rewarded for his work. In the context of our increasingly blatant fight, this was the equivalent of a rout. By now it was clear that what Tom couldn't stand about me was my giddiness, my lack of self-control. But I simply couldn't stop talking and talking, incensing him with my juvenile exclamation marks. 'Look at those lovely fields! Do you think I should get out of London more often? I'd really like to get out and get away more often. It's nice to listen to the local news when you're away, don't you think?' That kind of stuff. Meanwhile, the whole lodge was being summoned on what seemed like a half-hourly basis to raise a glass to Tom. *This* was what happened to someone wholly free of triviality! His films were so whimsical, so apparently uncharacteristic, full of fairy-tale images of crows distributing dandelions or inventors turning into wolves, that they were doubly powerful to all of us, sitting there next to their unsmiling, purposeful creator. I unreservedly loved those films. They were beautiful. His colleagues couldn't get over his Stakhanovite work ethic, his Thatcherite hours. His stamina.

And as Tom's girlfriend it seemed I was an object of respect. When Tom entered a room carrying with him his great freight of disapproval you could sense adjustments, certain tidyings and straightenings being made, physically and verbally. There was a great compliment implicit in being Tom's girlfriend. In having a boyfriend who could only be dealt with via trials of strength. A man who was strong enough to do without charm. Who held charm in *contempt*. It was Tom's hardness that kept me infatuated with him. The hardness which makes you desperate to leave the imprint of yourself on someone. Every woman adores a fascist, but it's never so much to do with masochism as with the urge to remake someone. And as the weekend went on, in conversation after conversation, in those somehow complicit groupings that a country house party throws up, there was always this subtext – how do you *cope* with him? It was an open secret, uneasily disguised as a running joke: we were all terrified of Tom. He was another distant idol, as worshippable as any snow-capped peak. Which I was supposed to have begun to understand something about on the beach in Wales. Slow learner.

On Monday we left for a tour of the Isle of Skye in a hired Mazda convertible, Tom paying and me driving because I couldn't pay and he couldn't drive. As you may not have gathered, because I have been concealing it from you, I am an exceptionally poor driver. You can't fault my driving for generating incident but you can occasionally fault it for driving. And that's in a 2CV with its dashboard gear-stick. I'd never driven a normal stick-shift before. So I coaxed the Mazda around a car park in three-foot spasms, like a Dostoevskyan sadist whipping a dying horse, while the car-hire rep and one of the hottest young animators on the scene today looked dubiously on. And so Tom's inexhaustible dissatisfaction with me now coalesced around the car, which was, like him, adult, non-trivial, and totally beyond my ability to manipulate.

We made our way west at fifteen miles an hour towards Skye, and the sigh accompanying each lurch and jerk restated my incompetence, my essential triviality.

'Oh, look – a bull!'

'And?'

Why didn't I just say, 'Let's go home,' and call the whole thing off? Because this was now a fight about strength and nothing else. And I was losing. You start off not wanting to lose someone and end up just not wanting to *lose*. But when strong people pick a fight with you, you'll lose. If you don't put up a fight, you'll lose. If you take the fight, you've already lost, because you didn't want to fight. All you can do is leave. And you can't do that, because that would be losing. So you stay, and you lose, because they're strong and you're not.

Across the water you could see the Cuillin mountains hunkered down under the cloud that lay over the northern coastline where the Gulf Stream makes subtropical coves blossom out of the rocks, like orchids on an alp. And in the clipped tones of the terminally aggrieved, with our metal mouths and glass eyes, we talked maps and facts and schedules. Just another couple in a ton of tin hating each other as a landscape of outstanding natural beauty scrolls by them under glass. I started to twitter on, inanely, about everything and nothing, slipping in the occasional dig. He was as silent as I had been to Dan. It was over. He just didn't love me. He didn't even like me, which, I remember realising, was why I found it so hard to hate him. It's too shaming to hate someone when, if you're honest, it might just be because they don't like you.

Tom took shelter in the radio and within the hour – something which had never happened to me before – we were listening to Antonia Quirke twittering on about Harvey Keitel. We didn't switch it off. Tom insisted on listening to me gush (I *love* Harvey Keitel) and was predictably, if justifiably, scathing. He began to babble in imitation of me, in a little Minnie Mouse voice: 'Ooh, and he's just gorgeous he's got such a sexy chest get that arse 'cos he's dead sexy he is he just is!'

Silently now, we approached a long white-washed, slate-roofed building: the Climbers' Inn.

'I'll go and check in; you park up,' said Tom, swinging the bags out of the boot. The car park was just an area of gravel to the side of the Inn and I parked up, but the car kept moving, as if it was being swallowed by the earth, as if it had fainted, falling forward like a heat-stricken guardsman. It pitched four or five feet down an overgrown bank and lay gently on its nose amid the nettles. I'd driven the car into a ditch. There was nothing to do except trudge in to face the music. Tom came out and walked around it, not looking at me, while the car gave off an aura of all the complex organisation, tedium, money and grief needed to make it right again.

'OK. You sort it out. I'm going for a walk.' And off he went, up a mountain, swearing.

Lost in a labyrinth of held and redirected calls, I despaired, and went to the bar of the Inn where, in a leopard skin tunic, leather sandals and wrist braces, a circus strongman was drinking. He was a near-ringer for Harvey Keitel. The same chest, the same low centre of gravity, super-dense, compact. He trooped out with me and several other interested drinkers into the car park and directed me into the car. The thing was, he said, referring to his outfit, that the Queen had come to the island on an official visit that morning and he was the strongest man on Skye, 'So I shook hands with Her Majesty. She was very small. About your height. Right, take the handbrake off.' He clambered down into the ditch, swearing softly about the nettles, and gestured at me to stay inside, as if I were his assistant, the lovely girl who gets sawn in half and then re-composed. He squatted to grasp under the bumper; his face bullfrogged at me through the windscreen, and then in one surprisingly fluid gesture we were delivered, like a perfect bon mot, like a baby, by a strong man.

Strength is the great virtue. And although it may be very banal to praise the proper usage of strength, it seems worthwhile to remind oneself of the distinction between strength renounced and strength mastered. Harvey Keitel is a world-consuming maniac much of the time in things like The Duellists or Bad Lieutenant. But I love the Harvey who has grappled with his mania and absorbed it and put it to use, the exhaled-belly Harvey of Smoke, so genial, so genuine. The Atlas who takes The Piano on his shoulders and then strokes it so soothingly. And even as Sport in Taxi

Driver, the child-enslaving pimp – his gentleness in dancing with Jodie Foster is the most mysterious thing, the most difficult to explain away, in the whole film. What is that gentleness doing there? You'd like to think he's ironising the villainous Sport. He's not. Keitel studied pimps for the role – and that gentleness, that strength and momentary tenderness is what he ended up bringing back. Could it be that Harvey Keitel, that most generous, hard-working of actors is – the last word you would ever think of applying to him – a gentleman?

5

Well, back on my boat behind Paddington Station with my tail between my legs, I was pouring out my creativity into elaborate plans for debt-restructuring, scrabbling for bits and pieces: doing the compressed listings for the Radio Times (The Godfather Part II: 'Crime drama with Al Pacino') and 'Forthcoming Events' for the Journal ('Bat-walk in Kensal Green Cemetery, 7 p.m.') and, once, moderating a discussion about fairy tales at the Institute of Contemporary Arts on the Mall by St James's Park. The boat, which to my irritation was called Wandering Lady, was moored on a stretch of the canal earmarked for redevelopment and there were few other stragglers left. Moorhens chided their new chicks in a continual, rather middle-class parental panic. Wharf beetles, taking five from chewing up the hull, came out to watch me with a companionable curiosity, twirling their antennae. I thought, I don't mind sharing. I don't like living on my own anyway. I bought an oil-burning radiator and looked into the possibilities of changing Wandering Lady's name. Desperate for anyone at all to fill the post after their Director of Talks had unexpectedly become pregnant, the Institute of Contemporary Arts rang up and warily offered me the job. It was time to get my shit together. It was my job to get the truth out there.

I had a programme of three talks or debates a week to organise, which meant I had to think up subjects and speakers, secure sources of funding for the department and look after its cheeseparing budget, establish relationships with relevant bodies, and compile a shortlist of credible prospects for the prestigious post of Scientist in Residence. Swivelling on my chair looking out through the plane trees at Churchill's ivy-covered old bunker, I thought: who's got a lot of time on their hands? Who has both artistic and intellectual cachet and an unstoppable desire to talk about themselves? Who could lend the ICA *glamour*? Who probably wouldn't mind doing it on the cheap? Who would I most enjoy mildly flirtatious email exchanges, intense little pre-talk discussions, and seven-hour drinking sessions with in the bar afterwards? And who got me into this mess in the first place?

Actors.

'How about a season on *spaces*?' suggested Philip Dodd, Director of the Institute, one day a week into the job.

'Yeah, space . . . Patrick Moore? Get an actor to introduce him? Alan Rickman. He's just been to space in Galaxy Quest.'

'A bit *populist*. Spaces in general, I mean – lacunae, vacua, charged absences. More that kind of area.'

Philip was a tall man who always wore a black overcoat and had an uncomfortable way of standing, as though he were crawling around the mic-stand of himself. He was an academic and presented the late night über-highbrow discussion show on Radio 3, Nightwaves, and as such was required on a daily basis to treat with equal enthusiasm the decline and fall of the Roman Empire and new developments in manga comic distribution. Or dare one say, with just a *little* more enthusiasm for the manga comics?

His worst and most frequent insult was that something might be 'a little South Bank'. Whatever the mainstream was, that's what the ICA wasn't. When I suggested that John Updike, who was coming to England in the summer, might be petitioned to talk, Philip was incandescent: 'I won't have that man in this building! Out of the question. Totally South Bank.'

I soon learned that something like **The Actor's Voice: Alan Rickman** would be considered ludicrously prosaic, whereas something like **Hollywood and the Other – European Villains in a Post-Cold War Mythology: Alan Rickman on Hans Gruber** might well stand a chance. The key was to have a *twist*. One of Philip's pet ideas was a series called **A Slight Disagreement** which would feature two or more artists coming together and disagreeing *slightly* on the work of Gerhard Richter, or somebody like that. But most of the time they didn't disagree at all – 'Philip, Catherine Yass doesn't disagree with Marc Quinn about Richter. They *both* think that sustained interrogation of a single work is valid.' 'Well, get someone else.' 'I'm trying. But they *all* think it's valid.' More often, the twist was about an improbable juxtaposition of speakers. A neuro-psychologist would be made to debate with an expert on climate change. An internationally renowned economic historian would be asked to find common ground with an architect and a tramp.

'Get Ziauddin Sardar to come,' said Philip. 'That book of his, Why Do People Hate America?, is coming out in paperback. And Phil Collins can chair it.' *Clever*, I thought. *Quelle twist.* But it turned out that Philip meant Phil Collins, head of the think tank the Social Market Foundation. I didn't have the foggiest what was going on.

'Get Incenseburger! Get Žižek! Get Irigaray!' Philip would say. It sounded like he was recommending perfumes. It all made me want to go home and curl up with The Once and Future King and Fairport Convention.

'Dear Dudi. Sorry to bother you, but I need to ask you a question. Do you know of a writer called something like Incenseburger?'

'Maybe you mean Hans Magnus Enzensberger? Saw an online trailer for Lord of the Rings. Not bad.'

Lord of the Rings. Sean Bean. **The Unbearable Lightness of Bean: Sean Bean on Kundera**. Too South Bank?

6

The only great difficulty of the job was that, being largely government-funded, we couldn't afford to *pay* anyone to come and speak. Possibly a bus fare, occasionally a train fare, certainly not a plane fare. This meant trading off the ICA's faded avant-garde glamour when inviting prospective speakers while simultaneously emphasising its reputation as a cutting-edge ideas factory. Which meant that you had to appeal not only to the speaker's goodwill (that faint guilty conscience which artists have about 'giving something back'), but also remind them of the importance of what they were being asked to contribute. Actors took fright at this second idea. They were too humble, they had nothing of interest to say, nobody would want to listen to them, they wouldn't dream of being so arrogant as to stand up in front of people and express an opinion as *themselves*. I simply could not get any actors to come. Coupled with this was the difficulty that people who come to give their time for free quite rightly expect to be treated like kings. And we didn't have the money for that either. Some brilliant guy would come down from Cambridge or wherever for no money, with nothing to flog, and be thrown in with, say, a lion-tamer who himself had come from Cornwall for free. Lots of lovely, intelligent, sincere people with no side, doing it for nothing. And the hospitality budget was £10 a night. If you had a panel discussion, that was two large glasses of white wine and four straws between them. For Gérard that's not even breakfast. I needed more drinks. I thought: *Fix the drinks and they will come.*

I showed Ilana around my desk, and took her to explore. 'MI6 used to be here. Fay Weldon was a secretary. She used to take baths among the box files.' We admired the moulding and the parquet floors together. My favourite thing was the twenties lift – it reminded me of Paris in movies. Like something in Frantic.

'When speakers ask you to let them know when their time is up, you can just tell them to look out of the window at Big Ben,' I said. 'Americans love it.'

I regretted saying that. I didn't want Ilana to feel like an alien here. Someone who had been embroiled in a foreign affair and was craving home. Meanwhile, I was learning to swim in the necessary lexicon. I had no idea what I was saying but I was staying afloat.

'A season on *Not* Being,' mused Philip. 'Not Being and Absence. We need a title.' I would email him back with things like **Whole/Hole: Who Are You, Anyway?** Or **Craving Authenticity: Selfhood in the New Voids.** Or just **Disappearances.**

I wrote to Kevin Bacon to see if he was interested in a talk I had provisionally entitled **Invisible People: Refugees and the New Underclass**. Philip was happy. It was *easy* being avant garde.

7

(1) Why does Sean Penn get on my wick?

    (a) because he's 'the best actor of his generation. Period. No contest. There is nobody as good. The range becomes frightening, actually' – producer Art Linson

    (b) because he has 'that underlying quality of "I won't live another minute unless I'm exciting myself and everybody around me"' – Cameron Thor, acting teacher

    (c) because he is 'the last outsider in his country, you know?' – Alejandro Iñárritu, director of Amores Perros

    (d) because he has a 'relentless intellectual curiosity' – Bono

    (e) because he's a 'genius' – Elizabeth McGovern

    (f) because he's 'brave' – Kevin Spacey

    (g) because he's 'brave' – Susan Sarandon

    (h) because he '*deserves* to be a legend, you know? I see Sean with the young Bob Dylan' – Anjelica Huston

    (i) because I have just finished Sean Penn: His Life and Times, a 450-page authorised biography by Richard Kelly from which the above quotes are among the more grudging assessments of Sean's wondrousness

(2) '"Courageous, courageous, courageous". That's what'll be on his gravestone. Why three times?' asks Garry Shandling in the book.

Why three times?
(a) because, obviously, that'll just look great in a cemetery
(b) because acting has been scientifically proven to be the profession requiring more courage than any other
(c) 'because he's *more* than courageous in my eyes. He's a man on fire'
(d) because eight times would probably be too much

(3) What picture is on the back cover of Sean Penn: His Life and Times?
(a) Sean and Madonna hanging out on the set of Shanghai Surprise
(b) a rather poorly executed painting by the author of Sean in a crimson surplice holding out his left hand to be kissed by a long line of celebrities, orphans and geniuses such as Shakespeare, Chomsky, Lord Byron, Jo the crossing sweeper, Chekhov, etc., while with his right hand he slays a bear on whose fur the legend 'LIES' is daubed
(c) Penn photographed from behind holding his Oscar on stage with his head bowed in deeply solemn humility while he receives a standing ovation

(4) Why am I suspicious of the reverence with which Penn's fellow actors regard him?
(a) because, although Penn has been consistently good, it strikes me as absurd, and nostalgic, to claim, as many do, that he has the same crackle coming off him as a Dean or a De Niro

(b) because actors love acting that shows acting, and Penn's characters are always contaminated by that atmosphere of hard serious work which he cannot wholly conceal. Although he's great in Carlito's Way. And Sweet and Lowdown. And when he was younger. Especially in Taps. Oh, and Fast Times. God, he's good in that

(c) because anybody consistently praised for commitment, integrity, bravery and daring is somehow doing too good a job of projecting those qualities

(d) because those qualities, admirable as they are, are not the most important things in acting

(5) What do you make of people whose inner rage and violence makes everybody in the room a little nervous?

(a) they're great – what's wrong with putting people on their mettle?

(b) they're bullies, whose supposed high standards are the expression of an abiding anger which leads inevitably to the cultivation of a Them and Us mentality which will then be described by friends as 'intense loyalty'

(c) they frighten me – I really must try my best to make them like me. Then I'll be safe

(6) Why is acting thought of as courageous?

(a) because it demands complete exposure of the self, abandonment of ego, total honesty, and can mean living inside the minds of psychotics and murderers

(b) I know, why is it? All those things could equally apply to a novelist, who gets a lot less sex and doesn't go on about it quite so much. Plus, what's more courageous, a guy who pretends to be a murderer or the psychiatric nurse who has to deal with the murderer or the policeman who arrests him? It's no more courageous than going to a therapist

(c) are you kidding? You try getting up there and showing all your tears and weaknesses. It just *is* more courageous to be Macbeth than to write him. By definition you are out of your depth

(d) because actors think it is

(7) Are they right?
   (a) yes
   (b) no

ANSWERS: (1) i (2) c (3) c (4) a, b, c and d (5) it's up to you, but you only get a mark for c (6) d (7) a and b

8

Summer came and stretched itself out like a fat man in a hammock. The great films came and went and withered on to video, moving through their spans at an unnatural pace, behemoths with butterflies' life expectancies. In Los Angeles, Dudley Moore was dying. I looked out at the Mall wondering, as I did about a dozen times a year, if I would see Wilson, who had left his passport and could have been in London all this time. I could no longer see Churchill's bunker through the planes.

'About the **Disappearances** season,' Philip said. 'Something on schizophrenia and identity, I think.'

'The whole … divided self thing, notions of gender, signifiers of race, those kind of things?'

'Excellent. Any suggestions?'

'Well, schizophrenia … we could get … we could do something called "Mirrors" or something like that – "Mirror Image". The, uh, duplicated image. Get Jeremy Irons to do it. He was in Dead Ringers.'

'Do we really want Jeremy Irons?' I could tell that Philip was trying to work out whether Irons was South Bank or not. The thing is, something could be ICA-ish to the extent that it was something that the ICA *wouldn't* do. It was doing his head in.

'What about Daniel Craig?' I said. 'He was a schizophrenic in Some Voices.'

'Oh, whoever you want, but *not* an actor. I've got to go.'

Philip was off to a screening of the new Woody Allen for Nightwaves. He had high hopes: 'Did you see Philip French? "*Woody back on form*: Woody Allen hasn't been at his best recently, but *Anything Else*, a return to familiar themes, is very funny"!'

It was clear that the key to running a successful Talks programme was sorting out the hospitality budget. I had taken to ignoring it and putting drinks for the speakers on my own tab, which I planned to take up with Philip some time in the future. I mean, when Susie Orbach, author of Fat is a Feminist Issue, cycles down from Hampstead and says, 'I'm starving!' you can hardly offer her a third of a gin and tonic. And I did believe my new approach was working. The ICA's bar is its masterpiece, with its late licence, its food, its generally febrile air. After an hour or so of free booze, historians and academics were falling over themselves to suggest topics they could come back and discuss and huge networks of colleagues and friends who would be only too delighted to talk themselves. An hour of pleasant discussion in central London followed by three hours of free drinks and convivial conversation – it was a no-brainer. I would get out of bed, pump out the bilges on Wandering Lady, cycle to the ICA, go straight to the post to see if any of my actors had responded, sneak off to the screening-rooms for a film, write up my Journal page while Philip wasn't watching, say 'digital revolution' a lot over the course of the afternoon, cycle back up to Paddington to pump out the bilges again, get back to welcome my speakers with complimentary drinks around six, introduce a debate called something like **Is Genre the New Mainstream?**, have a little sleep in the Nash room upstairs while it was going on, buy drinks all round from eight onwards and stay in the bar until half three in the morning because, like everyone else within a radius of half a mile – no, make that two hundred miles – I was keeping everything bowling along with amphetamines.

And the ICA bar really is a great place. There's a certain percentage of oblong-spectacled record-bag-sashed Hoxton types, of course, but also genuinely cool people, and the speakers and their friends, and the considerable number of borderline-mad people who attended the talks in the hope of getting picked during the Q&A session, and the crowd leaving the ICA's cinema, and the crowd who'd come to see a band in the theatre, and Nobel-winning scientists from the Royal Society across the road, and young, very clean-shaven, politicians up from Westminster, and tourists taking a break from Trafalgar Square, and pensioners, and drinkers and post-pubbers who knew about the extra hour, and basically everyone. It was like Rick's. Everybody came to it. Even Marcus.

You see a patch of shoulder or the way a waist turns into a hip or the quarter of the back of a head, and the eye remembers. Everyone says that smell has the greatest memory of the senses. But it's the eye. It's the eye. And the eye is the quickest too. Light travels faster than sound. So the shock hits you, always, too quick. Your heart has skipped a beat before you even know what you've seen. I was *eshtambaumflot.* And I thought, and this is true, for some reason I thought of Tony Roberts on his knees in front of a crisp machine shouting *Come out potatoes!* I also saw: Marcus coming back with ice creams at Bletchley Park to find his mother and mad aunts discussing my orgasms and their own and not breaking stride. He was with friends, of course, and hadn't seen me. And I decided to gather myself a little, my six years of smart lines and clinchers, before going over. And then I didn't go over. Another virtue of the ICA bar is its generous provision of hiding places, its nooks and crannies, and I was content just to watch him. His nose, which stopped him from being straightforwardly handsome – that was what everything depended on, I realised. Everything funny he had ever said and all his will were figured in his nose, the Denning nose which the Denning DNA had been faithfully turning out of its mould for sixteen generations.

I looked at him and felt very close to him. But I didn't go over. Because nothing would have been as intimate a trans-action as my looking at him, and his just receiving my gaze, unconscious of it. Like you feel intimate with Jack Nicholson during the opening credits of Five Easy Pieces, in which he is filmed chatting in silhouette by an oil derrick, laughing, gesticulating, moving lightly and happily, forty yards away and inaudible to us, but already the guy you've fallen for.

It was nice to see him again.

9

That year was a time of relationships. I was habituated rather than compelled, which is another way of saying I wasn't in love with several very nice people. 'Dating' was the word that had crept back into the English vocabulary – a self-protective and cold-eyed Americanism. Inside it was a flinch – and a sad suggestion of unwanted expertise. There was a sculptor I spent several weeks with who engendered no migraines in my mother and who was so nice, and not in a dull way either, that my eventual rejection of him, when it came, seemed bewilderingly directionless. It was the first time I had ever grasped the full ghastliness of the infinity of choice. The numberlessness of the loveable. It might seem that my hunt was getting a bit Bridget Jones, scuttling around like a mouse in the maze of the metropolis trying to find the right guy before the clock ticked down. But I felt no increase in my urgency. It had always been urgent, even at nineteen. I've never sniggered overmuch at that contemporary stock fool, the husband-desperate thirtysomething. Well, sure, there's urgency. But how blasé was your heart at twenty-three? At seventeen? At forty-two? How non-urgent is your search at sixty? At seventy-five? At ninety? Along the way there are sabbaticals and convalescences and even consummations, but it is never not urgent. One is *always* urgent. You're trying to find someone you can love.

At the ICA, I was a sort of cultural air-hostess. One of those smiling girls always ready to get you a drink but with no bloody idea why an aeroplane doesn't just fall out of the sky. It seemed that I was at the centre of an ever-shifting group of some of Europe's most radical thinkers and artists – for two reasons:

(1) I was buying all the drinks, all the time; and (2) my perceptions may have been distorted by the Dexedrine. Hans Magnus Enzensberger, for instance, turned out to be a poppet. Germany's greatest living poet was *fun*. Volker Schlöndorff was utterly charming! As a big fan of The Tin Drum and Swann in Love, which I had invited him to come and introduce so I could watch Jeremy on the big screen, I maxed out one of my more ignorable credit cards on champagne for him and pumped him for the answers to the big questions.

'What is Jeremy Irons' wife like? Are they happy? Do have some more.'

'Are they happy? I can't say. Sank you, I will. She looks . . . a leetle like you.'

It was around this time that Bianca Jagger came along to represent the Human Rights Foundation in a talk about child soldiers, a subject on which not even Philip could find anyone to disagree. And anyway, nobody would dare disagree with Bianca Jagger. You certainly don't ask her to get the drinks in. (*Your round, Bianca.* I don't think so.) Bianca's face bespeaks a barracuda-like intelligence. It *looks* as sharp as a steel trap, but in truth she may be no smarter than a fish. Hell, who am I to judge? Afterwards, in the bar, when I offered her a menu, she passed it in front of her unseeing eyes and said: 'Yes.'

'Sorry, Bianca, what will you have?'

'I'll have it.'

'What?'

'All of it.'

Two dozen plates arrived and were arrayed about her like an entourage. She ate a tomato. After that night I completely lost track of the bar bill, sticking two-thirds of it onto a couple of new credit cards and hoping that the rest would just go away. The speakers were having a great time, and couldn't wait to come back (although no actor had yet deigned to turn up), the talks were full. The only trouble was this niggle at the back of my mind that I was paying for everything. I was too frightened to bring it up with Philip. After some thought, I managed to devise a workable solution to the problem. I moved on to something called Desoxyn, and some pretty blue-and-white capsules which worked best if you remembered to drink a hell of a lot of wine. Also these big orange American pills which looked delicious mixed with the blue-and-white capsules and made me feel like Roberto Benigni receiving his Oscar. I was pleased to have met a dealer who sold such attractively colourful drugs. Some nights I couldn't get the front door of Wandering Lady open and would lie down in the prow of the boat, reassuring myself that beds were for pitiable dopeheads. I was so out of it I thought Vanilla Sky was good. I mean, man, *just say no.*

And all the time I was 'dating' and trying to develop, at last, some criteria to help me stop being a reed in the wind. What *did* I know? Talent, I was beginning to think, was overrated, and I would be happier with a man who knew himself, with a Mitchum rather than a Brando. On a merely physical level, I still liked men who would get fatter as they aged rather than thinner. Time is bulk, not evidence to be destroyed. I wanted someone with a torso like Alan Bates's, that great beautiful thoracic cavity, and his width of shoulder too. Decision made. Except a little more elegant in the forearms and hands; increasingly it seemed to me that the most beautiful parts of men were their forearms. Montgomery Clift's forearms in Red River, the muscles moving under the skin like arpeggiating piano hammers – with Denzel Washington's hands. In fact, all of Clift's arms attached to Bates's torso. With Donald Sutherland's hands, sorry. Beautiful. I also liked the long slow comical retreat of hair – Jonathan Pryce's or Morgan Freeman's, less phantasmagorical than Penn's or Willem Dafoe's plumes, although Gabriel Byrne did always have lovely hair. Posture of Christopher Plummer, and *Pacino*'s hair; that simply was the perfect. as if intelligent pinch in Bettany's nose. with Paul McGann's back. Can Fonda?

Klaus Maria Brandauer. Fiennes's eyebrows/Brody's eye-lashes. Mitchum w Phoenix's head – other way round? Alain Delon w better bottom half – Eddie Murphy? + Vincent Gallo's chin

James Mason, Michael Gambon,

Donat, Kurt Jurgens?

Mouth – McQueen/DENZEL/Brando/COBURN

Pacino's is just too vain, it's like an organ

Good. My beautiful creature begins to live! You just cannot put off decisions indefinitely! In fact, this was the attitude I brought to bear on the question of my mid-four-figure bar bill: I decided to avoid Philip and found an old pink folder and put the receipts inside. On the folder it said **Blanks: Denial, Amnesia and Crime**, a talk I was supposed to be putting together. In the evenings, the tour boat Jenny Wren would always have arrived at the same point in its *shtick* about the construction of the Regent Canal as it passed Wandering Lady: 'Every day the barges would carry coal from Bow,' the guide always said. 'Day after day . . . from dawn to dusk . . . year in, year out . . . relentless . . . relentless . . .'

Some time after Churchill's bunker had become visible again, I was talking to Jonathan Miller about the upcoming season and mentioned that John McCarthy was coming in to talk about travel.

'Who?' asked Miller.

'Oooh, you know,' I said, breezily, 'the *celebrity hostage*.'

Miller turned away and shared a look with A. S. Byatt while I hastened to assure them I'd only been joking. But it was too late, and so I excused myself and went and leaned against the cool loo-wall for quite some time, trying to think things through. The worst thing that had happened was that my mother had come down from Manchester the previous week for the march against the Iraq war and had called round to take me for lunch. Clambering off Wandering Lady, I had dropped the keys in the canal. *I'll get another set cut*, I assured her. But she had rolled up her sleeves and went to borrow a sea magnet from a neighbouring boat. Well, sea magnets are just big magnets like you see in cartoons on the end of a rope, which you use for just such eventualities, and my mother fished around in the canal patiently, waiting for a bite. After a while she brought up a couple of saucepans which she had given me at Christmas and which I had, faced with a particularly uncontemplatable post-bacon clean-up, simply thrown out of the window in a despairing panic. Bits of pork rind still clung to the presents along with weed and several of the weird, toxic-looking mussels you get in the canal. Oh, *shame*. I checked myself out in the loo mirror: my hair was insane, like Robert Plant's. Dear oh dear oh dear oh dear oh dear, as Jonathan had once said at the sight of another wreck.

10

A discussion on child abuse, introduced with a reading from Lolita by an actor, specifically Alan Rickman or possibly Jeremy Irons, as there was a link after all, or maybe Alan Howard? I wrote to all three, and Howard said yes. *Got one!* I've always been a great Howard fan, although he has never been really interested in the movies. He read Humbert Humbert in his great RSC baritone, with enormous stretches of ground covered between breaths. You saw the remnants of his great technique when, after swimming a mile on a single breath, he would, so to speak, switch on his five-minute reserve, and with nothing left for the vowels but a whisper, make the far shore on consonants alone. 'Never grow up' was 'Nev— Gr— p', that final *p* as plosive as a gunshot. There were intonations in his voice which made me think: they're going, all those notes, little passages of cadence that belong to a previous generation, dying out of our voices forever. Afterwards he hunted for 'ciggies' in the bar.

Rickman didn't even reply, though I'd pointed out that we'd spent ten seconds in the same room after a radio broadcast several years before. 'You won't remember me . . .' my letter had begun. You won't remember me. He could have written back 'You won't *forget* me . . .' You won't forget him. When you're eighty, you'll remember Alan Rickman. Rickman is a control freak. He is Pacino-esque in repose, an absolute master of verbal control, sucking everything towards him with his tractor beam. That he dedicated years of his life to a project about Franz Mesmer, the hypnotist whose name gives us the word *mesmerise*, strikes you as an interesting description of how well Rickman must know himself. He was an RSC boy and took his time to relax into the possession of the space he seems to need, where he does his best work, lolling like a leopard. You can see, or am I just making this up, faint traces in his seventies BBC Shakespeare stuff of someone who might have been a little gauche, a little physically clumsy and set apart as a sixth-former, and it helps you understand the melancholy touch in his dryness, as if dryness had never been his first option. And then later, with a little more space, he came into his own, blowing the top off London's head with his stage Valmont in Dangerous Liaisons. How can we sleep for grief that Rickman never got the part in the movie? Malkovich was brilliant, and let's not get into that now. Rickman would have been better. Would have become a megastar. You hear the classical training in his respect for the integrity of sentences. The pause he gives a full stop in a script would have any writer punching the air with gratitude. Rickman loves sentences. Rickman loves vowels – whenever he says a word beginning with a vowel, such as 'I' or 'ever', I get a little shiver at the almost consonantal edge he gives them. Because of course, as you already know, Rickman has the most beautiful voice in the world. Mesmeric.

The late music writer Ian MacDonald once drew a distinction between McCartney's 'vertical' melodies and Lennon's 'horizontal' tunes: 'Penny Lane' v 'I am the Walrus'. Rickman's melody is horizontal, unscrolling over long passages of sheer beauty, often resolving on a tonic note which can sound awful close to a weariness with his own power. And so everyone casts him a cobra, when his heavy-lidded drawl in fact contains all the colours of the rainbow. His best movie? Sense and Sensibility, playing the *romantic* lead. He's sixty now and you worry that the movies looked this gift horse in the mouth somewhat. But I love him. You love him. We all love Alan Rickman – the Mongolian eyes, the literate face, the gun-dog smile which he peels back to reveal teeth which actually glint. I have never seen anyone *actually glint*. And quite honestly, I am so faint with desire picturing him now that I can hardly type this.

So imagine my reaction when, a couple of days after the talk, I received an apologetic message on my answering machine (he was filming Harry Potter and couldn't get away) from the cobra leopard gun-dog himself which began, 'Of course I remember you, *silly* . . .'

I slept with the tape.

11

It wasn't specifically The Royal Tenenbaums that did it for me, nor was it The Fellowship of the Ring, just as it's impossible ever to find the moment of irretrievability in a failed love affair, but they will do as emblems.

I hate Lord of the Rings. And I'm a big fan of the book. But not so big a fan that I hate the film because it let down Professor Tolkien. And already I feel the need to tread delicately because of the touchy quality of its fans' admiration. Dare one suggest that it's merely the biggest of that contemporary type, the under-loved mega-hit? In the hellholes of the true movie-maniacs, on places like the ain't it cool news.com message boards, ferocious battles are waged with frightening acronyms: 'To say SW:ROTS is better than LOTR:FOTR is like saying LOTR:ROTK is better than SWOT:ANH. You f***ing asswipe!' (SWOT:ANH means 'Star Wars Original Trilogy: A New Hope' – in other words, Star Wars.) Even the LOTR True Believers sound shrill. I suspect that the rest of the people who liked it would never claim to have enjoyed themselves as much as they had during, say, Raiders of the Lost Ark, or even Butch Cassidy and the Sundance Kid. I think there is Denial going on here. I think there is a settling for less. I think that Lord of the Rings is one of those films which slightly uses up love for the cinema rather than augments it. I think that when I hear the statements 'But he also manages to make you *care* about the characters' or 'There are real emotions here', uttered in tones of grateful surprise, then something has gone not just wrong but insane.

My ideal Lord of the Rings movie, scene 1: Two hobbits are walking across a field in the Shire discussing Bilbo's forthcoming party. It's a real field. It's a real evening. Natural light. There is no music. You can see, well, whatever Tarkovsky saw in grass in Mirror, or Kurosawa in Ran, or Terrence Malick in Days of Heaven – whatever is there in that field. You can hear, well, whatever Antonioni heard in the thresh of the trees in Blow-Up – whatever some assistant director noticed when he was scouting about in that field. You can hear a blackbird, if it's there. There are blackbirds in the Shire. If it's not there, not. You can hear the hobbits pant as they talk – the field inclines slightly uphill. You can hear and see things rather than what someone remembers things are supposed to sound and look like. At the party, which reminds you of the wedding in The Godfather, or the ball in The Leopard in its eavesdropping upon fragments of reality, we are engrossed in the human comedy of the hobbits. Then something unbelievable happens. Astonishing. Bilbo *disappears.* As if Schindler had suddenly stepped out of Schindler's List. And we're off, into an

Hitchcockianly sinister conspiracy thriller chase, the world revealing and remaking itself at every new corner. You'd want big stars, serious actors, as Frodo and Sam. Chaplin maybe, or the young Daniel Auteuil. You'd want Frodo and Sam to wring you out like Hoffman and Voigt do by the end of Midnight Cowboy. You'd want, at the very least, Peter Lorre or Buscemi or even Edward Norton as Gollum. You'd want Frodo and Gollum to add up to a better study of the corruption of power than Citizen Kane. You'd want it to be a better film about addiction than Requiem for a Dream. You'd want the Inn at Bree sequence to be something terrifying out of a David Lynch, to do with the far edge of innocence. Bergman for the Scouring of the Shire, which Jackson ducked. You'd want Giuseppe Rotunno behind the camera, insisting on long, long master-shots. Led Zeppelin's The Battle of Evermore should be on the soundtrack – it ought to have a slightly trippy feel. Freaky, even. You'd insist on retaining those songs of Tolkien's which have scraps of English folk songs in them, with their funny implication that Earth has evolved from Middle Earth some-how. You'd want the book's metaphors for the apocalypse in France, where virtually all of Tolkien's friends were killed, to come out and really hurt you – you'd want it to be a film about world war; about Total War. (You'd want The Two Towers to feel like All Quiet on the Western Front crossed with Saving Private Ryan.) You'd *want* it to go over-budget, so you had some of the haggard chaos of Apocalypse Now. You'd *want* it to be disorientatingly inconsistent, like the book, with con-tinuity errors and a twenty-minute section which everyone thinks is unbelievably boring, and some people think is one of the greatest sequences ever filmed. You'd want the genuine interest in evil of Murnau's Nosferatu. You'd want it, via the Shire, to be a film about the denial of evil, about appeasement.

You'd just ignore the Three Men in a Boat silliness and the pomposity of the book and go straight to the heart of Tolkien's arrested development, his suppressed grief. It would be a film for 14- to 100-year-olds, not 12- to 25-year-olds. You'd want Sean Bean as *Aragorn.*

All of these things are there in that somewhat silly and poorly written book which is the world's favourite – and therefore the greatest of all adaptable 'properties'. And I'm sure Peter Jackson is a prodigy of organisation and management, but his movie is dead. The book, for all its flaws, *lives* – it's *wildly* alive – but the film is dead. It's not even particularly terrible, it's just very unambitious and mediocre. As Marcus once told me – 'Do *try.*' It's dead and distant from you in a very contemporary way. It's like trying to reach through veils to the thing itself. The veil of the score, which just never ever ever wants to shut up. It's muzak, terrified of leaving you alone with your own thoughts. The veil of the cinematography which cannot stop moving, which *fears* the ordinariness of a tree or a rock. And the veil of the CGI. That cave-troll in the Mines of Moria: I kept thinking, *this is a joke*, this is like Plan 9 From Outer Space all over again except this time they won't admit that it's useless. No weight, no mass, *no understanding whatsoever of the tempo at which living things move*, and less soul, if you think about it, than Ed Wood's octopuses. Of course, computer imagery is a tool or a medium so overwhelmingly powerful and all-changing that its early applications are obviously going to look a bit silly and misguided. But right now it almost invariably takes from actors. (Who are they, those deposed monarchs milling around the red carpets at premieres, as ignorant as any punter of the sights they're about to see? Are they artists, or do they ... do they not begin to resemble cattle?)

I'll make one point. When an actor – let's say Peter O'Toole – stands in front of a thousand people as their hero or leader, that is something which is actually happening to that actor. Which is actually happening in the world. The action is enacted, the actor is changed. A man from Connemara has commanded a crowd of Jordanians dressed as an Arab army, he is changed and so are they, and the moment has a double significance on film. Whereas Elijah Wood being bowed to by CGI Gondorians is not altered. We have no extra respect for him, no desire to be in his shoes on that day in that crowd, as they were never there and nor was he. He has learned nothing. CGI stops actors learning about the world. They will bring you nothing back from the world. And that's what actors are supposed to do – carry you things from the world; retrieve or create reality, whatever the genre. Even if you compare it with another action-adventure blue-screen kids' movie, Star Wars, it's still saddening to see the lack of freedom the actors in Lord of the Rings enjoy. You can see Harrison Ford and Carrie Fisher making up 'business' and fancying each other inside that Great White Space Worm. *Streng verboten* in Lord of the Rings. The actors are too hemmed in and hurried. Improvisations will not be kept. The camera will not be following *them* about. Their decisions are being made within too heavily circumscribed zones of freedom. Nobody's part will be expanded because they're good. Only Andy Serkis gets to act, as Gollum, and he isn't even there. So far, so typical. Nothing exceptional. Par for the course. It would seem a waste of breath to complain. But when the rest of the world starts talking about 'the best action movie ever made. Period' and 'one of the best movies ever made', I can't help but think: how did you get so distant from the things that really make you happy? How could you forget? I don't believe you.

Meanwhile Thomas Vinterberg had disappeared. Lisa Cholodenko made a barely straight-to-video mainstream flop. Todd Haynes made 'a work of enduring genius' called Far from Heaven which you could have been forgiven for thinking was pointless, boring and even fake. The great Von Trier made that utter, utter stinker Dogville, a film whose full badness took a year completely to filter through. Shane Meadows's standards dropped with the excellent Dead Man's Shoes. Charlie Kauffman looked increasingly like a likeable kook rather than the answer to comedy. I'm still not smart enough to work out whether Harmony Korine is a pain in the arse or not. I know what I think, though. The Great Editor, Paul Thomas Anderson, seems to diminish on every rewatching. And Wes Andersen's The Royal Tenenbaums was so self-satisfied, heartless and contemptuous of reality I wouldn't have left it on the telly to keep my dog company if I were going out (if I'd had a dog instead of a bunch of wharf beetles). Was it becoming a bad patch? Or even a drought, a bad decade? I was becoming a *Hungerkünstler*, craving a masterpiece too much and coming out grumpy and bolshie, trying to count up the cast-iron classics I'd seen since The Blair Witch Project in 1998 (which I still think is perfect although its obvious flukiness has injured its reputation). Vendredi Soir by Claire Denis, which you must see if you get a chance. Mulholland Drive, A Room for Romeo Brass, Read My Lips (a French movie with Vincent Cassel and a heart-stoppingly sexy last three seconds), Talk to Her – an Almodovar masterpiece straight out of the blue – and Twilight Samurai, a Japanese film set at the end of the Meiji era. Where were my zillion-dollar laser-battles and rom-coms? Where were my multi-car pile-ups? Where my Aliens, my Fargo, my Terminator 2? My LA Confidential, my Misery, my Starmen? My popular mainstream? *My 8's?* I was turning into one of the snorers. Shall I break the *omerta* and expose the true extent of somno-filmcrit? What the hell. Listen. Sometimes, down at the screening-rooms, you can scarcely *hear* the movie for the snoring. There are naps galore. Stick it on the front of the Sunday Times. CRITGATE. I was beginning to leave as soon as the first closing credit hit the screen, I was forwarding through tapes at home, I was developing that spooky feeling of precognition which all critics end up getting whereby they can watch the first half-second of a film and say, 'Oh no, it's *shit.*' What was going wrong? 1) An absence of genius. 2) Digital editing seemed to be turning out to be an enemy of acting. Stop bloody cutting! And give us our non-crane, non-dolly shots back. Give us our static mid-shots, our leisurely-strolling master shots! *Let's see them act.* Those poets of walking, running, kissing, everything. And 3). Well, 3) is that the answer lies in the convolutions of a biblically vast entertainment industry. There's a good answer to why? on pages 470 to 476 of Peter Biskind's book about Miramax, Down and Dirty Pictures. But once you start going down that road, once you have realised that 1) and 2) don't matter, once you start contextualising the movies within their industry, once it gets through to you that it's all all *all* about money, then you had better become a business journalist. It was time to quit.

It's a hard job being a film critic. I'm not joking. It's a hard job: not to get too angry, not to get too loving, not to become indifferent, not to become sated, to remember that your first job is to save people money and your second is to make sure that you damn well *ought* to be able to get people to see something you know they'll like. To keep the expectations and standards of your audience up – never to let it slip their minds what the good times really feel like. Neither to decline into a burble of approbation at everything that comes your way, nor ever to withdraw into a sulk, not to forget that your job is to encourage artists, to help and not hinder (this should be the Vow of Office!) and not to burn out. Pauline *Kael* couldn't manage that. But Peter Bradshaw and Philip French and Alexander Walker, the lifelong numb-bum guys who have stayed good for years: here's to you.

12

It was the noise that hit me first. A wave of noise as if the tropical heat of the Saigon night had taken the form of sound. Everybody in the room was yelling, caught up in the frenzy of easy, dirty money. Every hand waved a wad of dirty dollars, dirty francs, dirty *dong*, and at the table in the centre of the room sat two Vietnamese in white shirts, scarlet bandannas tied around their heads. I knew that table. Every night I sat at it, and every night instead of a click, I woke up. The master of this obscene ceremony called for silence, and, like a conjuror, showed the revolver's empty chambers to the crowd before inserting a single bullet. It only took two shots, which I guess was some kind of a mercy, but there was no mercy here, only death and money. And then I saw him, a white shirt stretched over his paunch, a bandanna around his greying hair. *Bobby*. The man I had come twelve thousand miles to rescue.

'Bobby, it's me! It's me!'

But there was something wrong with him, I could see at once. There was the dead look in his eyes which I recognised from Meet the Parents.

'Bobby? Say something. Talk to me. You know me. It's me!'

His whole body seemed stiff and reluctant as if with physical decline his zest for life had gone. He was wearing the ridiculous painted-on clown's smile I remembered from Analyse This. And Analyse That. He looked straight through me, walked straight past me. Despairingly, I grabbed the front of his shirt and pulled him to face me.

'Bobby, it's me, it's Antonia!' I pleaded, but there was no flicker of recognition in his eyes. 'Tell me: *It's Antonia.*'

'It's Antonia, so what? Antonia who?'

He tore my hand from his shirt and walked laboriously into the light and noise of the room. I could only watch him go through my tears. He had done this so often that his soul had withered and died. It was killing him. And one day very soon it *would* kill him. I pushed the Frenchman in front of me – 'I want to play,' I said. 'Tell them I want to play the American,' and he led me to a room where half a dozen Vietnamese sat eating. In the corner of the room I noticed a grimy wall-phone. *That must be it*, I thought, *that must be where he phones in his performances.* I pulled out a fold of notes from my breast pocket.

'*Cai nay la cai gi* . . . is how much?' said one of the eaters.

'It's seventeen and a half million dollars,' I said. 'It's what he got for Showtime with Eddie Murphy.'

It was enough. I made my way back into the stink of money and death where Bobby sat wearing his indescribable smile, looking bored. I was led to the chair opposite him. There wasn't much time.

'Listen to me, Bobby. Come back. Come back home. I'm serious. Don't you know how much we love you?' His eyes were dead. Negotiations for Re-encounter the Parents were being made hysterically all around us.

'I'm talking to *you*, Bobby. Don't you know that I was just being flip before when I called Pacino the best? It's you. It's always been you. To anyone of my generation it is you. And the reason they resent your decline more than those of your peers is that you were always so ungraspable that I think we couldn't believe you didn't have some secret access to acting which no one else knew about, like a chess grand master, like Kasparov – so good, nobody else in the world can actually understand his full talent. So it hit us hard when it stopped, because you were such a magician we thought maybe what was happening to you was crucial information about what it means to be an actor. And maybe it is. The resentment is just an index of your greatness. Like Heat, Bobby. You blew Pacino off the screen, but we keep hearing about *your* decline, not his. Because people of my generation set you apart: there's De Niro, and then there's the rest. Bobby! Come *on*. You remember? You remember the fifteen different smiles of the noble Travis Bickle? You remember the way Rupert Pupkin waited in reception? Remember? You have to remember! Remember *the time you played Russian roulette and the VC captain slapped you and you made your head explode from within, and suppressed it, and turned it into a laser-gaze of pure death, and then unpeeled that smile?'*

A flicker of recognition kindled in his eyes. The master of ceremonies was holding out a pen and a contract for a five-picture deal to play a divorced cop whose partner is an animated dog which surfs and raps.

'Pupkin ...' he breathed. There was a light in his eyes. 'I remember that name ...'

'*Maow!*' screamed the master of ceremonies. '*Maow!*'

'Come back!' I begged, grasping his hand, clinging to it like it might save me from drowning. 'I know we ask too much! I know that genius often makes it hard to love your audience so that when it goes you've got nothing, not even joy. Tolstoy retired into a gloom, and Shakespeare too. Probably. They'd had enough. But we cannot bear to lose genius because *nothing else matters* apart from more of its product. And now you've none left, we just don't want to see you around any more because you remind us of what we've lost. You goddam *depress* people, Bobby. You help Meet the Parents do 200 million, and, sure, you're quite fun, but deep down you depress the hell out of everyone. You're so goddam *depressing*! You're like Paul McCartney! So come back. No matter how ungrateful we seem! Come back. Because I think continually trekking to the well of the seventies golden age is sending us a little barmy, and I'm sick of making the journey. Come back, because *I love you*. Come back so that we can all be young again together.'

He tilted his head to one side and lifted his eyebrows. And then smiled his old, slightly offended, encouraging smile. His crow's feet concertinaed up in that ecstatic, mutually incriminating way, and he shrugged.

'Kid,' he said, 'you worry too much.'

13

Because you looked at me
Because you looked
Because you looked at me and thought 'I like the look of him'

Ah, yes, it's an impersonation of the poem which Quilty reads out to Humbert in Lolita. Which is itself nicked off something, isn't it? Eliot maybe.

because of your hands
holding a lamb,

He must mean that picture of me when I was eleven in a snowy field holding a black lamb as if more for my warmth than its.

because of your feet
naked on the accelerator and the clutch,
because of your voice
rewarding the right answer with a book

Christ, I didn't even know he'd heard me doing that. Doing competitions on GLR. Why had I never really read this before? Got it one night after a bit of a row. Scribbled down. Given casually. Hiding at the bottom of my shoebox. Once gave me a lovely little sonnet about Withnail. Lot of stuff to sort through, lot of old film stuff to put into storage.

And because to steal when you're poor
and restore when you're rich
is beautiful
and ought to be a slogan on T-shirts and bumpers and iced on to
the Queen Mother's centennial birthday cake.

Was he talking about those books I'd put back? Handwriting's a bit drunk. Lots more *becauses* coming up now. Getting a bit Dylany. Nice bit about sleeping.

and because you came to me wholly, wholly out of the blue
and did this, I'm enraptured –
I am shatteringly in love with you, I'm not joking –

You love the weak and you love the strong
And I'm both.

All these words I'm saying – don't you see they've never been said before? Can't you see? I'm crazy about you. I adore you. I'm madly in love with you. I can't believe that what anyone at this moment is saying has ever happened. *Has ever happened.* Nothing has ever happened. Nothing. This is the only thing that has ever happened. *Betrayal.*

Listen: I'm astonished
finally to find myself
up here in this high hanging valley
the solitary rare birds
the friendly lizards
the incredible purity of this water

Jonathan. Feeling it in my bones, neuralgically. Losing someone and finding them again after tribulations. Like in a movie.
    Jonathan.

14

I think the most harrowing thing I ever saw in my fucking *life* was a poster for the launch issue of Glamour magazine. It featured Kate Winslet wearing something casual and it said something like, 'Kate Winslet on Having it All: *I love my life, my man, my baby.*' She had, since the magazine had gone to press, left her 'man' – her husband, Jim Threapleton. But the poster was everywhere. All the way down the Finchley Road. On the tube. On bus shelters. And it was on the cover of the magazine, of course. Now, you probably remember how immensely popular Kate Winslet was at that time, what a byword for normality among actors she was. OK! magazine just couldn't get enough of her. She was in every week being snapped strolling around north London. And part of the reason for this reverence was the fact that her husband was not a musician or another actor or a hot young English theatre director who had just made a successful leap to Hollywood but a *civilian*. Jim Threapleton was a second AD, an assistant director, which sounds much grander than it is – it means you make sure the actors get to lunch on time. Which meant that the princess had chosen one of the people. And what drove and still drives OK! magazine nuts with hatred and envy of the celebrities it spends half its time fawning on (the other half is spent candidly venting that fury *at* them) is that the evil, talented bastards won't ever go out with the likes of us. So Jim and Kate held out a faint distant glimmer of hope for even the most humble of us, in the OK! scheme of things.

How sad when a marriage breaks up. But having to see this protestation plastered around town! *Being Jim Threapleton* and having to see this protestation plastered around town! Oh, it must hurt ... A *civilian*. Jonathan had once known Emily Mortimer when she was young and used to say that in any given room Emily had the most wattage. This book is not, though it might seem so, about being starstruck (I hope). *Civilians* tend to think that on the other side of the glass are a bunch of lucky people who have been selected by lottery to fulfil the roles of stars. But of course they're not. They may be horrible worthless human beings, unexceptional in every other way, but they have wattage. They're stars because they *are* exceptional in their own peculiar ways, by and large, although our culture would desperately – despairingly – like to think otherwise. That's not being starstruck, that's being honest.

I had never met a star. I once interviewed Christopher Eccleston. I had to go and talk to Ken Russell in his house in the New Forest, which was a pleasure. I saw Terence Stamp once in a bookshop in Manchester. I saw Sharon Stone in a grocer's on Parkway, stinking the place out with her charisma. I drunkenly told Peter Mullan he was great in The Claim about a dozen times in a row, and of course I had Alan Rickman's voice on my answering machine. But I had never met a star.

Back Row was winding down its series of actor profiles. Meanwhile, inside my pink folder the bar receipts were growing so thick that I transferred them into a box file, and then piled more folders on the top. I was only saved by a stroke of fate. Alexander Walker died. And somehow a lot seemed to go with him – a sense of continuity with Ealing and Gaumont, with Lindsay Anderson and producers in offices in Frith Street, with a time of fewer releases, longer runs, and yellow cashmere scarves. So it turned out that I was offered a job on the Evening Standard and an escape route from the ICA, which I took, managing to get away by throwing my entire fee for Jaws at the bar tab, hiding the other receipts in a plant-pot on the balcony and hoping (I'm still hoping) that that would sort of do. But like I've said, my heart wasn't really in reviewing any more and I didn't last very long at the Standard. If you've quit inside, you should quit. Nonetheless, Back Row coming to an end was a pain in the neck.

The BBC always suggested the actors and I merely concurred, or spiked the obviously boring ones, like Brad. One day, I was sitting on the stern of Wandering Lady feeling a little lonely because the wharf beetles had disappeared for another year. There was a great pale carp, known as the Ghost Carp, which you occasionally saw about, greenish in the canal, and I was half hoping it would swim over for some crumbs when the producer of Back Row called.

'Antonia. Would you like to interview Jeff Bridges?'

'What, *interview* him?'

'He's in town next week. He's doing interviews at the Dorchester.'

'Uhm . . . not my kind of thing, Stephen. Thanks for thinking of me, but no.'

'What are you *talking* about? You love Jeff Bridges. You've already done him twice. I know you love him. You're always going on about him.'

'Oh, I do, I do, yes, absolutely. I know *exactly* what you're saying. I *used* to love him. But I think you should get someone else to do it.'

'What do you mean, you *used* to love him? Since when did this happen?'

'Gone off him. I don't really like him at all these days. Overrated. Plus, I've never done any interviews. So thanks, but no. To be honest, I'm surprised you're even asking me. It's so *obviously* not my kind of thing. You know. Why are you trying to involve me in all of this, anyway, Stephen? It's *your* problem. It's *your* job. I mean, *get a grip, will you*? How *dare* you?'

A little later, I called him back and agreed to do the interview. It was in five days' time. I drove round to Video City and rented a stack of favourite Bridges movies. Not John Huston's Fat City (1972), not Bad Company (also 1972) and not Cutter's Way (1981), because you can never get hold of them. If any of those three are ever on TV, record them. They're all great, and nobody ever talks about them. But I managed a pretty good stack, because Bridges has managed a pretty good stack. In the afternoons I revised him in the BFI Library. I bought his blues *record*, which isn't bad at all (John Goodman plays on it). I wandered around his charming website. I had my hair straightened. I resisted getting some Dexedrine, and then got some, and then drowned them all in the canal. I accumulated notes. I had a pedicure in a Vietnamese parlour off West End Lane, and read about long-defunct marriages in very old back editions of Hello! Old divorces whose pain had, all these years later, been completely healed. The happy had become sad; the sad had become happy, and sad again, and happy again. I watched him resurrect the deer killed by hunters in Starman (1984) over and over, wondering about how protective of the animal he must have felt at that moment, filmed from the back in long-shot, standing over it for long minutes, waiting for it to wake from its drugged stupor so they could get the take. I bought an expensive blue-and-white-striped top which I thought would make me look French. I took it back. I marvelled at what he creates from a truly recalcitrant part in The Last Picture Show. I saw how one of the marks of a great actor is how little he changes in covering a range. Bridges has range in that way. I got my bikini-line waxed. I prepared late into the final night, condensing my notes for questions into a manageable number of pages. I wore a cream Chinese jacket embroidered with scarlet flowers over a plain white T-shirt with jeans over boots. The jacket was mysterious, the jeans and boots were practical. Practical plus Mysterious equalled Romantic, I had assessed.

I drove down to Park Lane on a white, wettish day, met Stephen at reception, went up to the suite, and waited among other journalists in a side-room until a publicist put her head round the door and said, 'Antonia.'

15

Kinerotiquana. It's an anagram of Antonia Quirke. Jonathan did it for me the other day. Kinerotiquana, with a hard *qu* as in 'Mozambique': Kine. Kinerotiq. Kinerotiquana. The whirl of sex and cinema. My life is kinerotiquana. I followed the publicist through the doors of the next room. I entered the kinerotiquarium.

16

He had on a white shirt and a pair of houndstooth check trousers. He stood up as I walked in and negotiated the intro-ductions between publicist, Stephen and me, very deftly. It was just a little bit of gentle pre-publicity for Seabiscuit. Nothing too onerous, not the full, gruelling junket that would come six months later. We had ten minutes.

We sat down side by side on the sofa and I brusquely shuffled my notes, not looking at Bridges, while Stephen set up. I was able to see at the periphery of my vision that he was studying me with that very patient, reassuring, curious, unreadable smile you'll know so well. *Careful*, I thought, *this is a guy whose face had you fooled all the way through Jagged Edge*. A film *predicated* on Bridges's ambiguity. (Reader, who *could* have been better in that part? You have one minute.) When I looked up, his head seemed enormous, at least the size of the back of a chair, say, about three feet wide by four feet high and solid as a bronze of itself. Nothing about his face, apart from this scale, was a surprise. He seemed to have carried it like an egg on a spoon intact from two dimensions into three. His famous hair, like the wake of his head. Those eyelids. The set of his mouth, as if he is hiding a crabapple on his tongue. He was, without a shadow of a doubt, the most handsome man I have ever encountered. I felt extremely unwell – my throat seemed clogged with painful tears. I wanted to go home.

'Just before we start on Seabiscuit,' I said, grimly, 'did you like playing opposite an alien more than you liked playing an alien? In K-Pax. I mean, you were wonderful as Starman. The scene in the diner when you eat the apple pie, and it's the first time you've eaten food. It's astonishing how you go from wariness, to learning the technique of eating, to joy, to gratitude, to greed. I mean like the whole spectrum in about two seconds.'

'Thank you.'

'The thing about playing an alien must be that you have to re-examine so much of your own technique as you did not by using a movement coach but by observing your own baby daughters over several weeks of pre-production, but of course you know that anyway. It wasn't actually the question I wanted to ask. OK. That bit at the end of Starbiscuit when Karen Allen looks up into the spaceship and the look on her face I just wondered what she's seeing in there. Oh, forget that, because you're not on the spaceship anyway.'

'There was no spaceship.'

'No, no. Of course there wasn't, it was a studio. But the question is, when you're playing an alien discovering human-ity, you must be working from your own responses. So my question is this. What do you think of humanity?'

'Well! I think ... sometimes it's good, and sometimes it's bad.'

'Ha ha ha ha ha ha ha ha ha. Ohoho oho oho! Ohhh! Ohhh, dear! Oh, you know that bit in Thunderbolt and Lightfoot when you have a stroke and you can't talk well, I read some-where that you injected novocaine into your own jaw to get that effect, is that true? I mean, of course it's true, it's famously true, of course, of course, forget that.'

'Well, there was this dentist –'

'I remember now it's totally true. So sorry to ask.'

'That's OK.'

'Stephen, would you mind very much if I went to the loo for a second?'

In the loo I ran the taps and washed my hands thinking if this were a movie I'd splash cold water on my face now but I can't risk ruining my make-up. The cold water was com-forting. *If I were called in / to construct a religion / I should make use of water*, I thought reflexively. *The incredible purity of this water.* I walked back with a new approach. To be more casual, chatty, to relax him, draw him out.

'We thought you were running a bath in there!' said Stephen as I returned. Bridges maintained a courteous silence. He was like a lion that had allowed itself to be captured, in that room. A talking lion. In a hotel room in London, the King of the Lions takes human form in order better to observe human behaviour and compassionately guide us to a higher path. He falls in love, by accident, with a journalist whom he imbues with complete understanding of the Laws of Nature, enabling her to write astonishing articles making the case for a fun-damental change in human behaviour. Yet the journalist is corrupted by the world and her articles fail. Though he must leave her to return to the savannah, she may follow him, transformed into a lioness, despite the fact this means almost certain extinction at the hands of an unchanged humanity. Starring Jeff Bridges. Yeah – he looked like *Aslan.*

'I just wanted to say how much pleasure your *record* has given me!'

'Oh really? Well that's *great* that you've listened to the album. You wonder if people in the UK are into this sort of . . .'

'And isn't John Goodman good on it? What's he like? No, sorry, not enough time. But you know that song Get Your Whip Out? Is that a personal song at all? Obviously it's personal, but I wonder who the person is with the whip? Is it you with the whip? Why the whole idea of a whip, I suppose I'm saying. What's the idea with you and these whips?'

I said goodbye to Stephen and got very drunk on red wine on my own in a restaurant in Shepherd's Market. When I got back to my car, it wouldn't start and I was desperate for the loo, so I found another car and went behind it and the car park attendant tried to throw me out. I was crying so much he changed his mind and sat with me in my car and confiscated my keys while I cried and cried and cried.

I love Jeff Sbridge!

17

If we hadn't had a conversation in the ICA bar ten days after the Jeff Bridges debacle, Jonathan and I would be divorced by now.

'. . . think Dangerous Liaisons is clever when it's not particularly, it's just a fucking brilliant episode of Dallas. Because it's not finished with a marriage, which is the *sine qua non* of all comedy, or rather romantic comedy, you know, as understood by Shakespeare, which is a fucking educative concept, the getting of wisdom and so on, the marriage as a terminus of happiness rather than its beginning, the comedy being the education of the foolish, and if you take that away all you've got left is sex comedy which either turns into pornography, or something Stanwyckian or just lifestyle bollocks which is what we've –'

'Jon, Jon. How did we end up here?' I said. 'What has Ilana being pregnant got to do with all this?'

Jonathan ceded that. He was wormolding with his food as he spoke. 'Yeah, sorry,' he said. 'I seem to be terribly *nervous* for some reason.'

And I was nervous too. It had been a fortnight since I'd read his old poem. He was no easier to get in touch with. But there's a near-telepathic sensitivity lovers develop, and he knew, just from the tone of my voice inviting him to the ICA, why I wanted to see him.

The ICA was screening Jaws and someone had had the idea that I could give a brief introduction and sort of turn it into a launchlet for my little book. It was August and there was no one around anyway. Philip had got wind of this, however, and had decided it was an event, and demanded a *twist*. I don't think he had at this time discovered the bar bill. So a nice Jungian analyst had been assigned to ask me two or three very difficult questions before the film started. Jonathan and I had slipped away after the first girl had been munched. It was very quiet in the bar. Quiet bars, quiet cafés, quiet restaurants. Depardieu and Deneuve in A Strange Place to Meet. The restaurant in Kramer vs. Kramer. The café near the end of Serpico. Jonathan had forgotten to bring me any flowers for the launch and I think he felt a little guilty about it.

'Well, I'm nervous too,' I said.

'Well, then. We're nervous. But they're probably fucking wrecks in Jaws.'

'Yeah.' It was a pretty weak joke – a nervous joke. It didn't carry us very far. I remember it threw us into a bit of a silence. I think we hemmed and hawed for a while, not long, and then one of us said – 'So, what do you think, "darling"?'

'About us, "darling"? What do I think?' said Jonathan.

'We could call if off, or –'

'Or, we could go to bed together, get married, grow apart, get divorced, remarry, grow apart from our, uh, spouses, get in touch again as friends, have a couple of, uh, walks along the canal and have this same conversation. We could do that and put this one off until then.'

Jonathan was like me. I knew him. He had a little movie camera following him around in his head. *He* might have said 'dead shark' at the station just for the effect of it every bit as much as me. He didn't want to have to stop and explain that 'vulpine' meant fox-like because it would spoil the effect of the scene he thought he was in. He knew all about the shadowlife of movies. The ghosts they litter the world with, the templates they suggest. The delight and the resentment and the ironic resignation and the *danger* packed inside the phrase *it's just like a movie*. And I was thinking – or rather I wasn't thinking so much as just overbrimming with memories – of resolution after much difficulty, of being reconciled after being sundered, of scales, after much foolishness, finally falling from eyes, of Pretty in Pink, Jules et Jim, The Vikings, Car Wash, Solaris, The Philadelphia Story, Ugetsu Monogatari, Top Gun and just about every other film ever made including One Million Years BC in which Raquel Welch and her caveman, after travails among enormous iguanas, are heartbreakingly reunited. Oh, Kinerotiquana!

The thing was, he was a hopeless romantic too. He said (and none of the words in this scene are exactly right. But they're pretty close. He said something like this as the bar began to fill up little by little): 'You can ruin your life trying to fit your life into your life story. *Anything* that goes on a long time is going to seem like an epic, you know. But I'm unsuitable. I never loved you at the same time as I loved my book. And I never loved my book at the same time as I loved you, which either makes me a crap lover or not an artist or means I'm right, we shouldn't be together. I'm thirty-two and I *actually have got* a sole flapping off my shoe. I fucking *hate* West Side Story and you love it. I'm unsuitable. And you don't love me. Not really, not any more. I let you down, as idols tend to do. Nobody wants to be a fucking idol. Apart from fucking idols.' Something like that. And these words weren't being interrupted by the last call at the departure gates or being yelled from pavement to fifth-floor window, nor were they drenched in a timely but unnoticed rain or inadvertently being transmitted to a global audience during a live TV press-conference. 'You're a born *pupil*,' Jonathan said. 'You always want to be the pupil. And it's not because you want to learn from each man either. Which I do think is *right* – the idea of your lovers being a process of elimination, an education towards Mr Right, is overrated. It doesn't happen in reality. You, you're just a crap pupil. You're not interested in learning, you just want to fancy the teacher. You're not *becoming*, you're perfectly happy *being* – if you'll forgive the jargon. So don't lose your fucking nerve. Don't start getting all *shaped* on me. Someone else's shape. Thinking how romantic this would *look*, when we wouldn't last six months. Don't settle for less. You remember that conversation we had on the beach?'

'About setting your sights too high. An idol will let you down . . .'

'. . . yeah, but how can you lower your sights?'

'But you've just said that all idols let you down!'

'Find one that doesn't. Don't lose your nerve. Just because you're thirty-one and it would look like a perfect ending. Die trying.'

He was smiling, to himself, at everything, because he knew he was right. Even though I could see it hurt him to be so. And I knew he was right, though it was like using the last of my courage virginity to walk past all the silly counter-arguments in my head, not catching their eyes. As Alida Valli walks down that windless woodsmoke-scented avenue past Joseph Cotten and out of The Third Man. More and more people were coming into the bar, sitting at tables ever closer to ours. It was becoming less intimate. There were people arriving but they could see we were having a bit of a chat and were holding back.

'And you know the worst thing?' said Jonathan. 'The worst thing is that we can still be friends. Because we're not in love. '

Now friends were coming over and saying hello and well done, and Jonathan ended up getting quite drunk and heckling a really terrible sort of live music event that set up in the bar called Laptops Live and making a bit of a fool of himself, throwing limes at them, and although, I admit, Laptops Live made some of the most terrible music I have ever heard in my life, I thought he was being a right arse, because he can be like that quite a lot of the time. I thought: you wouldn't catch Javier Bardem doing that.

18

The last thing that seems important to tell you, dear dear reader and thank you so much for your patience, is that I was sitting in Hyde Park the other day on the slope above the lake, waiting for my boyfriend, when I saw Albert Finney. My boyfriend wasn't there yet because I was deliberately early and Hyde Park – Hyde Park is the most beautiful widescreen panorama in the world. It's even shaped like a cinemascope screen. I always wanted to make a movie called 'Hyde Park'. A commentary-less couple of hours just nosing around taking in the sights. And I knew this was mad, because what on earth would the film be *doing* in excess of the park itself? Why would you go and sit in the cinema rather than the park? Maybe Woody Allen could make it – maybe it would be his return to form! People had given up saying by now that Woody was back to his best, and I didn't bother with Match Point or Scoop. In fact, I don't go to the cinema an enormous amount these days. Maybe once a month or so. I read more. (Prince Andrei in War and Peace, now *he's* a bit of alright.) As I write, the drop of almost a third in cinema attendances that took place in 2005 shows no signs of reversing. Something's gone drastically wrong. Although Dudi's got his chance to do something about it. He got a job in America adapting Walden for Disney and Brad wants to star (I remain a smidgen dubious about this project's ability to rescue cinema). What else? Let's see . . . I'm a godmother! Ilana had a baby boy with her new husband not long ago. He's called Max (the baby) and Jonathan showed up with a tetrameter sonnet that he'd knocked up for the occasion. He's doing OK these days, Jonathan, still perpetually ten minutes away from a dazzling success. And Marcus is still a brilliant Company Member: I imagine him propping up the bar of the Arden Hotel with Roger Allam. Janie and Aubrey and Chips and Duzz are all fine. Jim stopped drinking, got married and now has two children, apparently – I never saw him again after he left London. Mark's band picked up their guitars and became really quite famous. Tom is really successful (the bastard), Dan's happily married and Alun's still being very sensible and responsible on coke. The Camden New Journal is again the best local newspaper in the country now that I've stopped writing for it. And Wandering Lady – I finally did get around to changing her name. London went to live on a farm in Yorkshire, where I picture her running rings round the yokels like Autolycus in A Winter's Tale. I still have no idea where Wilson is. And Marlon Brando is dead. Brando – who they say couldn't sit next to someone without becoming them, who would unstoppably consume you as you talked – finally, at 350 pounds, choked to death. Brando, the eater of souls.

But my boyfriend. His name is – well, I think it would be rather indiscreet to go into personal details about him, don't you? What kind of a girl do you think I am? Yet I feel about him like I feel about Russell and Jeff and Robert and Al and Nikita and Javier. I don't want to lose him. I love him. Isn't love wonderful? Trust to luck.

He was annoyed to have missed Albert Finney, though. I watched Finney walk down the road by the lake, looking pretty old and still pugnacious in a light grey sports jacket and open-necked shirt, still very solid, still very much a drinker, not stopped or recognised by anyone, as far as I could see, and I only have this banal thing to say about someone who was never a genius, and never even one of my favourites: he looked like a force of nature. He bent the light around him, like stars do, and walked out of my line of sight behind some lime trees and into the Kinerotiquana in my head where all my boys live. My beautiful strangers. And that sounds almost creepy, does it not, as if I'm some old miser chuckling over my hoard of gold atmidnight or maybe some weirdo lepidopterist gloating over the display cabinets where all his beautiful specimens lie impaled, ruined, dead? But I don't think it is. Why? Because of the magic – the *magic* – of motion fucking pictures, that's why. I swear too much, I really do. Sorry. But *can you fucking believe it*, you can see people running and jumping and dancing and talking and being themselves. (And I'm not worried about the movies, if the bad patch turns out to be a permanent decline. Even if the movies don't stage a comeback, they ran a century. There are only two options, I suppose, with the things you once loved. You can either be bitter at their loss, or you can try and recollect them as you loved them. Recollect them. Love your exes. And you have to suspect that the movies will be back anyway, in one form or another, because, although they're not the greatest art form or the most intelligent medium or the most dynamic art – they're not a whole lot of things – nothing, nothing ever anywhere is as *romantic* as the cinema. No wonder we can't get over it.) You can see, what? You can see Elliott Gould in The Long Goodbye ('Ugly, boring travesty of a well-respected detective novel' – ah, Halliwell!). You can see James Woods down by the pool in Salvador. William L. Petersen bow-legged on the beach in Manhunter. Steve McQueen giving Jacqueline Bisset the once-over in her office in Bullitt. You can see Willem Dafoe hypnotising Laura Dern in Wild at Heart. Tom Bell's sins turning into pure pain in Wish You Were Here and Nicolas Cage in Moonstruck and Joaquin Phoenix in To Die For and Denis Lavant's unforgettable hate-dance on the empty dancefloor at the end of Beau Travail. And the pinches in the sides of Chris

Cooper's nose. And Chazz Palminteri! How could I forget him? What a thrill always to see Chazz Palminteri! And Liotta, of course: Liotta, light of my life, fire of my loins . . . And Billy Crudup standing on a roof in Almost Famous shouting, 'I am a golden god! And my last words are . . . I'm on drugs!' And you can see Lukas Haas as the little witness in Witness, telling Harrison Ford in a fearful singsong: 'But you don't have your gun!' (And, twenty years later, witnessing Joseph Gordon-Levitt's talent kick into gear in Brick.) And you can see – can you see? – Nigel Green as the colour-sergeant taking the rollcall after the battle in Zulu. And Ed Harris out-wintering the winter's day in the park in The Firm! Treat Williams sliding down a table in Hair! Romain Duris driving with the underside of his wrist in The Beat that My Heart Skipped! You can see Christopher Plummer in three-quarters profile having just torn a Nazi flag with weary contempt, an image that should be concretised on the fourth plinth in Trafalgar Square. You can see Richard Burton – oh, no, how could I have forgotten about Burton? It's like missing out someone like Burt Lancaster, or Richard Harris – *Harris*! That's it, the book is worthless. It's ruined. No Harris, no Yul Brynner, no Burton, no Cagney, no *William H. Macy*, for crying out loud. Oh, my God. No Philip Seymour Hoffman. And I fancy the *pants* off him. What's the point? I haven't even mentioned Jimmy Stewart. Or Bart the bloody Bear from The Edge; he should have been in it (I'm not joking, there's a bit on the DVD where you can see Bart relaxing on set, ruminatively munching a salmon and obviously husbanding his fury for a take – a pro).

Let's face it, as a comprehensive round-up this book is a comprehensive failure. But – Elisha Cook Jnr, aren't you just glad he existed? And Pacino and his hollow density. And Penn's hair. And Rickman's teeth. And Cruise's striving, and Cusack's tetchy lower lip, and Bridges's entrance in Thunderbolt and Lightfoot, where he strolls into the film as if he'd always been there, strolling around somewhere, and isn't fazed that a movie has just sprung up around him, and Jeremy Irons's throat, and Walken's face, and Crowe's mass, and Keanu's innocence, and De Niro's talent, and Brando's genius. And Gérard Depardieu's *soul*.

And this is the point. This is the whole bloody point of this book. (Apart from an attempt to raise awareness of Perforated Screening Mechanism Syndrome.) This is why I've been telling you all this in the first place. And it only goes to show how incredibly clever I am, because a proposal for this book ended up in the hands of someone who apparently said, 'Oh yeah, yeah, this might make quite a good *movie*,' and then I heard that he was having lunch with Drew Barrymore's producer and she had *expressed interest*. So, obviously it's quite a long way from some nice Californian saying, 'Ooh that sounds interesting, no salad dressing, please,' to Drew actually emoting with a wharf beetle on the big screen, but it's not impossible, is it, and in fact, if they did end up making the film, then Drew Barrymore playing me would actually be up there in some fantasy sequences which they'd probably work out so that my character would be like dreamily kissing the real Javier Bardem, who might well be pleased to turn up in one of those game little cameos that you get in a film like The Player where you turn up and play yourself, and in fact, come to think of it, it would be *precisely* the sort of film where word would get around and you'd probably have dozens of stars saying, 'Ooh, can I come and do a bit as me for like half a day?' until the producers would be completely overwhelmed by the sheer number of these fantasy sequences and they'd have to cut them down to a sensible sixty or so, of me (played by Drew Barrymore) actually kissing Jeff Bridges, Javier Bardem, Al Pacino, etc., etc. And at the very least they'd have to have me kissing Jonathan and Marcus, who might well be played by, well, you know, some reasonably dishy guy like Damian Lewis – or John *Cusack*. Now *he'd* make a good Jonathan. A *great* Jonathan! And that's all very well and good, *but the point is this*: and this is why the following is not so much a fond hope or a prophecy as a statement of already-occurred *fact*. Which is: if they make this film, then there is no way in the world that Gérard Depardieu is not going to hear about it, and people are going to ask him about it on chat shows and so on, and even if he says, 'Bof! I 'ave no read eet, eet sounds veir sillee,' still, some producer is going to think, 'Gérard's coming to England to do his new cookbook,' or whatever, 'tell you what would be good. Get that girl who wrote that book they're making a film of. She's a nutter, get her to come and be on a panel with him.' *Fact.* The peck he'll give me on the cheek when he arrives – that's already in the bank. That has already happened, so to speak. So I'll be sitting next to Gérard Depardieu on this panel and I'll lean over to him and say, off camera obviously, 'Gérard, you know how I feel about you. Would it be so foolish and destructive and wasteful to come to a hotel with me?' and he'll be saying things like, 'But zees is madness! I weel no be a partee to zees! I am *srough* wiz love,' and I'll say, 'How can you say you're through with love? You might as well say you're dead. How *unhappy* you must be.' And he'll say, 'Yes, yes, I *am* un'appy. I am old. My vitalité is ebbing, life is receding from me. You – you are yous.' 'Use?' '*Yous!*' 'Ah, *youth*!' 'Oui, oui! Yous! La jeunesse! Printemps! Les fleurs du printemps! 'Ow could I forget? Ze smell of YOUS, like ze sap which flows vert et sanglant through ze vines! I weel take you! But not to an hôtel, eet would be shameful. Tu comprends? Love is not shameful. Eet is like your English poet, a woman, bien sûr, a *woman*, she say 'er heart is glad: *Because the Birthday of my life is come, my love is come to me.*'

I am going to marry Gérard Depardieu. In a sense, I already have.

I am Madame Depardieu. Now, who are you, and what the hell are you doing in my chateau? Will you please leave *immediately*!

Thank you so much.